THE ENEMY I KNEW

THE ENEMY I KNEW

GERMAN JEWS IN THE ALLIED
MILITARY IN WORLD WAR II

STEVEN KARRAS

ZENITH PRESS

First published in 2009 by Zenith Press, an imprint of MBI Publishing Company, 400 First Avenue North, Suite 300, Minneapolis, MN 55401 USA

Zenith Press titles are also available at discounts in bulk quantity for industrial or sales-promotional use. For details write to Special Sales Manager at MBI Publishing Company, 400 First Avenue North, Suite 300, Minneapolis, MN 55401 USA.

To find out more about our books, join us online at www.zenithpress.com.

Printed in the United States of America

Library of Congress Cataloging-in-Publication Data
Karras, Steven, 1970-
 The enemy I knew : German Jews in the allied military in World War II / Steven Karras.—1st ed.
  p. cm.
 ISBN 978-0-7603-3586-4 (hb w/ jkt)
 1. Jews, German—United States—Biography. 2. Jews, German—United States—Interviews. 3. Jewish soldiers—United States—Biography. 4. Jewish soldiers—United States—Interviews. 5. World War, 1939-1945—Participation, Jewish. 6. World War, 1939-1945—Personal narratives, Jewish. I. Title.
 E184.37.A147 2009
 940.53089'924073—dc22
                    2009015510

Design Manager: Brenda C. Canales
Designer: Jennie Tischler
Cover: Matt Simmons

On the back cover: Soldiers from the 29th Division search captured German soldiers in France 1944. *Harry Lorch*

For the refugees of Nazism who wore the uniform of the
Allied Armed Forces during World War II

If we mean peace by slavery, then nothing is more wretched. Peace is the harmony of strong souls, not the fightless impotence of slaves.

—Baruch Spinoza

CONTENTS

PROLOGUE

Dearest ones all,

A collective letter is coming your way, one that will be of particular interest to all the Frankfurters, relatives and friends and foes alike. I have finally fulfilled the nightmare which followed me in my dreams, just like it followed you perhaps. <u>I was there.</u>

Captain Speckman, Brown, Wolf and I took the jeep this morning and rode. I heard the familiar dialect and I saw familiar sights. Slowly places and names came closer. I can't deny that my heart was beating a little faster. There was Frankfurt, or was it? On we went slowly, and I tried to absorb every memory. The tower of the Dom was still there, but the church belonging to it was only a skeleton, that is completely uncovered, so that the tower of the Dom stood all alone. The Schauspielhaus has disappeared; there is a tremendous hole in the ground where it used to be, only part of the stage-house has still some walls standing. The familiar sight along the Main River looked changed, it looked familiar and then again it did not. Whatever houses are still standing along the river's edge, are no more houses, just empty shells. The Gestapo Headquarters on Lindenstrasse is down, so are most of the houses there.

We turned slowly into Kaiserstrasse and towards the Rossmarkt. This used to be a fairly long block. But now it seems awfully short because between Frankfurter Hof and Rossmarkt all houses are gone, every one of them, to both sides of the street there is space filled with rubble. You can't walk on the sidewalks, they are roped off or filled with stone, not a single building is even as much as inhabitable. Most of the streets are impossible to pass, by foot or jeep. Then we went to Wiesenau to look for Oma's house. It is not there any more, don't worry over it, mom, Oma did not live to see the day. I went into a few houses and asked a few people for her name, it seemed to me she lived on number 54, but nobody knew her. She is not alive any more, I'm sure of that, mom; she is better off that way, believe me.

Our house, number 53, must have had a direct hit, because it is now a pile of twisted girders, stones and dust. The iron front gate sticks out from the end of the letterbox [which], strangely enough, lies on top of the pile. Just one wall is standing. The "house" looks as if somebody had taken a knife and cut it straight down, throwing everything on one big pile, but leaving the rear wall standing. It was very silent in Gruenstrasse, not a soul, the wind was waning some of the hanging window shades and made a weird noise, as if the bones of old times were shuddering, bringing back memories.

We traced our steps back to the synagogue. Strangest sight of all: It is complete, absolutely undamaged, copula and all, as if it was ready to open for services any moment. The houses facing it [are] all damaged, empty, burned out, but our synagogue is untouched. Of all things where else could God's unbelievable justice be more evident than here?

It is hard to describe the emotions that went through me, it's just like going home after many years and looking for the people you used to know and all you find is their grave. That's what Frankfurt is today, a graveyard, a vast terrible graveyard, a sign of Divine justice, of retribution, a sign of God's wonderful ways to lead us away from the Sintflut [deluge] before it could engulf us. Where else and where more would we have reason to sink down on our knees with tears in our eyes? I almost had them, and thank Him for all he did for us, that he led us away from it all to this land of Liberty, the United States of America. And where else could it be that I, born in that town, would return after so many years, as an Officer of a conquering

Army. I felt as if today I was the safe keeper of the many thousands of Jews of Frankfurt or Germany that came with me together in spirit to see what Justice eternal does.

Walter Rothschild
175th Regiment, 45th Division
United States Army

FOREWORD

Almost two decades ago when we began working on the final film for the United States Holocaust Memorial Museum's permanent exhibition, we revisited the riveting testimony of Gerda Weissman Klein and her husband, Kurt. Gerda was a Holocaust survivor who, after a death march of many months, was liberated in the Czechoslovakian city of Volary. Her liberator was an American GI lieutenant named Kurt Klein. When telling the story, Gerda said, "I looked into his eyes and said, 'I must tell you something . . . we are Jews.' And for what seemed like an eternity he stood there and then he answered, 'So am I.'"

Gerda weighed seventy-eight pounds, her hair was white, and she hadn't had a bath in years. Yet Kurt and Gerda grew to love one another, married, and raised children and grandchildren.

In the testimony Gerda's story seemed primary. The primary text of the Holocaust is the story of the victims, and the best way to understand their plight—to enter what we now call *l'univers concentrationnaire*—is to heed their words orally and even visually. Only thus can we understand, only thus can we come close to understanding.

And yet that is not the only story—the only narrative—of the Holocaust. Kurt was a German Jew who found refuge in the United States and sought with all his limited power to have his parents join him in freedom. He was unsuccessful and they were murdered at Auschwitz, according to the best of information that he could find. That part of his story was covered in the PBS series *America and the Holocaust*. Kurt was a German Jew who returned to Germany, the land that had killed his parents, had oppressed him, and was only too happy to see him leave, as forced emigration was the first of the German policies toward the Jews.

Mistakenly, I had not understood that Kurt, too, had a powerful story to tell, a story of not only victimization, death, and destruction, but also of exodus and return, empowerment and vengeance, of turning the tables on his former countrymen. He was the Jew as warrior, the Jew as conqueror, the Jew as liberator.

More mistakenly, I had presumed that his was an isolated story until I met a young and talented filmmaker named Steven Karras. Steve was working on the film *About Face: The Story of the Jewish Refugee Soldiers of World War II*, which told the story of the many men and women who shared a common past with Kurt, whose journey resembled his own. Cast out of Germany, often leaving their parents and siblings behind, they found their way to the United States and England where their adjustment was painful. They were regarded as immigrants in countries that did not welcome immigrants. When the war began, they were regarded as Enemy Aliens and were suspected of being "fifth column" spies for the motherland. For a time, it was beyond the comprehension of the U.S. and British governments that Jews deserved a different category. They had not only left their homeland, their homeland had left them. They had every reason to fight Nazi Germany—every possible motivation. They understood that World War II was a matter of life and death, good versus evil, a true clash of civilizations. At stake was the character of civilization.

Then, wonder of wonders, the governments of the United States and the United Kingdom realized what a unique resource these men and women were. Their intellectual level was generally quite high, their motivation intense. Their knowledge of Germany was native, and their linguistic skills were unequalled. Some were educated in the best German schools and raised by cultured and intellectual parents. Had the Nazis not come to power, they would have fully participated in German culture and commerce. Soon they were trained by the U.S. and British governments in elite units to be in intelligence, conduct interrogations, and run the occupation, which they did.

Their stories vary person to person, as they should, and yet each story has much in common with the others. For some, the army experience sped their process of Americanization. For others it created the sense of redemption, personal and historical. From unfortunate refugee, they became members of elite units at the forefront of the battle against Germany, respected and looked up to rather than disdained and looked down upon.

I am drawn to their stories in ways I understand and in ways I do not. My father, Saul Berenbaum of blessed memory, was born in Poland and came to the United States as a nine-year-old in 1919. He quickly became Americanized and volunteered to fight in World War II. He served valiantly, earning a Bronze Star and two Purple Hearts. We did not know of these medals until we went through his papers after his death, but we were raised on World War II stories and understood that this was a war he felt was his to fight. The Nazis were the sworn enemies of the Jewish people, and they were antithetical to every American value he cherished. World War II united both of his identities as a Jew and as an American—even though he had not lived under Nazi rule. So until I saw the interviews, until I read what these soldiers had to witness, I could only imagine how intensely they felt about the battle they were called to wage.

As a young man of draft age during Vietnam, I clashed with my father who, for a very long time, could not understand why that war was not my war. He could not see why it did not unite my identities the way that his generation's war reflected who he was, even as it transformed him. I envied the clarity of battle he had, the purity of arms that was so much more so for these men from Germany and Austria.

We must be grateful to Steven Karras for gathering this testimony, and even more grateful to the men and women who trusted him with their stories. In Karras' hands, their stories have come to life twice—once in the compelling film *About Face* and again in this memorable work.

Read not about Jews as victims but Jews as warriors, proud and defiant, determined, and fighting justly. Read also about their courage and the impact that their courage had upon their later life. Some embraced their Judaism and wore their identity proudly. Others learned from their experience in Germany that being Jewish was dangerous, so it must end with them. All embraced their new lands and gained confidence and power from their experience as soldiers. It shaped who they became. It healed deep wounds and opened up new horizons.

This is a book about Jewish men and women, immigrants and refugees, who knew full well the menace of Nazism, the promise and the betrayal of Germany, who experienced persecution and danger, who might have only been victims but whose fate was changed because they became warriors able to defeat their enemy. They were able to liberate the Nazis' victims—knowing that there but for the fate of circumstances go I—and hold the perpetrators partially accountable and run the occupation where they struggled mightily between the need for justice and the honorable desire for revenge. In the end, they gave much to America's freedom and contributed significantly to Germany's defeat—and not insignificantly to its rebirth.

—Michael Berenbaum
Los Angeles, California

Michael Berenbaum is a professor of Jewish Studies and director of the Sigi Ziering Center for the Study of the Holocaust and Ethics at American Jewish University. He was also the executive producer of About Face.

PREFACE

In 1999 I began conducting interviews with former German and Austrian Jewish refugees who had served in the allied armed forces for the documentary *About Face: The Story of the Jewish Refugee Soldiers of World War II*, which I produced. The subject had first piqued my interest when I was fourteen at Camp Menominee in Eagle River, Wisconsin. A friend of mine named Roger Fields from Riverdale, a neighborhood in the Bronx, mentioned to me in passing that his father, a German Jew, had fled the Nazis with his family to New York, changed his name from Dingfelder to Fields, and joined the U.S. Army. I was blown away to learn that not only did he return to Europe as a GI to fight the Germans, but once his unit got to Germany, he also drove to his hometown of Uehlfeld.

Having been raised Jewish and possessing an intense interest in stories of Jewish courage during the Holocaust—such as the Ghetto uprisings and the partisan groups in the forests of Russia—I had never heard anything like this, nor had anybody else I knew. I tried to imagine the tremendous sense of triumph and pride Fields and many others must have felt as part of the vanquishing army when they returned to the towns where the German population—their neighbors and former friends—had betrayed them, passively standing by and watching while Jews were humiliated, arrested, and forced from their homes. Then I wondered if those same Germans were shocked or frightened to encounter these Jews, no longer the cowering youth they had bullied and abused years earlier, who had returned in the uniform of the enemy.

Word of mouth about my search for interviewees spread after I posted an inquiry for such stories on a World War II veteran internet message board. An Austrian survivor by the name of Leo Bretholz, who lived in Baltimore, heard about what I was doing and introduced me to nearly everyone he knew who would qualify to be in the film. This led to an avalanche of contacts. By January 2000, my answering machine was filled with messages from men named Klaus, Fritz, Manfred, Gunther, Hans, and Otto, each of whom had thick German accents and enjoyed waxing nostalgic about their former units and wartime exploits. By February 2000, fifty men and three women had contacted me.

The stories presented within this book are based on these interviews which I personally conducted from November 1999 through May 2002, with some exceptions. Ralph Baer's and William Katzenstein's stories are drawn from their unpublished memoirs. Eric Boehm's story is based on a transcript of an interview conducted in 1988 with H. W. Mermagen. John Brunswick, Karl Goldsmith, Jack Hochwald, Siegmund Spiegel, and Fritz Weinschenk's interviews are augmented with material from their unpublished memoirs. Fred Fields was interviewed by Joshua Franklin in August 2008. Peter Masters' story is informed by his book *Striking Back: A Jewish Commando's War Against the Nazis* (Novato, CA: Presidio Press, 1997).

As I prepared for the personal interviews, one of my first tasks was to learn the British and American tables of organization, the orders of battle in the war against Germany, and which units were deployed from the first attack on German forces to the surrender. For this and other background information, the following sources were particularly helpful: *Afbau*, "The Truth About Refugee Immigration: A Few Amazing Immigration Figures" (July 15, 1939); Martin Gilbert's *The Holocaust: The Jewish Tragedy* (New York: Harper Collins, 1986); Walter Isaacson's *Kissinger: A Biography* (New York: Simon & Schuster, 1992); Arnold Pauker's *German Jews in the Resistance 1933–45: The Facts and Problems* (Berlin: The German Resistance Memorial Center, 1985); Joseph Persico's *Piercing the Reich: The Penetration of Nazi Germany by American Secret Agents during World War II* (New York: Viking Press, 1979); and Bryan Mark Rigg's *Hitler's Jewish Soldiers: The Untold Story of Nazi Racial Laws and Men of Jewish Descent in the German Military* (Lawrence, KS: University of Kansas Press, 2004).

My pre-interviews over the phone fortunately yielded a large number of units to choose from, so it became easier to prioritize certain stories. For example, when Siegmund Spiegel in Bal Harbor, Florida, told me he was in the 1st Infantry Division, I immediately knew I wanted to interview him. "The Big Red One," or the "Fighting First" as the division was called, had been a spearhead outfit that invaded North Africa, Sicily, and Normandy. As Spiegel had participated in all of these engagements, his rich firsthand accounts were extremely beneficial to my research. They helped me accomplish my goal of finding veterans from each campaign, demonstrating the refugee soldiers' ubiquitous presence in the allied war against Germany.

While the German-Jewish refugee community is now dwindling, it amazes me that it is nevertheless still as closely knit as it ever was. Cousins put me in touch with their cousins and friends with other friends living all over the country. Their knowledge of, and obvious pride in, each other's personal war histories are remarkable. I've been told: "Call Siggy Katz. He won a Silver Star after capturing fifty German soldiers," or "Call Harry Lorch. His unit held a Passover Seder in Joseph Goebbels' castle in Muenchen-Gladbach."

One remarkable and rather eerie encounter occurred one morning back at the New City YMCA in Chicago when an older gentleman named Herbert Kadden started talking to me in the locker room. When it became obvious to me that he was a German Jew, I told him about my film project. "I've probably already interviewed half the people you know," I remarked rather lightly. Then I randomly picked the name of a refugee, Otto Stern, who was one of my interviewees. The man in front of me became visibly emotional. "Otto Stern found my parents, who were in hiding in Belgium," he said. As a result of this encounter, I was able to reunite two long-lost friends for the first time in fifty years. Fortunately for me, those I interviewed who had served in the British Army all lived in the United States.

The biggest revelation that came out of my research was the veterans' overriding emphasis on the importance to them of having become allied soldiers. Acceptance into the allied military—not the fact that they were victims of the Holocaust—was *the* formidable life-shaping event of their lives. This fact indicated to me that the story I was researching was far more complex than I had expected and was not the revenge tale that had attracted me to the subject in the first place. It really was a story about identity as well as courage. In Germany, their national identity was taken away and they became hate objects and then refugees. Their military experience transformed them from victims into valued members of a victorious army, and finally their national identity was restored when those in the United States and the United Kingdom became naturalized citizens.

It is also the classic immigrant story of rebuilding one's life and the determination to live up to an adopted country's expectations. In the United States, the GI Bill offered refugee soldiers the education they had formerly been denied, and many thrived and became physicians, architects, chief executives of international corporations, small business owners, Wall Street scions, economists, attorneys, educators, inventors, entertainers, writers, public servants, and simply productive and hardworking citizens. As such, their trajectory is in every way a highly *American* story, as well as part of the story of America itself.

This speaks to an even larger lesson: individuals have the ability to choose whether or not to be victims, as well as the power to redefine themselves. Even more than the great historical significance of the stories themselves, this notion inspired me throughout my work on this ten-year-long project and continues to do so every day. With the tragedy as monolithic as the Holocaust, nothing will ever eclipse the fact that there was a near successful attempt to eliminate the Jewish seed from Europe. There are, however, stories of courage that continue to emerge within the margins of the greater story, and they should be told. This is one of them.

ACKNOWLEDGMENTS

I am indebted to all of the veterans and their families—wives, children, and grandchildren—who graciously answered my many questions; shared their stories, family documents, photographs, and memoirs; opened their homes to me and my colleagues; or answered queries via letter, email, or telephone.

Special thanks to Gayle Wurst at Princeton International Agency for the Arts for quickly taking a shine to me and this largely unknown subject, for finding a home for this book, and for her friendship.

I am particularly grateful to the people at Zenith Press: Richard Kane for recognizing the value of these stories and taking this project on, Steve Gansen for taking the time to help guide me through a new process, and Scott Pearson for his real-time direction and his inimitable humor.

I am profoundly grateful to Fritz Weinschenk, Marty Peak, and Frank Helman of the Otto and Fran Walter Foundation for championing this project and granting the necessary resources for research, travel, and interviews—as well as access to the foundation's rich archive of oral histories—so that this book could be written. This was a dream realized, and I can only hope that I have lived up to their generosity and expectations.

Special thanks to Rose Lizarraga, my co-director on the documentary *About Face*, for her hard work around the clock (and globe) for the past seven years—interviewing and scouring archives for relevant material in Washington, D.C., New York, and London's Imperial War Museum—and for her continued dedication to getting this important story told.

Most especially I would like to acknowledge Dr. Michael Berenbaum for his valued advice, guidance, and approbation; Julia Rath, an early colleague who was enormously helpful in seeking out willing interviewees, many of whom appear in this book; and Ilko Davidov and Carmen Cervi at BulletProof Film in Chicago for their technical help, recording the interviews in many cities and managing the archival materials.

Leo Bretholz enthusiastically contacted dozens of his veteran friends on my behalf in the winter of 2000 and, along with wife Flo, was very hospitable whenever I visited Baltimore. Joshua Franklin, an expert on the subject of German refugee soldiers and whose grandfather, Walter Spiegel, was a refugee and GI in the European Theatre, generously shared his research with me and conducted a videotaped interview with Fred Fields in Riverdale, New York.

For their warm friendship, opinions, sound advice, and frequent correspondence, I wish to thank Sig Spiegel, Peter Terry, and Walter Reed.

Warren Leming in Chicago was a tremendous help in translating German articles and documents.

I would like to thank my friend Christa Fuller for her insights into all things German and historical, and for sharing the many wonderful anecdotes about her late husband, Samuel Fuller, both as an infantryman in the Big Red One and as a film director in Hollywood.

For their love and support, I wish to thank my family: my mother Rita Kanne and her husband Jeff; my father Sheldon Karras and his wife Karen; and my brother Michael Karras, his wife Jennifer, and their kids Noah, Reese, and Blythe.

Lastly, I am most grateful to my wife, Andie, whose humor and love sustains me.

INTRODUCTION

Many people often think that they know the history of the Holocaust and that they have heard all the stories. Each story is different, yet each story seems the same. These particular stories, however, are different. True, like most Holocaust memoirs, they are divided into three: before, during, and after. The before segment reads like many memoirs about the wonderful days of one's youth, the well-integrated life of Jews in Germany before Hitler and the Nazis came into power. Then the story describes the growing oppression, persecution, loss of status, and collapse of self image as a German Jew—but suddenly this narration veers off course and introduces a new element. These Jews left Germany while there was still time. Often they left by luck or fortitude, but they were living outside of Germany when the Holocaust began.

   This is not the story of powerless Jews or helpless refugees, though many were the latter for a time. It is the story of men and women who were drafted by the Allies and returned to their native lands as empowered soldiers on the vanguard of war. This inspiring turn in the narrative of the Holocaust is told through twenty-seven firsthand accounts taken from interviews and memoirs of German- and Austrian-born Jews who served in the Allied

1

forces in Europe and North Africa. Though seemingly indistinguishable from the ranks of millions of other American or British troops, they were Jewish refugees. They had recently suffered persecution and discrimination and had escaped from almost certain death in Nazi Germany—only to return and fight the Nazis and strike back with a sense of fury for what had been done to them. They faced the shock of the Holocaust, knowing full well that had they not left in the nick of time, they would have been slaving in the camps, they would have been the skeletal remains, and their families (or more members of their families) would have been murdered and would have disappeared into mass graves.

In the aggregate, each story paints an unfamiliar picture of how the U.S. and British military valued and took full advantage of the unique skills, motivation, and experience of the German Jewish refugees. They had firsthand knowledge of the enemy, a nuanced understanding of the psyche of the German people, detailed knowledge of the country, and, of course, skills as native speakers of German. Each personal story reveals never-before-heard experiences of refugee soldiers in wartime: their varied roles in the gathering and use of military intelligence, their contribution to elite units like the British Commandos, being entrusted with running the occupation of Germany and Austria, and their prominent and fitting roles in frontline interrogation units interrogating the very Nazis who had once persecuted them.

Most of these young men (and women) were born into middle or upper-middle class families, and many came from small towns and villages like Fürth or Lehrberg, as well as large cities like Munich or Vienna, located across Germany and Austria. Each veteran experienced life differently after Hitler came to power and has varying sagas of escape. Some parents had foresight and were lucky enough to get out (or at least get their children out) of Germany in the early days of the regime; yet many remained and suffered the hardships of years of discrimination, second-class citizenship, and a brutal campaign of state-supported violence and propaganda that incited anti-Semitism throughout the country, turning neighbor against neighbor. While some Jews emigrated with their families intact, others were forced to leave alone, devoid of companionship or support. All, however, understood one thing about themselves and one thing about the Nazis: they knew that they had gotten out just in time and they knew how menacing this regime was, thus how imperative it was to defeat it.

The refugees had varied war experiences; each had different perspectives and emotions and served in various non-combat and combat roles. Ironically, these former victims of Nazi terror landed on beaches during the Normandy invasion, only a few miles from the ports where they had boarded ships to go the United States or Britain four years earlier. Some captured or guarded former classmates and neighbors and interrogated high-ranking Nazis such as Hermann Goering, Josef "Sepp" Dietrich, Julius Streicher, or Jurgen Stroop. Others occupied and governed their hometowns or liberated family members from death camps. When coming face to face with their tormentors, these soldiers grappled with the decision of whether or not to exact revenge, as their judgment was far more complex than that of the average soldier.

BEFORE THE WAR

In the years leading up to the rule of Adolf Hitler, Germany had been a place most hospitable to Jews; Jewish communities in Germany went back to the early medieval era. Even when Europe's different monarchs expelled Jews out of their countries, they were never completely driven out of Germany. In the Rhineland, Jews had been settled there for hundreds of years, had achieved legal equality from 1870 on, and were woven into the fabric of German society. Thus, Germany was a country in which Jews felt at home and relatively safe.

In World War I, around a hundred thousand German Jews—a high percentage, more than one in six—fought for Germany on all fronts. Some 78 percent of these saw frontline duty; twelve thousand died in battle, over thirty thousand received decorations, and nineteen thousand were promoted. One of the great ironies is that the officer of the 16th Bavarian Reserve who recommended Hitler for the Iron Cross First Class was a Jewish captain named Otto Guttman.

It was Adolf Hitler's initial intention to drive every last Jew out of Germany—to make Germany *Judenrein*. As a consequence, the Nazis implemented a number of policies designed to create a national atmosphere so hostile and unstable for German Jews that they would have little choice but to emigrate. The first of these measures was the nationwide boycott of all Jewish businesses on April 1, 1933. Dispatched in small teams and hovering around storefronts, the Sturmabteilung (SA)—better known as "stormtroopers" or "brownshirts" because of their black and brown uniforms—were vicious street thugs who took pleasure in intimidating and assaulting defenseless

Jews at the slightest provocation. During the boycott, the SA defaced Jewish property, painting Stars of David and *"Jude"* (Jews) on the windows and buildings of Jewish-owned supermarkets, department stores, legal offices, and medical clinics. They held signs that read, "Germans, Defend Yourself, Don't Buy Jewish Goods," and goaded enthusiastic crowds into joining them in reciting popular anti-Semitic mantras like "the Jews are our misfortune."

In 1933, German Jews numbered 564,519, less than 1 percent of the overall German population of 65 million, yet they were far more prominent and visible than their numbers. In Berlin, almost half of all doctors and lawyers were Jews. Nationally, 16 percent of Germany's dentists were Jews. There was also a disproportionate presence of Jewish students and professors in universities, medical schools, and law schools. The high visibility of Jews as a distinct element in German cultural circles, such as in cinema, music, and literature, further contributed to the feeling that Jewish accomplishment had gone too far and that Jews were over-represented in German society.

In spite of the high-profile intimidation of the April boycott, it hadn't made the impact the Nazis had hoped it would. Nevertheless, it had struck a major blow to the diminishing morale of German Jews. Most had experienced discrimination in their lives, but this was different. Here was a regime with such monumental power and authority that it could turn modern anti-Jewish rhetoric into state policy, all the while emboldening the Jew haters of an entire nation.

One week later on April 7, 1933, the Law for the Restoration of Professional Civil Service expelled Jews from the civil service, including professors at state universities and government-employed physicians. On May 10, Hitler's one hundredth day in office, mobs of pro-Nazi students stormed administration buildings, lecture halls, and libraries of universities all over Germany, purging bookshelves and burning books written by Jews or others deemed enemies of Hitler's Reich.

Jewish children were equally affected by these policies. The Law against the Overcrowding of German Schools and Institutions of Higher Learning limited the amount of Jewish students in state schools. It was the first of many stages to force Jewish children out of the German school system. Siegmund Spiegel, then a teenager in Gera, Germany, and later an infantry sergeant in the U.S. Army, was one of those students: "In April 1933 my father was called to the Gymnasium [high school] and told, 'Mr. Spiegel, take your son out of our school, we want the school to be *Judenrein*'—and that was the end of my formal education at the age of fourteen."

Jewish youth who remained in German schools were constant targets of ridicule and abuse by teachers and non-Jewish children. Karl Goldsmith was one of the few remaining Jewish students attending a German school in Eschwege, Germany. He recalls, "I was in the third class of the Gymnasium when it became brutal. . . . My teacher, Mr. Almerodt, one day simply ordered me in front of the class and caned me with the words to the class: '*So verfrugelt han einen Jude*' (This is the way you beat up a Jew). For this episode, which I never forgot, I ordered him to pull weeds in the Jewish cemetery in 1946 when I was back in Eschwege in charge of Denazification for the U.S. Army."

In 1935, the Nuremberg Laws were introduced to segregate Jews entirely from the rest of German society. Some of these laws were symbolic and inconsequential, such as the Reich Flag Law, which forbade German Jews to fly the official state flag, the swastika. Others impacted on the very status of Jews, such as the Reich Citizen Law, which stripped Jews of their German citizenship, and the Law for the Protection of German Blood and Honor, which forbade Jews from marrying or having sexual relations with non-Jews, or employing non-Jewish women under the age of forty-five in their homes. Most importantly, the laws defined Jews as a racial, as opposed to a religious, group and used race to separate them from the general population. If one had two or more Jewish grandparents, or was a practicing member of the Jewish community, it was sufficient to define their legal status as a Jew and discriminate against them as such.

Historically, the distinction between Jews and Christians was religion. Conversion to Christianity often provided Jews with an entree into the social, professional, and political circuits of Christian society that had been traditionally denied to them. Gustav Mahler, a Viennese Jew, is a well-known example. His conversion to Catholicism allowed him to accept the coveted directorship of the Vienna Opera in 1897.

Remarkably, the Law for the Protection of German Blood and Honor impacted those who had long since intermarried with Christians, had converted to Christianity, or had completely disavowed their Jewish past. The definition of Jews here was racial, based on bloodlines, not on the values they accepted, the traditions they embraced, or the religion they practiced. Under the Nuremberg Laws, Germans of the Jewish faith were now only Jews. As a child in Berlin, Adelyn Bonin had been baptized and raised as a Lutheran by her parents, Otto and Lilli Bonin, and was unaware of her Jewish heritage: "When Hitler came to power I returned home one day with a swastika on my coat and my father told me, 'We have to have a long talk.' He told me that I was Jewish, and this was devastating to me."

The Nazis' legal separation of Jews from the rest of German society was seminal in driving them completely out of the German economy. Aryanization of all German businesses—the euphemism for taking over Jewish businesses—allowed the Nazis to manipulate and extort Jews by liquidating assets, stocks, and companies over to German companies at prices far lower than their worth. Additionally, Jews were increasingly driven from nearly every professional field; by 1935 physicians and lawyers who had continued to practice after 1933 would never work again. In rural areas, Jewish cattle dealers, farmers, and land owners were forced to sell their property. Fred Fields, a future U.S. Army interrogator in Lt. Gen. George S. Patton's Third Army, was a nine-year-old in Uehlfeld, Bavaria, when his father, a wealthy cattle dealer, was forced to sell his property: "We had to turn over our house, acres of land and meadows which we leased to other farmers, and sold everything for nothing, one thousand marks, which was the price of two cars at that time. The Nazis took away my father's ability—like most Jews—to make a living and my family had to resettle in Bamberg for my father to find work."

The psychological toll on the Jewish youth during this period was significant. Their friends with whom they had forged strong bonds suddenly joined other students in taunting them, even throwing rocks at them. They felt betrayed by the government, by society, and most importantly by neighbors and friends. From street corner kiosks, newsstands, and radio broadcasts came vile propaganda that resonated with average Germans. Park benches were forbidden to Jewish youths, as were school assemblies, community swimming pools, museums, cinemas, libraries, and, by 1938, education itself. Not only was their world outside of the home unsafe, but parents could barely protect themselves or their children.

In Schenklengsfeld in Central Germany, a town with twelve Jewish families, Werner Katzenstein became an easy target for his classmates: "Most of my friends began joining the Hitler Youth. At that time they started calling me a 'dirty Jew' and the insults soon escalated into violence and that includes beatings. I remember many trips home from school that included bloody noses and broken glasses."

Only gradually did Jews come to the conclusion that there was no future left for them in Germany. Bernard Baum, who came from Giessen, Germany, remembered that his father, Theodore Baum, a decorated veteran of World War I had anticipated problems early on:

> My father was a very bright, intelligent, well-read man, and politically liberal by orientation. He was a World War I hero and was awarded the Iron Cross. He read *Mein Kampf* in 1930, and when he finished that book he turned to my mother and said, "If this man Hitler comes to power we're leaving Germany." So, in January of 1933, when Hitler became chancellor, my father got the papers to leave. Some of his Jewish friends pleaded with him to stay and would ask him, "Why are you leaving? You won the Iron Cross; you've got a successful dental practice and are living well." My father replied, "Because I've got three sons."

For other German Jews, the decision to emigrate was difficult to make, especially among heads of households. Not knowing another language meant professionals couldn't qualify to work in their chosen professions in other countries. This impacted most directly on those whose professions were dependent on language skills. Musicians and architects, even filmmakers have a universal language, but lawyers, for example, do not. Some professions have rigorous licensing requirements, and experienced lawyers and physicians knew that it could take years and additional education to obtain recertification for fields in which they had a lifetime of experience.

The young, who once imagined intellectual and professional careers, instead prepared for mobile professions that they could practice anywhere, but finding a country to take them was difficult. Even though the horrible news of boycotts and anti-Jewish decrees continued to filter out of Germany, countries were still ambivalent to the plight of the Jews. The United States had imposed a quota system in 1924 with a limited number of visas available for refugees from Germany and Austria, and did nothing to lift any restrictions on immigration. Not until 1938 was the full quota of immigrants admitted to the United States.

Immigration officials erected what historians have called "paper walls." Hopeful immigrants had to locate citizens in countries who could provide affidavits for their families, assuring immigration officials that the potential émigré could find work and not become a public charge. In addition to Likely to become Public Charge (LPC) documents, immigrants to the United States required a Certificate of Good Conduct. Teenagers and young adults learned physical trades and became plumbers, tool and die makers, mechanics, and cooks to make getting out much easier.

The emigration crisis had reached its boiling point in 1938, resulting in the largest emigration wave of Jews. On March 12, 1938, German troops crossed the Austrian border and marched into Vienna. What had been a five-year gradual buildup and intensification of anti-Jewish policies and discrimination in Germany came in a shocking instant to Austria's 183,000 Jews. The Nuremberg Laws were immediately implemented, and Jews lost their Austrian citizenship overnight; Aryanization of Austrian businesses yielded the same results as it had in Germany and spontaneous violence against Jews erupted all over Vienna.

Peter Terry, the son of a well-known surgeon living in Vienna, remembers: "When you looked out the window, you saw horrible scenes— people being arrested, mostly Jews being forced on their hands and knees and made to wash the pavement while Viennese Nazis spat on them and shouted insults." SA men made a sport of randomly pulling religious Jews out of crowds and shaving their beards. Pregnant Jewish women were ordered to run in circles until they collapsed in exhaustion. In the months following the Anschluss, five hundred Austrian Jews committed suicide.

Nazi officials in Austria accelerated forced emigration at such a breathtaking pace that by the summer of 1938, approximately ninety thousand Austrian Jews—one in two—had fled the country. Peter Masters, a future British Commando, was fifteen years old and one of those who fled in 1938: "My aunt in London got fourteen people out, of whom I am one. When I think back to what went on in Vienna on a day-by-day . . . it sends shivers down my back because there isn't the slightest doubt that you would've been murdered if you'd stayed any longer than we did. The ultimate fate was never in doubt."

APPROXIMATELY 150,000 GERMAN AND AUSTRIAN JEWS had been fortunate enough to escape by the summer of 1938; 8,000 made it to Great Britain, 40,000 to Palestine, and 55,000 to the United States. This mass immigration sparked an international refugee crisis and posed major problems for countries that maintained very strict immigration laws. In July 1938, President Roosevelt convened (without attending) a gathering of thirty-two countries and a host of relief organizations (many of them Jewish) in Evian, France, to discuss the plight of the Jewish refugees. Although there was sympathy toward the Jews in Germany and Austria, quotas and restrictions stayed the same, and doors remained closed to hundreds of thousands of Jews.

In October 1938, the Nazis expelled seven thousand Jews living in Germany who had Polish citizenship, but the Polish government refused to readmit them to the country. In early November 1938, Herschel Grynszpan, a German Jew studying in Paris, received a letter from his mother informing him that they too were among the deportees. Despondent over the news, Grynszpan walked into the German Embassy in Paris with a pistol and shot a junior embassy official, Ernst Von Rath, who died later that evening. The Nazis used Von Rath's murder as an excuse to launch a highly disciplined and coordinated pogrom against the Jews, otherwise known as the Kristallnacht, or the Night of the Broken Glass. In two days, seven thousand Jewish businesses were ransacked and looted, windows were smashed, Jewish cemeteries were desecrated, more than a thousand synagogues around Germany were torched and burned to the ground, and almost one hundred Jews were killed.

In the town of Ludwigshafen, Germany, across the river from Mannheim, Eric Hamberg, who was sick with a fever, watched the tragic events unfold from his bedroom window: "SA men went up to our neighbors' apartment and took that nice family's bedding, threw it all out of the window and into the street, and then set it all on fire. I saw people laughing and dancing and being so happy that the Jews were getting something that they didn't expect."

The Nazis entered homes, dragged men out of bed and arrested them; thirty thousand Jewish men, ages sixteen to sixty, were shipped off to Buchenwald, Dachau, Gross Rosen, and Sachsenhausen concentration camps. They turned out to be the fortunate ones. They were told they could be released on the condition that they somehow procured a visa and proved to the Nazi authorities that they could leave the country in a short period of time. This put tremendous pressure on wives and relatives to find a way to get their husbands and children out of the camps.

Jews who had second-guessed and agonized over whether or not to emigrate were now desperate to leave. Applications for visas piled high in the offices of foreign consulates in every major German city; frantic Jews waited hours in lines that stretched around buildings and city blocks to plead their cases. Detached, unsympathetic consulate generals—known to deny applicants for any number of reasons, no matter how trivial—had the power over life and death. Medical records that revealed any history of surgeries or ailments were often grounds for rejection. Karl Goldsmith, who went with his family to the U.S. consulate in Stuttgart just after Kristallnacht, describes the indifference of the consulate general and his staff: "This was degradation at its worst. My father who had had cancer two years before I was born and had surgery was told by the vice council that he could not go to America. You cannot imagine the absolute fear, horror, and terror this produced in my family. It was a horrible experience for me, a seventeen-year-old boy to see my proud, sixty-year-old father degraded, insulted, pushed, and treated like dirt."

Steven Rose from Frankfurt, later in the U.S. Army Counterintelligence Corps, remembers a similar event at a U.S. consulate: "I had a cousin, a girl about the same age as me, who walked with a slight limp. Aside from that slight limp there was nothing wrong with her. Well, they denied her a visa and she became hysterical and then jumped out the window and killed herself. From then on, I had a personal vendetta against the Germans. I hated the bastards."

After the tragedy of the Anschluss and Kristallnacht, 180,000 German Jews fled to many of the countries that would take them. The British government offered some relief when it agreed to open its doors to 10,000 unaccompanied Jewish children via a rescue initiative called the *Kindertransport*. The United States, with a German-Austrian immigration quota of 27,370 per year that had never come close to being filled throughout the early and mid 1930s (reaching only 42 percent in 1937, the most yet at that time), allowed 50,000 German Jews to immigrate after Kristallnacht and before entering the war. The quota fill rate hit 100 percent in 1939.

SAFETY

When most former refugees recall their arrival in the United States, Great Britain, or Palestine (then a British Mandate), they speak of the immediate sense of relief after stepping off the boat and the comfort of knowing they were finally out of danger.

While the Depression in the United States continued to cast a dark shadow and jobs were difficult to come by, Jewish relief organizations—such as the Hebrew Immigrant Aid Society (HIAS) and the American Jewish Joint Distribution Committee (JDC)—labored to help refugees find jobs and accommodations. Nevertheless, for most it was a glorious time; refugees explored their new environments with great wonderment and enthusiasm. For Kurt Klein, a refugee from Walldorf, Germany, New York made quite an impression:

> I had seen New York City in films and photos, but I could hardly believe that I was there. Of course to a young boy that part was an adventure—to get out of the environment not only because of the perils imposed on me and my family, but just to travel to a place like that seemed immensely exciting to me. It meant that much more to me to see New York and discovering all it could offer. Even a subway ride was exciting.

For the younger refugees, it was a chance to make up for all of the lost years from their youth— they went back to school, learned English, and began to assimilate. Their vocational training received in Germany paid off in many cases, and getting jobs helped lift some of the burdens for those supporting their families. The refugee communities that desired to maintain roots while adjusting to their new environment settled in scattered, but closely-knit, communities. New York had its Washington Heights (called the "Fourth Reich"), Chicago its Hyde Park, and Los Angeles had yet another thriving Jewish community. Edmund Schloss, a refugee from Jesberg, Germany, whose family settled in the Hyde Park section of Chicago, enjoyed the familiarity of maintaining ties to the refugee community: "Within Hyde Park we had a big circle of friends and relatives and life became very comfortable. One could walk up 53rd Street and only hear German being spoken." The German newspaper, *Aufbau* (to rebuild), circulated among refugees and was an important source of news. During the war, the *Aufbau* dedicated a section to refugees in the armed forces entitled "Our Boys in the Army," which listed all who were fighting overseas, in Europe as well as in the Pacific.

Refugees closely followed the events in Europe with great concern. There was little doubt that war with Germany was imminent, and even the refugees who had considered themselves pacifists knew war was the only way to stop Hitler and possibly save their families.

Despite the Jewish refugees' feelings about the war, American and British immigration policy had yet to understand the unique antipathy that German Jewish immigrants felt toward their homeland or recognize the important skills they possessed. Those who had fled the Nazis were still categorized as Enemy Aliens, nationals of countries at war or in conflict with their host countries, and were not spared the rampant suspicion that their presence might prove to be an internal threat to their country's national security.

In Great Britain, there was increasing concern over a fifth column and suspicion that Nazi spies were hiding among the Austrian and German immigrant population. After France fell to Germany and the Luftwaffe began pummeling industrial cities in bombing raids over England, killing thousands of civilians, the British government rounded up male refugees it called Friendly Enemy Aliens and placed them in internment camps on the Isle of Man. In his book, *Striking Back: A Jewish Commando's War against the Nazis*, Peter Masters writes:

> Although we sympathized with our British hosts' concern about the threat of a fifth column of infiltrated spies posing as refugees, we also knew that we were the real thing: refugees. We had no trouble at all telling friend from foe, and we would have been happy to help our jailers identify any suspect elements among us, had there been any. We who had hoped to fight the common enemy were being held as prisoners by our own side, probably for the duration of the war—our war! What we wanted was to help.

Circumstances were not as extreme for refugees in the United States, though they did experience setbacks because of their status. In many cases, refugees had to turn in cameras and shortwave radios to authorities. Perhaps the greatest restriction was being prohibited from enlisting in the military until, in 1940, the Selective Training and Service Act was passed by the United

States Congress. The act required all men, including enemy aliens, eligible for military service to register for the draft. To their great delight, refugees were drafted into the military as early as 1940. In Great Britain, the privilege of enlistment was eventually granted to refugees, but they could only serve out the war in labor battalions in the Royal Pioneer Corps. Although a setback for those eager to get into the fight with Germany, it was a way out of the internment camps.

Revenge was a driving force motivating refugees to serve in the army, especially among those who had lived through Kristallnacht and spent time in a concentration camp. Refugees instinctively felt that if anyone should be inducted into the military to go and fight the Nazis, it should be them. John Slade, a thirty-four-year-old banker from Frankfurt, was working on Wall Street when he was seized with the urge to go to war: "I decided that if a guy from Oklahoma could fight against Hitler, then I, too, must fight." Amidst vestiges of suspicion of their national origins, this was a fighting chance to prove their loyalty and learn more about their new country. In the United States, it was also the fast track toward becoming naturalized citizens, something that refugees desired and strived to obtain. Nevertheless, it was their duty to serve the countries that had taken them in.

The Allies came to recognize the many strategic advantages in making use of the refugees' German language fluency—including the many local German dialects—as well as their motivation and willingness to help the war effort.

In the United States, fledgling intelligence agencies, like the Office of Strategic Services (OSS), singled out refugees who were only too keen to help provide any vital information that could be of use to the war effort: their knowledge of various regions and cities, locations of industries, factories, famous landmarks, Gestapo headquarters, train stations, and ports, as well as names of regional Nazi party leaders and mayors of towns. Joseph Persico, author of *Piercing the Reich: The Penetration of Nazi Germany by American Secret Agents during World War II* further explains, "Intelligence agencies even wanted the clothes off the refugees' backs. They wanted their wristwatches, pens, razors, wallets, luggage, and their underwear. The quality, fabric, and workmanship of a suit, could indicate the state of the German economy. The kind of steel in a razor might reveal something of German industrial processes."

Once the war came to the United States, refugees already in the military were pulled out of the ranks and placed in division intelligence sections. Early in the war, British intelligence—coming out of North Africa and France via Force Françaises de l'Interieur (FFI, or French Forces of the Interior)—was the best source of information for refugees to learn proficiently. Subsequently, they became instructors and taught officers and enlisted men basic German, German Army commands, and how to identify German uniforms, ranks, and insignia.

Not long after U.S. forces landed in North Africa and helped drive the German army off the continent, the U.S. government decided to centralize its intelligence operations in Hagerstown, Maryland, at Camp Ritchie. Between 1942 and 1945, thousands of refugees from the Nazis passed through Camp Ritchie, where they received highly specialized training that included learning the German table of organization, order of battle, interrogation of prisoners of war (IPW) techniques, combat exercises, field maneuvers, psychological warfare, and counterintelligence. Once out of Camp Ritchie, graduates filled the ranks of intelligence and interrogation units that were attached to different outfits all over Europe, and ultimately in American Military Government in Germany at the end of the war. Needless to say, a great many refugees served only in a combat capacity and ended up in frontline outfits; while they spoke German and could be a great source for translation and ad hoc frontline interrogation when needed, they also fought just like any other soldier.

CONVERSELY, JEWISH REFUGEES IN GREAT BRITAIN were sought out for their obvious linguistic advantages over the average British "Tommy." In 1942, Chief of Combined Operations Vice Admiral Lord Louis Mountbatten convinced Winston Churchill to create a unit of German-speaking soldiers of exceptional initiative and self-reliance and include them in the roster of No. 10 Inter-allied Commando/Special Services Brigades. They would become No. 3 Troop, 10 Inter-allied Commando. However, it was Churchill's idea to call them "X Troop," or the "British Troop;" it was a unit shrouded in mystery because of the very high concentration of German and Austrian Jews. Consequently, troops were ordered to Anglicize their names, create false personal histories, and don Church of England dog tags to conceal their identities in the event of capture. Unlike refugees serving in the U.S. Army, refugees serving in the British Army were not given citizenship. Since they were German nationals and not British citizens, they were not protected by the Geneva Convention and the Germans had the right to execute them in the event of capture. They became reconnaissance and weapons experts, but most importantly, they were remarkably skilled frontline interrogators.

Ultimately 3 Troop would not be known for its collective action as a unit; many were deployed alone or in small groups to units in and behind the frontline in the islands of Crete and Sicily and mainland Italy, and they also participated in the Dieppe Raid in occupied France. The troop was disbanded and its members were attached to other units just prior to D-Day.

Great Britain's Friendly Enemy Aliens steadily trickled out of the Royal Pioneer Corps and did eventually see action in North Africa and later the European Theater of Operations (ETO), as did those who entered the British Army in Palestine and other countries in the British Empire. By 1940, approximately 280,000 Jews had left Germany and 117,000 left Austria. Nearly 13,000 German and Austrian refugees—men and women—served in the British Armed Forces. Of the 95,000 German and Austrian Jews who had immigrated to the United States, it is estimated that 9,500 fought in the U.S. armed forces—the second highest concentration of German/Austrian refugees serving with the Allies.

The extraordinary, if not unprecedented, circumstances that led to this impressive number of Allied refugee soldiers during that period was best summed up by historian Arnold Pauker, a former German refugee and soldier in the British Army: "It is terrible to have to say this but in one respect we German Jews were quite lucky that Hitler came for us first. This meant that the majority was able to flee or immigrate in time, and among this number the younger generation was heavily represented. When the war broke out, there were many of military age, who had been waiting for an opportunity to fight against Nazi Germany."

Chapter 1

SIEGMUND SPIEGEL

GERA, GERMANY

1st Infantry Division
North Africa, Sicily, and European
Theater of Operations

*Siegmund Spiegel was one of three children born to Jacob and
Sara Spiegel in Gera, Germany, a town just south of Leipzig.
His older brother, Norbert, left for Palestine in 1935; his sister,
Betty, went to the United States in 1936 and Sig followed two
years later in 1938. His parents were deported to Poland in 1938
and were last heard from in 1940. He was drafted into the U.S.
Army in 1941 and assigned to the 1st Infantry Division. He is
pictured above in North Africa, 1942.*

When Hitler took over, Nazi Stormtroopers paraded up and down the streets of Gera, my hometown, singing: *"Wenn's Judenblut vom Messer spritzt, dann geht's nochmal so gut"* (When Jewish blood squirts under knives, then all goes doubly well). It seemed as though we were always sitting at the edge of our seats and there was constant crisis. We could no longer associate with our school friends because they were Aryans and we were not. So naturally, strong bonds were made between the Jewish boys. Finally, in April 1933 my father was called to the Gymnasium and told, "Mr. Spiegel, take your son out of our school, we want the school to be *Judenrein.*" That was the end of my formal education at the age of fourteen. We knew that while we were born in Germany, this was no longer home and it would never be. So, I looked around for a job because it seemed the only way one could exist was to learn a trade and work with one's hands. So I learned to be a bricklayer.

My brother, Norbert, and I were ardent Zionists. He became very active in the Hechalutz, a Zionist organization in Germany, and from the age of eighteen he assumed high leadership positions in Berlin. In 1935 my brother was to emigrate from Germany to Palestine. On the evening he was to leave, we were gathered at home having our last supper as a family and prepared to take him to the railroad station (to Trieste, Italy, where he would board a ship for Palestine) when suddenly my mother collapsed from a stroke. Obviously, it was because her first child was going to leave and she knew all too well that she may never see him again. Yet the decision had to be made—he had to leave and save himself. Upon our return from the station, we ultimately had to commit our mother to a hospital from which she was thrown out a few days later. They did not want to take a Jewish patient, and so we found a Jewish hospital in Leipzig, where I, too, had to say goodbye to her a few years later.

My sister left for the United States in April 1936 just after taking her last exam for her doctorate. At the age of sixteen I became the sole bread earner in my family, working as a bricklayer apprentice until I left in August 1938.

I reached the United States as a refugee in the fall of 1938; the ship landed in Hoboken, New Jersey, just outside of New York City, and my sister picked me up. On the subway into the city, whenever my sister asked me a question I would look around and quietly answer her until she said, "You don't have to be afraid anymore, you can talk openly. You don't have to look around to see if someone is watching you." That made a real impression on me, aside from the dirt of New York City.

That October, my parents were rounded up and deported to Poland because they had not been born in Germany. They had come from Galicia, which had become part of Poland after World War I, so that was where they were sent. My mother could not walk at the time and was permitted to stay in the hospital in Leipzig, but my father still had to leave. She opted to be with my father and they were both shipped off.

The war in Europe started in 1939 when the Germans invaded Poland, and my parents were fortunate enough to get to the Soviet-occupied area of Poland; so, we were still able to communicate with them. However, when the Germans overran that part of Poland and invaded Russia in 1941, communication quickly broke down and we no longer heard from them.

I became obsessed with joining the American army once war broke out in Europe in September because it was important to me to fight against Nazi Germany, the country of my birth. At first my application was declined on the basis of not being a citizen of the United States. I was an "Enemy Alien." But, being told that I could volunteer for the draft, it gave me an opportunity to pursue this goal, and I found myself inducted on November 12, 1941, before America entered the war.

Because the army felt it necessary to keep me, an immigrant from Germany, "under surveillance" for fear that I might be a Nazi spy, I was not given the privilege of joining the combat engineers, which I had chosen as my branch of service, but was assigned to receive my basic training in the infantry. At the same time, the 1st Infantry Division, "the Big Red One," needed personnel, so I was sent to Camp Blanding, Florida, as a member of a heavy weapons platoon.

Hardly a week had passed when I received the order to appear at the G-2 Section (Intelligence) of division headquarters (HQ). It was obvious that my personal record indicated my German background and my facility with the language made me a candidate to serve in the division's intelligence section. No sooner had I been assigned than I was sent on detached service to a training school of II Corps, to act as an instructor to members of the 1st Infantry Division, the 36th Infantry Division and the 1st Cavalry Regiment to teach some of their intelligence personnel German commands and drill them in German, as well as teach them identification of German uniforms, ranks, and insignia. I was promoted to technician fourth grade (sergeant's stripes with a "T"). Back at division, I immediately went into study of the German "order of battle" in which I became highly proficient.

After I became a fixture in the Big Red One's G-2 Section, I was asked to attend a dinner of the division HQ's noncommissioned officer (NCO) club. It was a rather prestigious club made up mostly of longtime members of the division staff, many regular army men, and a few draftees. There were very few Jews among them, and certainly no one who spoke with an accent. I specifically recall a master sergeant of one of the division sections (G-3) who distrusted me, not only because I was Jewish, but also because I was German and spoke with an accent.

After many drinks and dinner, and general cajoling, I got up and asked to be heard. I expressed my thanks for having been asked to attend and said that I was proud of being in the U.S. Army with this group, but especially proud to be with a group that was helping me, as I was helping them, to fight and hopefully to defeat the German enemy from whom I was fortunate to have been able to escape. There was roaring applause—a standing ovation. After much handshaking and as we were ready to leave, I passed a group of other higher noncoms, and heard that particular master sergeant say to the others, "You know, this guy is all right." I must say that the inclusion meant a great deal, but it didn't make me elated, which I didn't feel until I had the chance to confront the Germans.

WHEN THE DIVISION WAS READY TO LEAVE for Europe, it suddenly became apparent that I was not yet a citizen. The army at that time would not take noncitizens overseas, so while at the staging center at Fort Indiantown Gap, Pennsylvania, I was restricted to my office. After several hours an MP escorted me to the G-2 Section. Lieutenant Colonel Porter, my commanding officer, told me that at Gen. Terry de la Mesa Allen's request, the FBI had conducted an investigation of me as to my trustworthiness, since it was the general's wish that I leave for Europe with the division. He pointed to a man in civilian clothing who was sitting at a desk and who then interviewed me for some time, having interrogated all my colleagues previously. Upon conclusion of the interrogation, he announced to Colonel Porter that I would not be a "traitor to America." The following day, I was taken in a command car to a federal court in Philadelphia, where at a special session, I was sworn in as a citizen on July 29, 1942. The following day the division left for New York to embark on the *Queen Mary* for England.

No sooner did we arrive in England and were quartered at Tidworth Barracks, an old English military base, than intensive planning commenced for the invasion of North Africa. After extensive maneuvers off the coast of Scotland, we rendezvoused with an even larger armada out of New York in the mid-Atlantic, slipping at night through the Straits of Gibraltar into the Mediterranean, and past Oran, in a ploy to keep the Germans off-guard. Then we turned back to hit the beaches near Oran. My own baptism of fire occurred at the break of dawn on D-day, as I approached North Africa in an LCA (an assault landing craft for about forty men) with members of the advanced echelon of the 1st Division's general staff. The LCA, having hit a sandbar, stopped abruptly and lowered its front ramp, thus instantly signaling us to jump off. I hit a low spot and found myself in water up to my armpits. At that time, even the money belt I was wearing—carrying $20 Canadian gold pieces to be used if necessary to "buy" tactical information from the locals—helped weigh me down, in addition to my rifle, ammo, and field pack.

I never would have thought that the first "enemy" confronting us in Africa would be the French Foreign Legion, which after three days of intensive combat finally severed itself from its Vichy government ties, and later became our valiant ally. Our 18th Infantry Regiment lost hundreds of men during this three-day encounter. The cemetery in St. Cloud near Oran attests to the severity of the combat.

As soon as the initial engagement with the French Foreign Legion was completed and we were consolidating our forces in Oran, the campaign to oust German Field Marshal Erwin Rommel from Africa made us push east, through Algeria into Tunisia. To describe the Tunisian Campaign, its rugged terrain, its fierce battles—from the battle near El Guettar in the south, where we had no air night fighters to protect us from the constant night attacks by German JU 88 planes, to the loss of much of our armor at Kasserine Pass—until conclusion of the campaign would fill volumes. Our foxholes, protecting us from the deadly shrapnel of antipersonnel bombs, were literally the size of a grave. The toughness of the soldiers of Hermann Goering's Fallschirmjaeger Regiment and their arrogance after capture was proof of the Nazi's superbly working war machine.

The winter in Tunisia was wet and bitterly cold; it even snowed from time to time. At one point I came down with a severe cold and ran a temperature and was sent to the nearest field hospital, which was in the adjacent British sector in a large tent in which battle casualties, sick and shell-shocked soldiers, shared the space. It was a zoo. I still see the British nurse in front of me shaking me at about midnight to wake me up to take the sleeping pill that she had neglected to give me hours earlier. Needless to say, the screaming of the shell-shocked cases then kept me awake all night.

As the 1st Division moved east, our G-2 Section had attached a captain from the French Foreign Legion, he being a "specialist" in the treatment of the natives, together with two French sergeants. His name was Captain Mellish. He was an officer in the Imperial Russian Army in World War I, who had escaped to France during the Russian Revolution and then joined the Foreign Legion. Unlike other officers, he did not care much for "spit and polish," but instead wore American olive drabs (ODs) and a helmet liner, and had a Luger pistol tucked in his belt.

In most instances, he was the one who had contact with the local Arabs, in connection with obtaining information about German positions. On one such occasion, right near the front lines, I saw him talk to an Arab who had come across the German lines and pay him for the information he seemed to have just received, and the Arab turned and was obviously heading back to cross into enemy territory. Right after he had turned, I saw Captain Mellish pull out his Luger, shooting the Arab. When I confronted him with what he just did and why—after all he had just obtained information—his answer simply was: "The Arab is no good. He sells me information and he sells the enemy information." That was a real lesson to learn.

As we entered the outskirts of the city of Tunis, I saw many old natives squatting near the road begging, some of them holding out recognizable charity canisters. I stopped short after I recognized some of them to be Tzeduka (Charity) boxes used by Jews collecting for charitable causes. I couldn't help but being totally overwhelmed and I emptied my pockets.

The campaign finished and I had received orders to fly to Algiers for detached service at Allied Forces HQ (AFHQ), General Alexander's HQ, where I was to meet British Major Marsden. He was conducting examinations of captured German documents to extract tactical and strategically important information, wherein my experience with interrogation of prisoners and examination of documents captured in the field was to aid in this project. Then, Sicily became our next objective.

The 1st Division was designated to invade Sicily in August 1943, with the landing to take place near Gela at the South Coast. Again, approaching the beach on an LCA in the early morning hours on D-day, the reception was a hot one: German artillery had zeroed its 88 guns, located in the mountains beyond the beach, on our sector. I vividly recall the blasts as I jumped off the LCA and ran ashore. The enemy fire was so heavy that all of us sought cover by making ourselves as little a target as possible. Flat on the ground, I found myself, as most others, using my helmet to dig deeper into the sand in order to survive. Quite some time passed until the enemy fire weakened, and we advanced stealthily among the bodies and war material abandoned or destroyed until we were able to reach cover at higher ground.

It was Sicily that ultimately produced some of the heaviest fighting we encountered. Crack troops of Rommel's Afrika Korps, which had managed to escape Africa, had consolidated their positions in Sicily to still offer resistance. Having retreated from Africa to Sicily, the German supply lines were shortened. The Italian mainland being adjacent to the island, supplies flowed more easily. In Troina, I came across letters in a bunker we had just overrun in which German soldiers were writing home of the heaviest fighting they had been exposed to and expressing their doubts if ever they would see their home again. One of these letters was so remarkable that I translated it immediately. It was sent back to Washington, and some time later I received a copy of a War Department publication wherein this translation was published.

Our prisoner of war compound was in an open field, separated by barbed wire and guarded by MPs. The Italian prisoners were kept separate from the Germans. Among the German prisoners, the enlisted men were separated from the noncommissioned officers, who in turn were separated from their officers. On one occasion just days into the campaign, I went to talk to a master sergeant of a chemical warfare battalion. He was middle-aged, a family man, totally devoid of the arrogance of his commanding officer. As I approached him, I heard his major call to him in German across the barbed wire concertinas, urging him not to give me any information. I called back to him in rather rough German to mind his own business and keep quiet. When he continued harassing his master sergeant I responded in much harsher language. When he still was not convinced that it would be best for him to remain quiet, I alluded to him, in no uncertain terms, using a language unbecoming an officer, to mind his own business. At that point he became so enraged that he demanded to talk to the commander of the "pound."

When my captain slowly meandered down toward the enclosure where the officers were kept, I heard him ask what the problems were. Then the German major excitedly stated that he is an officer and he demands respect, and that this sergeant, pointing toward me, had insulted him and that he demanded that I be punished. At this point, our captain, the pound commander, pointing toward me asked him, "Do you mean him?" The German responded: "*Jawohl*" (Yes). The captain then sarcastically answered, "Impossible, he doesn't even speak German." On another occasion a fanatical Schutzstaffel (SS) prisoner blew smoke in my face and I gave him the back of my hand. I was a tough little guy.

Another time I got furious at some GIs who were handing their cigarettes to the prisoners. I said, "What do you think this is, a tennis match? A few minutes ago these men were trying to kill you. Let them smoke their own garbage." Needless to say, it was gratifying to see Germans humbled.

The Jewish holidays came around and since the 1st Division, being made up mostly of men from New York, Delaware, and Massachusetts, had a large contingent of Jews, among whom was Lieutenant Colonel Gara, the commanding officer of the 1st Engineering Battalion, and many others. The chaplain of the 18th Infantry Regiment, Captain Stone, was a rabbi from Massachusetts. For Yom Kippur, a motion picture theater in Licata was used for services, and truckloads of men came from various parts of the division. Some half dozen or so noncoms from division headquarters went by truck early in the morning to attend services. At around noon, these services were recessed to be continued later on in the afternoon. Those of us from HQ walked the streets of Licata and saw a very nice-appearing, clean-looking restaurant. It bore a sign in the window: "Off Limits to United States Troops." Nevertheless, we went in and were only too happily greeted by the owner, who indicated to us that the reason this sign was in the window was that the U.S. occupying forces did not want to deprive the local population of any food. Yet he said that there was plenty and he would be happy to serve us.

No sooner had we ordered wine and pasta when the door opened and in came two MPs, one being Sergeant Eddy, whom all of us knew very well. He was apologetic, saying he had to take our names and serial numbers and report us. Needless to say, we lost our appetite. I already saw in my mind the disappearance of my sergeant's stripes. Later that evening, I received a telephone call from Major Lancer, the division provost marshal. It was Major Lancer with whom I had developed a mutual respect over several months, since I kept a situation map as a hobby, showing the war's progress throughout Europe, including the Russian front, based on intelligence reports reaching us daily from English, French, and Eastern European sources, and he wanted to be kept abreast as to the war's progress. He started the conversation as follows:

"Sergeant, do you know what I have on my desk?"

My response: "I am afraid so, Major."

He continued, "I wouldn't worry about that, but how you as a Jew could be in an off-limits restaurant, eating on Yom Kippur, that you have to make up with your Maker!"

One of the more memorable events during the Sicilian campaign was when General Patton had slapped one of the men of the 1st Division, after calling him a coward while he was awaiting admission into the field hospital, having been ordered there by one of his superiors. This had caused a national uproar, resulting ultimately in an order from Washington that Patton himself had to apologize to the troops for this behavior. When the campaign was over, one afternoon the entire division was ordered to assemble on a large field in South Sicily, to await the general's arrival. Before he came, the chief of staff of the 1st Division, Colonel Mason, mounted the platform and issued the following command: "There will be no booing when the general gets here!"

Patton came wearing his pearl-handled pistols on his sides, mounted the platform, and in rough language talked of himself as only being interested in the objective, of being the person who does not pussyfoot around things and, in his wish to get things done, he may have overstepped the bounds of common behavior, but he should not be blamed because it was done in this spirit. As a whole, he spoke down to the men, making them feel as if he thought their intellect would not allow a normal tone of conversation. After this "apology" was rendered, I went back to our base, into the "war room," where I found myself in the company of Lieutenant Colonel Curtis and Major Gale. When Major Gale asked Colonel Curtis what he thought of Patton's speech, the colonel—a most refined West Point graduate, a real gentleman—responded, "Paul, listening to the general's speech, to me, was as if I heard my own mother use the word 'shit.'"

During both the African and Sicilian campaigns, as well as later on, I corresponded with my brother, Norbert Spiegel (AKA Nachum Golan, the commander of the famous Golani Brigade during Israel's War of Independence). He had joined the British Army in Palestine in 1939 as a member of one its Jewish outfits and became the sergeant major of its 1st Battalion.

When I found myself in Africa, so did he, and Rommel was between us. When we left for Sicily, he was still in Africa, but then participated in the invasion of Italy. When I finally left Europe for thirty days of R&R in April 1945, his unit came from Italy to Belgium, where he then participated in the liberation of the Bergen-Belsen concentration camp. Thus, two brothers in Allied Armies, fighting on the same continents, yet never reaching each other, had all correspondence being funneled through the army post office (APO), reaching us weeks after they were written, though the distance separating us may at best have been a hundred miles or less, It took twenty-five years from the time I had last seen him in 1935 until we finally were reunited in December 1959.

Having determined that the invasion of the Italian mainland went satisfactorily, our division was reassigned to Great Britain. Thus in the late fall of 1943, we prepared to leave. Much to all our amazement, we were to board the *Reina Del Pacifico*, a British merchant ship that had carried us from Scotland to the invasion of North Africa. Being tired then of mutton stew three times daily, the rumor that she had been sunk had circulated shortly after the African invasion, not to anyone's regret, but here she was again to carry us back to England.

Reaching Britain, Gen. Terry Allen, having been relieved in Sicily to return to the U.S. to train the 104th Division, which he later brought back to Europe for its famous drive into Germany, was replaced by Gen. Clarence Huebner, who took command of the division. It was under him that even members of the general staff had to participate in frequent "close order drills." Needless to say, he had observed a certain degree of sloppiness of military bearing of our troops, who too often had stared in the eye of death during combat. This did not endear him initially to those seasoned veterans, but obviously he knew what he was doing. It appeared it was necessary to instill properly soldiering demeanor.

There in England, I delved heavily into reports of the German order of battle, to a point where information of many German units was at my fingertips, even to the point of how many men were left in certain companies and what morale problems existed between a certain company commander and his men. Frequently, such information totally disarmed some prisoners of war when being confronted with it by me.

While also there, I had the opportunity to go to London from time to time, where not only had I located a girl from Gera (my hometown) who had escaped to England, but also frequented Jewish service clubs with other comrades. The Jewish community of England reached out to Jewish soldiers from other countries, enabling them to spend the Sabbath or other holidays with a family.

In the late fall, I was sent to Plymouth, a port city in the south of England, to work in some of the chief planning offices for operation Overlord—the invasion of Europe. It was there that we worked closely with British, Canadian, and French counterparts, incorporating naval, air, and ground forces specialists. Detailed studies of what were later to become Omaha Beach, Utah Beach, and other sectors were studied in most minute detail. This planning not only pertained to the U.S. targets, but incorporated British and Canadian sectors as well.

Sometime in April 1944, I received a call from the British Military Intelligence office. It came from Major Marsden, whom I had last seen in Algiers at the conclusion of the North African campaign. He was concerned with establishing a special section within the G-2 branch of Supreme Headquarters Allied Expeditionary Forces (SHAEF), General Eisenhower's command. The G-2 branch would evaluate enemy documents to rapidly extract both tactical and strategic information. He wanted me to join this group.

It was just about that time when an order came from SHAEF that higher headquarters could not initiate the transfers of personnel from lower headquarters, and thus deprive field units of valuable personnel. He asked me to phrase a request for transfer, indicating that an opening existed for me in his unit, wherein my contribution to the war effort would be of higher overall value than remaining at division level, thus also giving me a personal opportunity to advance in grade. So I submitted my request to the chief of staff of the division, Colonel Mason. The following day I found it back on my desk, Colonel Mason having written across in red pencil, "Disapproved." I called Major Marsden and informed him of this.

Just about that time, when we were working feverishly to prepare for the invasion, it seemed SHAEF Headquarters had succeeded in convincing the chief of staff to allow me to transfer. Thus three days before the invasion, I left the 1st Division to travel to London and go to the offices of the G-2 Document Section in the Kensington area of London. The place was swarming with noncoms of higher grades than my own—master sergeants, technical sergeants, staff sergeants—in addition to enumerable young officers. When Major Marsden spotted me, he shook my hand vigorously and said, "Sergeant, I am delighted you made it here. You are the only man with field experience. You will lead our advanced echelon into Normandy." This was certainly not what I had expected. I had finally looked forward to sleeping in a bed with sheets and, after two exhausting campaigns, had thought that I would spend some time in the rear.

Now it was up to me to establish contact with the forward headquarters of First Army, in order to assist in instant evaluation of enemy documents falling into our forces' hands. I was assigned to a three-man team to leave for Normandy with one jeep. We landed in Omaha Beach days after D-Day, unattached, unsupported, groping our way, supplying ourselves from wherever we ran into combat units. I carried an order originating from SHAEF that read:

"Restricted"

To Sergeant Siegmund Spiegel 32190831, Headquarters Detachment SHAEF

1. This is to certify that the above named enlisted man has been directed to proceed by rail on or about June 1944 from present station to Southampton, England, reporting upon arrival to the Port Commander for surface transportation to carry out an Assigned Mission.

By command of General Eisenhower:

E. C. Boehnke Colonel AGD

Adjutant General

We tried as far as possible to make contact with the Canadian First Army and the British First Army, in addition to our own units, relaying whatever gathered information we had laterally. We occupied a farmhouse as our temporary headquarters, which just had days before been evacuated by a German Army unit that had attached a battalion of Ukrainians serving in the German Army. No sooner had we gotten there than we got a hold of the personal diary of German Field Marshal Kluge. What a revelation! It described in detail his arguments with Hitler, contradicting Hitler's wishes in execution of the defense of Normandy, and some of the methods demanded by Hitler as being militarily impractical. The entire book was translated overnight, typed on stencils, run off, and distributed laterally to the various units confronting Kluge, forwarded to the rear, and sent back to England. Within a *day* (almost impossible in those days), broadcasts emanating from England destined to reach German troops quoted excerpts from this diary verbatim. Ultimately, Field Marshal Kluge died by his own hand.

Early in August the breakout of Normandy occurred. After the fall of St. Lo, a city for all intents and purposes totally destroyed, the lines became fluid. It was then that on August 7, 1944, having learned that German Army headquarters near Mayenne had been overrun, our team was to proceed to the Third Army G-2 Section. By the time we reached there, the frontline had again changed, and instead, we were to head toward Falaise. As we approached Vire, even small arms fire became hectic, and our infantry troops lay in ditches near a road intersection. We stopped and checked with an MP as to the current situation. He indicated that we could not proceed through the village but would have to bypass it.

We made our way down into a valley on a one-lane farm road when the "burp" noises of German submachine guns became nearer and nearer. It was there that I observed to Captain Curts that the valley was "too still." Even with the noises from small arms fire, it gave this whole scene a feeling of eeriness. I even recall using the German word *unheimlich* (eerie, uncanny) then. Just then all hell broke loose. Maybe seconds, maybe minutes, had elapsed when I found myself raising my head and looking around. Our jeep stood mangled across the road and me twenty yards distance from it. Captain Curts was lying on the road, his legs inside his combat boots swelling, seeming to burst the leather. The corporal, Trombley, was crouching in a ditch and bleeding profusely from his right hand where shrapnel had penetrated it.

At first impulse I thought we had a direct hit from an artillery shell. I crouched over the captain, trying to administer first aid to whatever extent possible, while Trombley was tying a tourniquet around his own arm. I remembered that just nearby, where we last had talked to the MP, there was a forward first aid station. I tried to make my way back to get them to evacuate the captain and the corporal. In the confusion of combat and operating strictly on instinct, I must have crawled the wrong way, further into German territory; I suddenly noticed a stack of mines not yet buried, and some hastily covered. I knew then that we had hit a "Teller" Mine (thirteen pounds of explosives). I turned quickly, even certain of hearing German voices near me, and made my way back.

I found the first aid station where the medics immediately wanted to evacuate me, but I insisted on leading them down to the scene of the blow up. We were all brought back and immediately taken farther back to where ambulances were ready to take casualties to the nearest field hospital. My carbine was lost, but I had to surrender my .45 pistol, which I carried at my side for some time. I was sent to the field hospital, where I was admitted with multiple contusions and injuries to my left knee and ribs, blast burns, and shock. The captain's legs were both shattered.

There I was on a cot, in a tent when the German counterattack was underway (it captured one of our field hospitals). Convoys of ambulances brought heavily wounded GIs in, and they remained on their stretchers set on the barren floor. When I saw this happening, I called the hospital administration officer and asked to be discharged, since my condition was not anywhere as serious as the men who didn't have a cot.

That morning, an orderly came with a batch of *Stars and Stripes*, which had just arrived from England. In it I saw a brief item that got me very excited: the Russian army had liberated Lwow, a city in Poland where I last knew my parents had lived. Of course, I was not aware then of what had happened in the interim to Jews, including my poor parents, who were massacred in Lwow by the Germans in the summer of 1941. Just then a Red Cross girl entered our tent asking us whether we needed writing paper, razor blades, or whatever else she had on hand to distribute. I asked her, "You are with the American Red Cross, right? You have contact with the International Red Cross?" When she nodded her response, I showed her the article in the paper, gave her my parents' names and last known address in Lwow, and asked her to immediately initiate steps to locate them through the International Red Cross. She looked at me as if I were shell-shocked, not having expected that a wounded soldier would worry about something happening on a front far removed from current combat in Western Europe. I assured her that I had all my senses and got her assurance that I would hear from the Red Cross. Sixty years later and I am still waiting.

I was sent back to England to recuperate on a C-47, which practically skimmed the waves of the English Channel, even to the point that spray hit the windows. When I asked one of the crew why he was flying so low, he explained to me that if he were to fly at the normal altitude, his silhouette would appear in the sky and either German fighter planes or even U-boats could shoot him down, whereas when he skipped the waves, the plane made no silhouette. We were able to reach Dover, and then the plane gained altitude to scale the cliffs.

After one week I returned to London and, immediately thereafter, back to Normandy to rejoin my unit. In the interim, Paris had been liberated. Our unit moved into an apartment on Avenue Fock, one of the more attractive avenues in Paris emanating from the Etoile and the Arc de Triomphe. The house we had occupied, as in most other instances, had just been vacated by German officers. To the best of my recollection, the owners of the building either had to flee or were deported by the Germans because they were Jews.

For a few days, we were much concerned with rounding up French collaborators with the Germans, and German officers who were attempting to continue to live underground in Paris. On one such mission I had teamed up with a lieutenant commander of the U.S. Navy, a middle-aged, midwestern schoolteacher who appeared to have received his commission through somebody he knew, rather than what he knew about intelligence matters. He relied fully on my guidance in telling him what could and could not be confiscated as we searched businesses and the homes of those who had worked closely with the Germans. Our stay in Paris did not last too long, since the front moved rapidly eastward.

From there it was onto Rheims, where it was sad to see the cathedral surrounded by sandbags to at least a story or higher to avoid the destruction of this historic gothic masterpiece by the instruments of war.

As soon as the first major German city, Aachen, was in the process of being captured, three of us from my team immediately went in. What a strange sensation: much destruction; white sheets and rags hanging from windows and from building ruins; and to me, personally, a feeling of deep satisfaction. While at that time I did not know what fate my parents and the millions of others of Jews had met, there was a satisfaction in seeing the "invincible" Third Reich having suffered a major defeat on its own soil. Not too many civilians were in town. Destruction was all over. Being on the west side of the Rhine River, it had been cut off from supplies reaching it from east of the river. Those civilians who we interrogated all swore that they would not have put up resistance had it not been for their being forced to do so by the Nazi officials. Unfortunately, it took quite a while before the river finally could be crossed.

As THE LATTER PART OF DECEMBER NEARED, the Germans commenced an all-out attack in the Ardennes with the aim of cutting through to Antwerp, thereby separating the American forces from the British. This began to be preceded by their dropping German soldiers in captured American uniforms behind American lines and attempting to raise havoc in our supply distribution.

Our MPs were alerted that any small group of soldiers or any army vehicle traveling alone would have to be stopped to ascertain that the men in American uniforms were actually Americans. Some of the Germans spoke English so well, some even without an accent, that trick questions were used to trip them up. For instance, some of the men stopped were asked to recite the words of the latest Frank Sinatra hit record, or to name the team who won the baseball championship, against whom they played, and by what score. This caused a problem with some of the men on my team, most of whom spoke with an accent. In one instance, one of our jeeps had attached to it a captured German trailer. When it was stopped by the MPs, one MP jokingly started a conversation as to "how many German soldiers are you hiding in the trailer." The staff sergeant, who spoke with an accent that could be cut with a knife, responded, "If you donn't belliff us, vy donn't you look in de back." It took some doing to convince the MPs whose side he was on.

The German attack proceeded rather rapidly. Our troops, who until this time never had been forced to retreat, suddenly found themselves overwhelmed. The retreat, in many instances, had practically become a rout. Especially rear echelon units that suddenly found themselves confronted by enemy forces, rather than having combat troops protect them, left much equipment behind and retreated. Finally the Germans were halted in their tracks. The few days between Christmas and New Year's in Brussels were comfortable. New Year's morning in Brussels droned from the enumerable airplanes, bombers, and fighters flying over the city toward the Bastogne area to stop the German attack and relieve the encircled American troops. The B-17 and B-24 formations, flying high, escorted by swift-flying fighter planes, left a magnificent pattern of vapor trails streaking the clear blue sky. It didn't take long for the back of the German attack to be broken and the ring around our encircled troops to be opened by our ground forces, helped by the aerial poundings.

By this time, I had close to three years overseas with no furlough and certainly the longest time overseas of our SHAEF unit. Toward the middle of March, the orders were cut for me to report to Le Havre for shipment back to the United States. When I got there, the military encampments around Le Havre were filled with tired and exhausted combat troops ready to find some rest in the States. We boarded a merchant ship outfitted as a hospital ship carrying seriously wounded soldiers from the front. Those of us who were well were made to help take care of the injured and sick soldiers. Being a senior noncom, the other duties assigned me were very light: I was to take care of feeding those men who had wired jaws, mostly caused by bullets or shrapnel having broken or demolished parts of their faces.

After several days on the Atlantic, an announcement came over the PA system that said, "Gentlemen, we just slipped inside the submarine net surrounding Boston Harbor!" Even remembering this particular moment still gives me the chills. It was at that moment that I felt as if a ton of weight was lifted off my chest. I didn't realize that I had carried this "load" with me ever since I encountered enemy fire and didn't leave me until, at that moment, I felt secure. After debarking we were taken to Camp Miles Standish to receive new uniforms. I called my girlfriend Ruth and my sister Betty in New York to tell them the news that I was back.

The next few days were hectic, to say the least: friends had to be called and seen, and above all, I had enumerable lists of families of comrades who asked me to be in touch with them, make a personal call, and even a visit to assure them that they were okay. On April 13, hardly a week after my return, Ruth and I were married, and on June 7, 1945, I received my discharge from the army. The reason: "Convenience of the Government."

At the beginning of World War II, I was young. I was eager to fight, fight as a Jew against Nazi Germany. I could not have lived with myself had I not played an active part. Having now, on many trips to Europe, revisited so many of the places which then held my life in the palm of their hands, and having had a chance in retrospect of sixty-plus years to reflect on the events played out over my close to four years in the service, I am thankful to have had the opportunity to relive them. Although circumstances and daily happenings make me at times wonder if it was worth it, the answer always comes back, as clear as can be: I wouldn't want to have missed it!

Siegmund Spiegel is a retired architect and the recipient of many awards for housing, planning, commercial, and institutional projects in New York State. He cofounded the Black-Jewish Coalition of Long Island and the Nassau County Holocaust Commission, and was the designer of the Holocaust Memorial and Education Center. Spiegel maintains an active schedule, even in his retirement in Miami, and continues to write articles for architecture magazines and lectures frequently about the Holocaust and human rights violations.

Chapter 2

JERRY BECHHOFER

FÜRTH, GERMANY

938 Field Artillery Battalion,
U.S. Army
North Africa and European Theater of Operations

*Jerry Bechhofer came from Fürth in northern Bavaria. He
was seventeen when he came to the United States in November
1939, just two months after the outbreak of war in Europe.
His last home in Germany before emigrating was Frankfurt
am Main. He received the Bronze Star in Germany, 1945
(above photograph, Bechhofer at right).*

We have my father's family documented back to the sixteenth century. At that time, the family came from Herrieden to Bechhofen in middle Franconia, Germany. Until the beginning of the nineteenth century, most Jewish families in southern Germany did not have family names. A decree of Napoleon declared that every family must choose a last name. In 1813 our family took the name *Bechhoefer*—translation: someone who lives in Bechhofen.

My father was born in 1888, one of thirteen children, my mother in Langenselbold in 1898, one of five daughters. Around 1902, my father became a baker in the town of Kitzingen. He was drafted into the German Army in 1914, served until the end of World War I in various countries in the East, and became a prisoner. Trying unsuccessfully to escape, he had to stay an extra year and came back to Germany in 1920. He met my mother—the boss's daughter—while working in her father's establishment, and they married in July 1921.

I was born in 1922, the same year my father started a hides and skins trading business in Fürth, Bavaria.

My first school attendance was in the Jewish community school in Fürth, a town which is famous because my classmate, Henry Kissinger, comes from there. We went to school together in Fürth. He was in the second grade and I was in the third, but we were in one classroom. My brother was a playmate of his; we were buddies and played together quite often. In 1931, due to adverse economic conditions, my parents moved from Fürth to Bechhofen. When I came to the school in Bechhofen there were only three other Jewish children, so naturally all my friends were not Jews, and relations with them were normal. Most of the people my father did business with were non-Jews. We had no problems with any of them. From 1935 to 1936, I attended the Jewish Preparatory School in Burgpreppach (near Bamberg).

After Hitler came in 1933, we watched with ever-increasing apprehension how people emigrated. Emigration became more difficult, especially to America, because of the infamous quota system. Strangely enough—or maybe not so strange—my father's business was doing relatively well after the Nazis came to power, which made immigration not such a great necessity. My parents, like many Jews, thought and hoped that the ever-increasing Nazi anti-Jewish propaganda would subside. How wrong not only we were, but the whole world!

At the time of Kristallnacht, my brother Fred and I boarded with a woman in Fürth. We heard window panes of a store near us shatter during the night, but knew nothing until three Brownshirts came to our door and commanded us to get ready to go with them. They marched us to a central place in the middle of town, where all the Jews—old men, young men, women, and children—were assembled. No announcements of any kind were made. Around 10:30 a.m. the men were told to march to an assembly hall, which had been donated to the city of Fürth by the Jewish Berolzheimer family as a library and intellectual retreat. Then women and young men under the age of eighteen were told to go home. All men over eighteen were escorted into the main hall, where some were taken to the stage and beaten. Most of them were brought to the train station and shipped to the infamous concentration camp in Dachau.

I was courageous enough to make my way to our synagogue, which was burning. I imagined that I saw my own tallis (prayer shawl) go up in flames. In Frankfurt, my father escaped being arrested probably by bribing a Nazi functionary.

The full extent of the crime of Kristallnacht settled on people's awareness only months and years later, and what followed still remains incomprehensible for many. The Nazis put out the story that this whole Kristallnacht episode was a spontaneous reaction of the German people because a minor official in the German Embassy in Paris had been shot. How untrue that was. I became aware of this when we (the U.S. Army) captured the documents that told each Nazi party official how to conduct the actions on the night of November 9 and the day of November 10. It was all planned with typical German precision.

Soon after November, there was no more work for me in Fürth, so I went to join my parents in Frankfurt. I spent a good part of the ten months there earning money to prepare the kind of lists that the Nazi authorities required from each prospective emigrant, detailing every piece of household goods they intended to take with them abroad. Religious life went on in makeshift synagogues, since all the actual synagogues had been destroyed.

At the time of our emigration, the easiest way to make passage to America was via Italy. We boarded the Italian liner, *Saturnia*, in Trieste and landed in New York on November 17, 1939. When someone lands in New York, they don't have much time for thinking, you just savor the experience. We went to midtown Manhattan to see everything. That's exhilarating. But there was always homesickness for my mother and family. It's a miracle that the rest of the family came in May 1940, literally on the last boat out of Germany.

Settling in New York was not very difficult, thanks to having relatives and compatriots close by, physically and spiritually. Jobs were very hard to come by in the winter of 1939–1940, and I spent most of my days actively trying to get jobs. My father, thanks to his training as a baker, secured one relatively soon, but it was a night job. I eventually became a messenger for Arrow Press on Eleventh Avenue.

In retrospect, we think of how fortunate it was that in the eighteenth and nineteenth centuries in many parts of Germany, only one son in each family could inherit his father's business or trade. That left many sons only the choice to emigrate, and many came to North America. My father's father did not want his children to leave. He told them "water has no boards to cling to."

In night school at George Washington High, my fellow classmates were to a great extent refugees like me. Few had much opportunity to get to know people who were born in America, except through work.

There is a difference in describing one's impression of a new country. A casual visitor certainly would describe his impressions and absorption of living and ideas differently from one who had to leave his old country behind and now this is all the country he has. Age also makes a difference. I was between seventeen and eighteen living in the Bronx, working in Manhattan, and reading the papers, and I got far more of an impression of what the new country was like when I started to meet "real" Americans in the army, for which I volunteered at the end of 1942.

Those of us who think about it are aware of the enormous gratitude we owe the country that saved us from inevitable destruction of which we, however, became aware only after the war. That sense of gratitude probably motivated me to volunteer for service. Like all other young men, I registered for the draft, as did my brother Fred. He was called; I wasn't. Trying to find out why I did not get called, I was told there were no papers. I had my draft card, but nothing happened. I said to myself: "The draft board has to fill a quota. If I don't go, someone else will have to. He may be a married man; he may get killed in my place." After an examination on Governors Island, I was pronounced healthy enough to serve and, in January 1943, became a member of the armed forces of the United States. One of my first "official" acts was to apply for U.S. citizenship, as did all refugee soldiers.

On the train ride that took us from Camp Upton, New York, to Camp Robinson, Arkansas, I saw a fellow engaged in heavy-duty learning of a Hebrew book. I asked him his name and where he came from. His name was George Aumann and was from Frankfurt where most of my mother's family had roots, and his familial relationship to me was that one of his aunts had married one of my grand-uncles! He and I and two other observant boys garnered a six-man bunk for ourselves, which was very pleasant. After basic training we were separated.

As for training, it is hard to say if it is ever really sufficient, but that is due mainly to the fact that most instructors have never experienced firsthand what they are expected to teach. But under the circumstances and because of time and personnel restrictions, it seemed adequate.

After basic, we were told that we would be shipped overseas, which could mean Europe or the Pacific. The staging area was Fort Dix in New Jersey. While there, preparing mentally for battle, I told my superior officer that I had a choice not to go abroad because I had not yet been made a citizen. In typical army fashion, my citizenship application, just like my draft board papers, was not to be found. My superior officer was Capt. John W. Frazier; in civilian life he had been a Philadelphian lawyer—high society. He made a telephone call to a friend, a federal judge in Philadelphia and told him, "I have this young man in my outfit who needs to become a citizen in a hurry."

The judge said, "Bring him in." Captain Frazier packed me in his jeep, drove to the courthouse in Philadelphia, and half an hour later I was a proud U.S. citizen. That night, my army comrades made a party to celebrate my citizenship. I must admit, I did not encounter any anti-Semitism in the army. I'm not saying that it didn't exist; I just didn't encounter any, and not among the officers either.

Two days later I joined fifteen thousand other soldiers on a crowded ship eastward. This was August 1943, the time when German U-boats prowled the Atlantic Ocean and sank a number of ships, killing many soldiers and sailors. A few days out, there was an explosion on our ship that killed an engineer and made the boat inoperable. So instead of sailing alone in a convoy of thirty or forty vessels, protected by a phalanx of naval vessels, our ship was left behind in the middle of the ocean, guarded only by one single little destroyer until the needed repair, which took close to half a day, was completed, and we could rejoin the convoy.

We were not told where we would land. When we passed through the Straits of Gibraltar, we guessed it would be somewhere on the northern coast of Africa. It turned out to be Oran in Algeria. Rommel had been defeated a few months earlier, and North Africa was clear of Germans. We were in tents, prowled only by natives who stole whatever they could. It is a Muslim's dearest wish to be buried in white, so our white bed sheets were easy prey. Another way the indigent population enriched itself was by performing laundry service for the soldiers. The army did not deliver laundry service, we needed it, and the natives needed the money.

After several weeks of training in the desert, we were informed that we would start our drive to Tunis on the day of Yom Kippur. I asked for permission not to have to travel on that day and join my unit the next day, but to no avail. I spent the entire day in the back of a truck. Late at night, I managed to get something to eat.

From Tunis we sailed across the Mediterranean to Naples, Italy. Bombing had heavily damaged Naples, and the "pier" where we landed was an overturned ship. We were quartered in a school in the north of the city, but we did not stay there long. Our next stop was the real front, a valley opposite the Abbey of Monte Cassino. A few months later, Cassino became a fierce battle, and the abbey was greatly damaged. On that first day in combat, we had our baptism of fire by being bombed at close range—by our own bombers. One of my comrades was wounded seriously enough not to be able to return to combat. I jumped into a foxhole providentially left by the Germans who had been there before us and was not hurt. I can still remember the sound of a large bomb hitting the ground about forty yards from me.

When our high command realized that Cassino was a difficult location to overcome, they decided to get closer to Rome at Anzio. We were taken off the front, brought to Naples, and boarded boats for the short voyage north to Nettuno and Anzio, about twenty-five miles south of Rome.

After a successful and relatively bloodless landing, we settled near the town of Anzio and dug in instead of pushing farther toward Rome. Every night, a single German bomber came over to bomb us. Nothing happened to us, but other people were killed constantly. That "folly" threatened to push us into the sea in the middle of February 1944, but thanks to favorable weather, our Air Corps were able to saturate the German lines with bombs, and we survived. We had to sleep in foxholes for three months, and more than twenty thousand soldiers lost their lives in the Anzio beachhead, until we broke out at the end of May and drove into Rome. The Germans had left, and the Roman population greeted us enthusiastically. That was on June 5. The next day, June 6, was the invasion of the coast of France.

Among the Jewish families who survived the war in Rome and Italy— thanks in part to the Vatican—was a family named Rothschild. The wife's maiden name was Lehmann, whose sister had been my classmate. They asked my advice as to whether they should take advantage of the special offer the U.S. government had made, to let a number of refugees come to America without any particular papers. I advised them positively, and they settled in Washington Heights.

In August 1944, the invasion of southern France took place. The Germans had either not anticipated it or didn't think it would be massive. At any rate, there was little resistance, and we advanced to north of Grenoble in a few weeks. I spent the days of Rosh Hashanah in Epinal, where the small Jewish community had survived and had come back from where it had been during the war years. This was the so-called unoccupied part of France, where matters were relatively easy for Jews.

Until then, except for the three months on the Anzio beachhead, my war experience was not too difficult, but the winter of 1944–1945 was a very hard one in Europe, and we in the Seventh Army were in the Vosges Mountains of France, across from the German border. Because of snow and rain and the lack of proper boots, and the prohibition of wearing rubber overshoes, many troops suffered frostbite and frozen feet, a condition that lasted for life. I was fortunate not to suffer. It was in one of these forlorn places where two "Germans" surrendered, and I was able to interrogate them. But these fellows were not even Germans. They were southern Europeans, impressed into the German Army, and knew virtually nothing. Surrendering was probably the high point of their career.

The battle of Bastogne, north of us, was the real turning point of the war. The famous German General Von Rundstedt had almost succeeded in overrunning the American troops in the southern part of Belgium. Again the U.S. Army's intelligence work was not too clever, but our troops held out and hoped for the snowy winter weather to lift, so that our bombers could do the job as they had done at Anzio ten months earlier. And they did after the famous General McAuliffe replied to the demand of the Germans to surrender with this one word: "Nuts!" A few days later, our bombers saturated the ground with bombs, Bastogne was free, and the Germans retreated back into Germany.

Toward the end of the war, I was transferred to the intelligence section of the Seventh Army headquarters. One of my assignments was to monitor the observations of the reconnaissance planes. Their reports came by radio to me. Several times they reported that there were large masses of people on the main roads, and they asked whether they should go down and strafe them. The choice was up to me. I did not think that the Germans would have their soldiers walk en masse as targets for American planes, so these must be different people. My answer was no. Fortunately that was the right choice, because these people were the remnants of concentration camps who the Germans had driven out for a death march. Many were sick and weak and many died on the road. At least some were saved and were not bombed by the Americans.

We got into Germany the night before Pesach—there's a picture of me reading the *Ma Nishtana* at a Seder table in Kaiserslautern. It's a tremendous thing to get back four years, five years later as a conqueror.

Toward the end of the war, we were in Augsburg, which was Seventh Army headquarters, and Goering was brought in—he still had his riding crop. I was right next to him when he was brought in; he went upstairs, and I went right after him. Goering went to shake the commander's hand, and Captain White did not shake it. To be able to do this to your enemy, and to conquer him, gives you feeling of power, gratitude.

There were many family members trapped in Germany, but we did not know the extent of the massacre until after the war. At one of the first Sabbath services in Augsburg in southern Germany, I met a Jewish woman and her daughter who told me they had been in the gas chamber in a nearby concentration camp. I asked what happened. She said that the gas did not work that day. That incident was the first eye-opener for me. I then tried to do as much as possible for the people in the displaced persons camps as I could. One such occurrence was when my parents sent me a telegram that my first cousin, Leopold Popowsky, survived and was in Feldafing camp. My first attempt to pick him up was unsuccessful, but a week later I got him to live with me, supplied him with clothes and a job, and a year later had him come to New York.

EVIDENTLY, MY PARENTS DID NOT ANTICIPATE the war or the attempted annihilation by Hitler of the Jews in Europe. If they had, they would have made more thorough attempts to leave Germany earlier. We should have been bright enough to know that Hitler would not stop with Austria and Czechoslovakia. Besides us, 95 percent of the people who thought about it did not expect the war either. Neither did most Americans, except when the Japanese attacked Pearl Harbor.

When that despicable act happened, a sort of kinship was felt between refugees from Europe and the American public. We were now in the same boat.

In May and June 1945, shortly after the war had ended, two important things happened: I was appointed second lieutenant, and I received the Bronze Star medal for meritorious service. I continued work in Seventh Army headquarters in the beautiful city of Heidelberg, where for once the U.S. Army had planned it right. They knew that the Seventh Army headquarters were going to be in Heidelberg, so they did not bomb the city. By February 1946, Congress prevailed on the armed forces to reduce their overblown military might. In the process I was shipped home and discharged. I could have stayed in the reserve and did so, but after a few months it became too boring. I was anxious to make a fresh start.

I also had an offer from one of my colonels, Colonel Radam, to join the CIA, which had been formed not long before and where he had a commanding voice. He had me come to Washington and tried to sell me on the good life in the new organization. Fortunately, I made the decision to "serve" with a nice religious civilian community in Washington Heights, New York, where my parents had moved from the Bronx during the war—a very good decision that would become apparent many times in my life. I met my future wife at a weekly gathering of our Youth Group in Washington Heights. At first I was cowed by her father, Joseph Breuer, who was the founding rabbi of our congregation and the grandson of the famous Rabbi Samson Raphael Hirsch, a formidable man to know. We were married in 1950.

My thought about my time in the military is this: I never would have been called if I didn't volunteer. It may sound trite, but the army made a man out of me—to become independent, to think, to lead, and to communicate with people, which is a great advantage in life. Most people who have been in the army have a little bit extra. And I also served my country.

After the war Jerry Bechhofer went into the computer processing business and developed and installed integrated computer systems for companies in the New York and New Jersey areas. He passed away at the age of eighty-six, shortly before this book went to press.

Chapter 3
ADELYN BONIN

BERLIN, GERMANY

502 Mechanized Ambulance Corps Auxiliary Territorial Service,
British Eighth Army
North Africa and European Theater of Operations

*Adelyn Bonin was the oldest daughter of Otto and Lilli Bonin.
She left Berlin alone in 1937 for Palestine (where the photograph
above was taken), then a British Mandate. When the war broke
out, she enlisted in the Auxiliary Territorial Service, the women's
branch of the British Army, and saw action as an ambulance driver
during the battle for El Alamein.*

*After the German surrender in North Africa, her unit,
the 502 Mechanized Ambulance Corps, Auxiliary Territorial
Service, British Eighth Army, was deployed to Italy and then
stationed in Rome before moving up to Austria for occupational
duty. In Gratz, the Red Cross informed her that her parents had
been deported to Auschwitz, where they perished in 1943.*

When Hitler became chancellor in 1933, I just thought it was the most wonderful thing. My classmates and I all ran around the streets and said, "Heil Hitler!" I bought myself a swastika and put it on my coat. That evening when I came home, my father saw the swastika and said, "We have to have a long talk." And he told me that I was Jewish.

I had been baptized a Lutheran, so at first reaction, the news was devastating. My second reaction was: I've got to find out what it is to be Jewish. I had no idea. I didn't know what a Jew was, so I made it my business to learn, but there were no Jews in my neighborhood or in my class.

I was in my very early teens when the law was passed that you had to leave school if you were non-Aryan or Jewish. Then I occupied myself more and more with the idea of what it meant to be Jewish. I met with a famous rabbi in Berlin, learned about Judaism, and soon joined a Zionist youth organization. In Germany, I wasn't wanted; I was told I was inferior. On the other hand, Zionism told me nothing of that. It spoke of hope, a future. It was something that any young person really would embrace at that time. I wanted to leave and go to Israel, which was Palestine back then.

All of this I had to do much against my father's will. He thought Hitler would be over in a few months and what I was doing was terrible. But I finally said, "What do you have to offer me here?"

Finally, my father said, "Okay, you can go." So I went with a youth movement, Aliyah, and promised to come back after two years—but of course there was no coming back.

I spent my first two years at a kibbutz and I didn't like the life at all. I was small, not very strong, and didn't take to growing oranges or working in a vineyard. I did not see a future for myself there.

It was shortly after I arrived in Tel Aviv that I saw the first posters: "Join the British Army." Since Palestine was a British Mandate and Great Britain was at war with Germany, it didn't take long before I volunteered. I was accepted in the British Army's Women's Auxiliary Territorial Service (ATS) at the beginning of 1942.

First of all, every girl wanted to be the girl on the recruitment poster in a beautiful uniform driving a car. That was just the height of my ambition. I wanted to be a driver, but I knew that everyone else would want this too. So, before I joined up, although I didn't have very much money, I said, I'm going to a driving school. I learned to drive a car, and then I thought, Well,

I'd better learn how to double clutch and drive a truck, too.

After about a week of ATS training in Sarafan, they said, "Who wants to be a driver?" Of the five hundred there, three hundred raised their hands. Then they asked, "Who has a license?" That put it down to about three. Then they said, "Can anybody double clutch and drive a truck?" I was the only girl with her hand raised.

I became a camp driver. About four weeks later, my officer asked me, "Bonin, do you speak English?"

Well, I didn't speak very much, but I knew enough to understand that, so I said, "Yes."

She asked, "Do you want to be an ambulance driver? They do frontline duty."

"Yes, yes! That's what I want!" I told her that I spoke English fluently, so they sent me along with three or four English girls to this British outfit, the 502 Mechanized Ambulance Corps, ATS, part of the British Eighth Army in Alexandria.

Then life changed completely because I was no longer in a training camp. We were encamped the way the English used to live in India in the time of the great British Empire, with servants and everything. The British are a different race, I think. Everything is different about them. So, I learned English very quickly and adopted a high-class British accent. Mixed with my German, it must have sounded very strange to anyone who might have heard me. The other British soldiers knew that I was German, but it didn't bother them. Funnily enough, my roommate was from Czechoslovakia, and we both spoke German to one another and it seemed to go unnoticed.

Alexandria was only about thirty miles from the front, and we were bombed every night; as Rommel came closer and closer, we started to push at El Alemein in the western desert. The British won the first battle and that turned the tables for the first time; it was actually the turning point because the British made a stand.

There were some Palestinian girls in Egypt, but none of them were at the frontline. There was only our unit, with three or four British girls. Our unit's job was to get to the line in our field ambulances and bring the wounded back to the big hospitals where they could be treated. The ambulances were built for four, but we could actually fit five stretcher cases.

Combat was scary, but when you're young, you think nothing can happen to you, and all you want to do is see and experience new things. Also, we didn't have time to be scared. I would call combat "organized chaos." That's what it was, because I can't imagine the English ever getting excited about anything. Even as we heard bombs coming over and in front of us, and there were tanks with manned machine guns moving back and forth, at all times it was met with a typical British calmness. Let's say that the Scottish bagpipes were coming up to the front. The MP would stand there directing them this and that way, and were often right there to show units coming to the front their positions. That was organization.

Being part of this enormous undertaking, this enormous machine that moves forward, you—in your convoy, in your ambulance—are just like a little wheel. It's a tremendous feeling. I never doubted even in the worst time of retreat that the British would not win. They were so sure of themselves.

Of course, we saw horrible things, like men without limbs, or with stomach wounds, which are the most horrible ones. One time an ambulance was brought in by one of our girls and another driver. As she opened the door—I was standing next to her—a soldier's head fell out. We saw a lot of bad things, but they happened every day and we really didn't think very much about it.

On one occasion, a corporal jumped up on my ambulance, ordered us to put in five stretcher cases, and shouted, "Back to Alexandria," which was only a few miles away. Moments after we left, there was a sandstorm. It was not for very long, but when it was over, I noticed that the driver in the other ambulance and I were going in opposite directions! Who had turned? What happened? Which way was Alexandria? There were no roads.

Of course, we didn't want to let the wounded know that we didn't know where we were going. We jumped off the ambulance and said, "Let's take the middle," which was right between the two frontlines. We heard all of these shells going over us, and we thought something was very, very wrong. So we veered a little to the left, and after about twenty miles—which is already too long with wounded in the back of a very hot ambulance—we finally saw some tents and cars. I thought, Well, this is it. If they are Germans, we have to get these people to a hospital or something.

Fortunately, they were the Free French. When they saw two women driving up, it was just the greatest stir for them, and they wanted to take us to their mess. I declined, since we had to get back to Alexandria. We came home about four hours late, and there was a big board in the reception room that said we were missing.

We were not like the ordinary ambulance drivers. We would try to make the guys comfortable, and apparently there was talk that we were so good that we soon developed a reputation. On one occasion, this wounded fellow who was pushed into the ambulance lifted his blanket, looked up, saw me, and said, "Ah, 502. Thank goodness."

After Africa, we went to Italy and landed at the very heel. We drove our ambulances to Naples, and then to Rome, where we would be stationed. And we had a very, very good time in Rome. It was still an open city at that point.

Pope Pius XII gave daily audiences to the Catholic soldiers, and I wanted to see the pope too. Now, the audience was not as it is today. The room was not much bigger than my living room today, with a podium. He stood and greeted us. Since we were the only three or four girls, and we were standing there in the front line, he came to us first and began to bless us. I was just about to kneel, because when you're in Rome you do as the Romans do, but when he saw the Palestine insignia on my lapel, he wouldn't allow me to kneel. He said to me in Hebrew, "Where are you from, my daughter?"

I said, "I was born in Germany."

He began speaking in German to me, and I was just flabbergasted. Here he was, speaking Hebrew and German. Finally he said, "I hope you and your family will be united soon." I thought that was very nice, so I thought a lot about that pope for many years. Since then, I have heard other things about him, and I don't think so much about him anymore.

I couldn't write to my parents anymore because the war was on, and so I bought my first diary book the moment I joined up. I thought, I can't write letters to them but I can write the diary, so when I see them, they can read everything that happened to me. When I was in Italy, I started saving all kinds of underwear, pajamas, and all the other things you can get in the hospital, because I wanted to give them to my parents when I saw them. The more we moved north, the more I thought the day was coming when I would see them—but I never did see them again.

At the end of 1944, we were posted outside of Venice, and that was where we met the first camp survivors who began to tell tales, all of which we could not believe. It was impossible. The English were not very forthcoming with news; they knew about the camps, but it was not publicized. By the time we got to Gratz, Austria, I was a sergeant in charge of a platoon. I contacted the

Red Cross to try and find out about my parents, uncles, and cousins. It took several months, but then this letter came that said my parents were on this and that transport, and their final destination was Auschwitz.

I forged on through though. I always found all through my life that work was the best cure for anything.

I still have an attachment to Germany, in as much as I teach German literature and history, as well as the language, which really has nothing to do with what happened during the war. The Hitler part, and even the war, is a small, small part of German history. German history is really a very glorious history, with fantastic writers. The world can look, and Germany can look, with pride on that which happened before, and with pride again at what has happened since the war. Many of my Jewish friends cannot understand this, and they cannot make peace with it, but I have made peace with it.

Adelyn Bonin immigrated to the United States in 1947. She returned to school, earning her BA and MA degrees at the University of California and her doctorate at Nova Southeastern University. From 1959 to 1983, she was professor of German at Orange Coast College. Her autobiography, Allegiances, *was published in 1993. Bonin now resides in Mission Viejo, California.*

Chapter 4
ERIC HAMBERG

LUDWIGSHAFEN, GERMANY

84th Chemical Mortar Battalion
Italian Campaign

Eric Hamberg was born in the town of Mannheim, across from its twin city, Ludwigshafen am Rhein, where he attended school. Immigrating to England not long after Kristallnacht without his parents, who remained trapped in Germany, Hamberg arrived in the United States in 1940; for two years he worked as a cook before being drafted into the army in 1942.

I had a very happy childhood; we had money, we had a nice home, my father owned a big store, which I was supposed to take over when I became an adult, which never happened, and an apartment house on top of it which had about sixteen apartments. We also had another apartment which was five stories high in which we lived on the second floor. I had nothing to worry about. I never really suffered. Even though I was the only Jewish boy in high school, I was never called a dirty Jew. But then things started changing.

By the time I graduated in 1937, every one of my schoolmates belonged to the Hitler Youth. By 1938, things were very hard for me, because my father had already lost his store, our houses were taken away from us, and my sister went to New York. The night of the Kristallnacht I was very sick, but I remember going to the balcony and looking down, and across the street was a Jewish store. They destroyed the store, they broke the windows, and they threw everything out in the streets. The brown-shirted SA men went up to our neighbor's apartment on the second floor and took that nice family's bedding, threw it all out into the street, and set it all on fire. I saw people laughing and dancing and being so happy that the Jews were getting something that they didn't expect.

I also saw people who cried, and not only Jewish people, but most of the people were very happy. As sick as I was, I just couldn't understand that. The next day, the SS men in black uniforms came to pick me up. I was running a very high fever. They were decent to my mother, but said, "We have to pick up your son."

She said, "He's sick, you can't take him out. He's running a temperature and has God knows what."

They said, "Sorry, get him dressed." She pleaded with them to call our doctor, who fortunately at that time was a Gentile doctor. So, they called him up and he said, "You want to take him out, why don't you shoot him right away? He'll never make it to wherever you're taking him because he's got pneumonia." So they left me and that was one of the things that saved my life. It also showed us that it was high time to get out. My father had a friend in England. They used to correspond on Rosh Hashanah, Yom Kippur, and send Jewish New Year cards. In one of his last letters, my father wrote, "Please, if you can, find out if my son can get out of Germany." In the meantime, I had gone to a Jewish hotel for two years as a cook apprentice. I figured knowing a profession would get me out much easier. However, the wife wrote back and she says, "Unfortunately, your friend died."

So, I wrote to twelve different British hotels to give me a job as a cook and get me out of Germany. I sent each one my report card from school and a letter of recognition my boss had written. Six hotels offered to help me and I got out in June 1939, three months before the war started. I was in England for a whole year, and then eventually immigrated to America.

It was a strange thing, getting out of Germany. My father rode with me on the train until we got to Holland. I didn't know if I should laugh or if I should cry. I was happy that I was getting out of there, and I was sorry to leave my parents behind, but to me, as a young fellow, it was almost like an adventure.

I got to the United States in 1940, and five days after coming, I got a job as a cook in a nightclub. Two years later I was drafted into the U.S. Army.

I was sent to Camp Rucker, Alabama, and was trained as an operator of a heavy mortar weapon—4.2-inch chemical mortar they called them.

I was very happy. I was hoping and praying that I would be sent to the European theatre and not the other one. We were sent overseas in September 1942 and landed in Oran, Africa. There, they put us on a hill outside of Oran called Canastel, which was nothing but a big rock. We put our tents up, and after a few weeks they took a report of how many people were in the outfit called Enemy Aliens. They would not let us fight until we became U.S. citizens. After a while, my outfit was transferred to Tunisia, to be part of the invasion of Sicily.

When we got to Sicily, they took twenty-six of us who spoke very poor English and attached us to an outfit that was already fighting there. For some reason, the outfit we had initially been assigned to had been held back in Africa. I never knew why. So, when we got there they made us mule bearers, taking the mules up the hill with supplies and bringing them down. At first it was uneventful, and then the Germans started attacking. Someone shouted over to us, "Hey you! Yeah you, going up the hill, you're going to be litter bearers. Get your asses up there." They didn't give us a Red Cross armband and they took our guns away. We went up the hill, and sure enough we were right in the fight.

I remember hiding behind a tree when the Germans kept shelling us. This might sound ridiculous, but I swear to God, in that tree was a little hole that I crawled into as much as I could, and I fell sound asleep during the battle. When it slowed down, I woke up and there were wounded soldiers all around and one of our men had already gotten hit. We took one fellow, four of us litter bearers, and carried him about four hundred yards until we realized he was dead. We saw a captain, who asked, "Who are you guys?"

We responded, "Well, we're Enemy Aliens, sir. We're over here to fight the war against the Germans, but they haven't made us citizens yet."

He said, "You're not citizens up here? Get the hell out of here!" So we carried that man down. It took us a day and half because it was on a rocky hillside and to carry a man that weighs about 190 pounds was pretty rough. We got to the bottom and they put us back with the mules. When the campaign in Sicily was over, they sent us back to Africa.

On the way back to Africa, our Liberty ship got torpedoed and it limped the rest of the way. Then they sent us back to the same hill we came from in Canastel, Oran. *Finally* an officer said, "Today fellas, you're going to become citizens."

They took us to a big tent that they erected. While we were sitting on benches on the outside, one by one they called us in to talk to a U.S. department official. Then I was called in and he asked me some very basic things like, name, town of birth, age. At the very end, he said, "Now comes the most important question I have to ask in order for you to become a citizen, and think very carefully about this: Do you mind fighting against the country of your birth?"

When I heard that, I laughed. I told him, "You're a little late."

He laughed too and said, "Yeah, I heard what you guys have been through in Sicily."

So I became a citizen right then and there and was sent to join my outfit in Anzio. I got there on an LST (landing ship, tank). We jumped off into the water and marched to the first village called Campo Di Morto—the Camp of Death. My unit was the 84th Chemical Mortar Battalion; our insignia was a yellow and blue field with a dragon with a death head and on the bottom it said *Cabe Fumo*. We were assigned to a mortar platoon; each platoon had four heavy mortars. It took four men to actually fire a mortar. One man attaches the explosives in the back of the mortar shell, one puts the instrument on the top of the barrel, and according to the place that we were shooting at, one guy would find the target coordinates, adjust the weapon accordingly—up down, side to side—and then one guy would take a shell and throw it down the barrel.

We were attached to whatever infantry outfit that was fighting in the area. When one infantry unit was pulled out, we stayed and supported the next one. In Anzio, we supported the 3rd Division, which also happened to be the division that Audie Murphy, the most decorated soldier in World War II, belonged to. We supported the 45th, as well as one of the great outfits, the 82nd Airborne. We also worked with the 442nd, the Nisei combat team, comprising many tremendous Japanese American soldiers; most of them were short in stature but extraordinarily brave. This unit was not that long in Italy, nowhere as long as we were, but they wound up with more decorations, more Purple Hearts, and more people killed than any other unit because they just felt that they as Japanese needed to prove they were Americans. I had a lot in common with them.

The first mortar shell I ever fired, when I came to Anzio, was a white phosphorus shell that landed in a ditch with five German soldiers in it. When some troops came back from the field, they said, "Hey, you fired the shell down there? Nice shooting buddy, you got five of 'em." I felt a little queasy in a way, but then I figured that I am fighting a war and I am here because I wanted to be. Also, I felt that this was my job, and this was my way of coming back at the Germans for what they did to me. I didn't know at that time if my parents were alive or not, because they were trapped still in Germany and living in a hell under the Nazis.

But I was a Jewish boy fighting against an enemy that I knew, an enemy that was responsible for arresting, deporting, and killing my people. Refugee soldiers who were drafted or volunteered fought against the Nazis with fervor, because they were our hated enemy and were responsible for us losing friends and relatives in concentration camps, through terror and beatings long before the ovens came. I still had vivid memories of Kristallnacht a few years earlier in 1938 and the pleasure most Germans got out of burning synagogues and businesses, dragging Jews through the streets. Fighting the Germans went very deep for me; I wasn't going to give an inch.

Anzio was like sitting in a shooting gallery. The high ground was totally controlled by the Germans who could shoot down at us anytime from the mountains where they were dug in, and they did fire at us constantly. All we could do was hide behind houses and in our foxholes.

Just before the breakout, I was wounded. I had been digging a foxhole and was bent forward hacking away, when a shell landed just short of the hole and I was buried alive. Since my buddies were there, they got me out right away. When they pulled me out, they sent me to a hospital where I stayed for the rest of the week before I came back. Collectively, my outfit was in Anzio for 160 some days. We had no chance to take a bath. If you were lucky, you filled your helmet with water, and washed yourself off a little bit, but you couldn't take a bath. I'm sure we smelled to high heaven, but we didn't realize it anymore because we got used to it. It was a life that only a young person could take. We didn't care if we spoke nice or not nice. When you're in the army, the word with an "f" was every third word.

When we left Anzio, we knew that all roads lead to Rome, so we didn't mind the dust, even though breathing was difficult. We also didn't mind the snail's pace we had to travel—nothing mattered. We were going to Rome after so many months of waiting, fighting, and hoping. We were dirty and tired, but we were a happy group of men.

On that truck bound for Rome I saw a German colonel coming down the hill. I stopped the truck, and captured and interrogated him. It felt beautiful to me—a little sergeant interrogating a big-shot colonel with maps on him and plenty of information that I passed on. He seemed very happy to give himself up. For him, the war was over and I certainly was glad that he was out of it.

One story that is not so pleasant for me to tell occurred when we were attached to an outfit comprising some real fuck-ups. One night two Germans came out of nowhere with their hands up and surrendered to me. I was on guard duty at the time and couldn't leave my post. So the GIs from this unit said, "Hey, you got two 'Heinies' there? Don't worry, we'll take them back for you." So, they took them back under guard, but five minutes later I heard two shots and saw the same GIs walking back toward me with smiles on their faces. "Sorry, they tried to escape and we had to kill 'em." That really bothered me.

At any rate, on the way to Rome we received the roses, the kisses, the cheers, and other greetings of the Italians on the history-making day of June 5. That's when we marched into Rome. We stayed a whole month. I never saw the Coliseum and I never saw St. Peter's, but I had a good time. It was the thirty days that our battalion had dreamt of—sidewalks, electric lights, spas, rest camps, girls, company parties.

After that, we continued going up the Italian countryside, every so often stopping for battles. There were always small and fierce battles. Italy has a lot of small towns—Cisterna, Atina, Wolmonterone—and a lot of them are in the mountains. We had to climb the mountains and drag the mortar behind us, so, it wasn't an easy thing to fight a battle in a mountainous terrain. During the winter of 1944–1945, we were in the middle of Italy when we were called over to the West Coast. There had been a breakthrough by the Germans, and this seemed to be one of their last pushes where they broke through.

During one of those battles, we occupied a cave that was being shelled very badly. At one point, we left the cave to set up our mortars to fire on the Germans, who were advancing quickly toward us, and one of our sergeants got wounded very badly. He had a big piece of shrapnel in his lung, which collapsed, so I ran out with my medic and carried him to a ditch nearby under fire. We got him into a ditch and we waited; as a matter of fact, I laid myself on the top of the guy that was wounded because it was a shallow ditch. When the shelling was over, we bandaged him, picked him up, and took him back to the cave, which we evacuated later on.

We went all the way up to the Arno River and then we went to Volterra, where we got a week off. It was a beautiful little town and it was completely intact. Every roof had a Red Cross painted on it, so we didn't bomb it. It was like a spa; it was like a place that people went for the mineral waters and all that sort of things. Then we went to Florence.

On the morning of May 2, 1945, I was a staff sergeant and platoon sergeant, and it was my job to divide up the rations and keep track of everything. I was in a house doing the things for the rations when an order came in for a firing mission for my mortar. Since I was working, my buddy, Joseph Weiler from Brooklyn, who was a mortar sergeant, said, "Eric, you stay here, I'll take care of the gun." We did that a quite often. He went down, I heard him fire about two shells and then I heard an explosion. I knew that second that it was my gun that exploded, and I ran down to the three guys that were manning the gun. My best buddy Joe was killed instantly by a piece of shrapnel that went between his eye and his ear and into his brain. One of the guys was slightly wounded, and the other guy was all right.

I just held Joe in my arms and I couldn't say anything, but he took my place and that's the way we were. Throughout the whole war, Joe and I shared the same foxhole, we shared the same tent, we did all the bad things and all the good things together. This was around two o'clock on May 2. All of a sudden, the bells started to ring, from all the churches around us, from across the lake, next to us. I asked, "What's goin' on?" The war had been officially over at twelve o'clock and nobody told us. Joe was killed at two o'clock in the afternoon. If we had known, it wouldn't have happened. We absolutely did not need a fire mission, but whatever it was, he was gone.

I was staying at the outfit, because of what they called eighty-five critical points. Critical points combined the amount of time you were in service, how many battles you were in (for each battle you got a certain star), and how many decorations you had. These were all tabulated, and if you had eighty-five or more, you didn't have to go to the Japan side to fight another war. I was taken out at ninety-eight points at that time. So we sat around in Italy, took it easy, and waited until finally in October they put us on a boat home.

In the meantime, I wanted to go look for my parents in Germany because we were already near there. I went to the captain and told him my story, and he said, "I'll give you my jeep. Take it, but I can't give you a pass." At that time, the law was that if you were outside of Germany after the war was finished, you were not allowed on the inside. He said, "I know how you feel. I know what's going on, but we don't know where your parents are. If you knew where they are, maybe you can find them, but if you get picked up in Germany without a pass, they will say you stole the jeep and I can't say I gave it to you because it's against the law, military law anyway."

He continued: "Look, you're a staff sergeant now, a decorated soldier. Why don't you wait? You'll see them later." So, I stayed in Italy and I came home in November 1945. I had a long journey across the ocean and came back with a beautiful suntan. My sister had gotten married and had a little boy, and I found out that she had been contacted by our parents. Our father had been in a concentration camp, he was in Theresianstadt. My mother had been sheltered by a Christian family who knew us very well, and since she was blonde, she could pass as German very easily. I started getting things rolling to get my parents to America. They came on June 24, 1946. I remember the day, because I got married exactly five years later to the day on June 24, 1951.

I remember my father when he came out of the concentration camp; he weighed sixty-eight pounds. When he came to America, he was very undernourished but between his wife, his children, and our love, he finally came back to life. Once he had been a very rich man, but then had been reduced to nothing. In the States, he worked for a while in a factory; I got him and my mother an apartment and I took care of him. My father wouldn't talk about the concentration camp except to say that when he was there, "I kept myself alive. I worked in the kitchen, peeling potatoes." That was funny in a way, because whenever he caught me in the kitchen at home in Germany, I would get a slap. He would say, "Boys don't belong in a kitchen." In Theresianstadt he told me that he would stuff the potato peelings in his pocket and another fellow would stuff onion peelings in his pocket; in the evenings, they would go back to the barracks and make a potato onion soup.

I said to him one night, "You know papa, your son, that little German refugee boy, became a staff sergeant in the war. I was so proud of being an American soldier and I was up for a battlefield commission, which means that would've made me an officer right in the fields." I had already been a forward observer and I'd say my battlefield commission came through eight days after the war had officially ended. One thing that they didn't need, though, was another young second lieutenant.

"But if the war had lasted eight more days," I said, "Your son would've been a second lieutenant in the American army, can you imagine that? I would've stayed then."

Then he looked at me and said, "If the war had lasted eight more days, my son, the second lieutenant in the American army, wouldn't have had a father." But it was a dream I had. For years and years, I still had dreams during the night that I had gotten the commission.

So, those were my war years. I got married to a beautiful woman and had three beautiful children. Sixty some odd years later, I'm very grateful that I'm here, and I'm extremely grateful that I made it out of Germany and survived the war.

My army experience was in a way a dream that came true. When I left Germany, I didn't know what was going to happen. I tried to go into the English army, but it wouldn't take me because I was an Enemy Alien. I wanted to prove myself. I was a small kid, however, I was always the kid that dared and tried everything. I wasn't afraid. I wasn't afraid to die. The camaraderie, the fellows cannot be matched by anything, but I was damn good American

GI who had a score to settle and was lucky to accomplish some form of revenge—or should I say *my way* of *wiedergut machung* (repayment).

Memories of combat were hard for me for years. I had dreams where I woke up screaming about somebody getting hit, or somebody getting killed, or having no protection during a battle, until I realized that I was in bed.

Eric Hamberg owned and operated a beauty salon in New Jersey until his retirement. He and his wife, Sonny, live in Union, New Jersey.

Chapter 5

BERNARD FRIDBERG

HANOVER, GERMANY

Eighth Air Force, Twenty-Five Bombing Missions
European Theater of Operations

*Bernard Fridberg was born in Hanover, Germany, in 1922
and lived there until he was thirteen years old. His great uncle,
Emil Berliner, who had invented the gramophone and had
immigrated to the United States in the 1800s, kept close ties
with his German relatives. Inevitably, Berliner's family was
instrumental in providing affidavits and vouching for Fridberg
and five of his cousins who came to the United States without
their parents in 1936. He is pictured above in 1944.*

I had had firsthand experiences with the Germans, so I was anxious to get even with them a little bit; as I started to fly missions, I did feel that way. After I volunteered to serve in the U.S. Army Air Corps, I was sent to gunnery training and then to Salt Lake City, where the bomber crews were put together, and that's where we met our pilot, co-pilot, radio operator, and gunners. There were ten men to a crew. From that point on, we were essentially together day and night—the enlisted men especially. Everybody knew where I had come from and that I was Jewish, but I never experienced any anti-Semitism at all. We all would become very close knit.

After six weeks of training they took us to Kearney, Nebraska, where all of the B-17 crews met and received their assignments, whether they were going to the Pacific or Europe. B-17s by their nature were earmarked for Europe, whereas B-24s were normally used in the Pacific Theater. To our chagrin, they gave us machete knives and mosquito netting; we were going to the Pacific. But at the end of the day, they recalled that gear and gave us equipment for Europe. Bangor, Maine, was the last place we would be stationed in the United States. From there, we went to Newfoundland and then to Europe. We took off for Belfast one night, and it was a bad night; the weather started to turn real bad. Unfortunately, out of fifty-two planes, more than ten didn't make it because of the weather and some had inexperienced pilots. We were very fortunate that our navigator had training with Pan Am—the only airline that made transcontinental flights—before the war. We were lucky to have his experience. We flew on radio silence.

We got to Ridgewell, England (outside Cambridge), where the 381st Bombardment Group was located. We were replacements. I had cousins from Germany who had escaped to London, so I would visit them from time to time.

The missions that we flew were long, usually seven or eight hours, on oxygen over ten thousand feet. By the time we were done with the missions, we were debriefed, then went off to bed. The days started by being awakened from a deep sleep—all of our energy was spent each day— and told that we were on again for another mission. That's how it went. There wasn't much talking; the enlisted men, like me, would head to the plane, while the officers would go to a tent to be briefed on our mission for the day. Even without being told, we could gather where we were going by the bombs that were already in the bomb bays. If we were going to bomb bridges or factories, we would have detonation bombs. If we were off to bomb Munich or Berlin, the firebombs (smaller than the others) were in the bomb bay and as many of them as possible. The ammunition was already there for me, and I would make sure that everything was in place and ready to go.

There would be about three hundred planes going over together; once we gained a certain altitude, we would go around in circles until other bomb groups, stationed all over England, joined us at a certain point over England. Then the lead group would start flying over the North Sea, and we would get in formation.

The first mission for me was over Berlin, the toughest one of all, on May 19, 1944. The one thing I remember is the flak. The German gunners already had a pretty good idea of what altitude our bombers flew when releasing their bombs, which was around twenty thousand feet. All of this would happen very fast; being a gunner I would fire at the German Messerschmitt planes as soon as they came into sight. I would see the swastikas on them. There were lots of narrow escapes. We had a plane shot up to such a point the hydraulic system wasn't working, and we had to take our parachutes and attach them to the side of the plane to slow it down for landing.

The second mission that I was involved in was one of the toughest missions in the war. We lost a large number of planes. One crew that lived with us in our Quonset hut (there were two crews per hut) was gone the next morning. These are things I don't like talking about, because I almost feel guilty for having lived through it.

Obviously, I never knew the details of what things the Nazis were doing to the Jews below, as far as death camps were concerned—we found that out much later. However, I felt a great deal of hate toward the Germans at that time when I was twenty-one; what I did know was that my family had lived in Hanover for centuries, and then all of the sudden I wasn't a German anymore. I wasn't allowed to swim in public pools or go into parks or enjoy things that non-Jewish children did. Essentially, they took our country away from us. So, I felt good about what I was doing in the air force.

Between May 19 and July 18 we had flown twenty-five missions. The last mission we flew was to bomb Peenemünde on the Baltic Sea where Wernher von Braun did the research on the V-2. Before we got there, however, we had engine failure. We were able to drop our bomb load and then made it to a small airbase in southern Sweden, which was neutral.

When we landed, we were under the supervision of the Swedish Army. Since we only had flight clothing on us, the army was nice enough to outfit us with civilian clothes and put us in boarding houses, where we stayed for four months until November. It wasn't internment, but we couldn't go anywhere we wanted. We were able to go into town and some of us had Swedish girlfriends, but we still had to sign in whenever we came back. Eventually, we were flown out of the Stockholm airport before the end of the war. Ironically, there were German planes with swastikas beside ours on the runways, but we were put in an unmarked C-47 and flown over German-occupied Norway to Scotland.

After twenty-five missions, I received the Distinguished Flying Cross. These memories do still seem vivid to me; the best part about it is that I feel that I did my part, even though I never think I am a big hero. The big heroes are the ones who didn't come back. The experience never leaves you. You're never the same and are a different person for having lived through it.

Bernard Fridberg was the president of a large typesetting company in Falls Church, Virginia.

Chapter 6
FRITZ WEINSCHENK

MAINZ, GERMANY

293rd Joint Signal Assault Company
European and Pacific Theaters of Operation

*After his induction and basic training, Fritz Weinschenk trained
as a radio operator and volunteered for the 293rd Joint Signal
Assault Company. He is pictured above in England, 1944, where
he received further training. He landed in the second wave on
Omaha Beach on June 6, 1944, and remained in Normandy
until August, when his unit was reorganized and sent to the
Pacific Theater for the invasion of the Philippines. In 1946, he
returned to Germany, where he served in the American Military
Government and was involved in the Nuremberg Trials.*

The first time I saw New York was from the ship *Aquatania*, which had just docked in New York Harbor. The city was in a muggy haze; there were skyscrapers and traffic, and I was terrified to leave the boat. That was my first impression. My family lived in Brooklyn and we were very poor. My father never made any money here, for he had no skills other than the wine business with which he did so well in Germany, and my mother knitted dresses. We had to be supported by the Jewish Joint Distribution Committee, which gave us rent money and food. I will never forget that as long as I live.

However, we were very happy and became much closer knit as a family than we were in Mainz, and we survived. I went to school during the day and worked at night. When I entered Manual Training High School, I didn't speak one word of English. The only words I could say were "I go to America." Two years later, I was an exemplary student and graduated with honors.

In 1938, I went to City College and became a history major. I was very interested in what was happening in Germany and read up on everything. I worked at the New York Public Library, so I had access to all of these German newspapers. I didn't necessarily hate the Germans, but I certainly didn't have any love for them either. My attitude toward them was always one of intense curiosity, because I knew not everybody was a Nazi and that there was another Germany. That was my firsthand experience. A lot of Germans went along with Hitler because of job needs and having to follow the crowd. If they didn't join the party, people were relegated to miserable existences—people with families to support. So, I knew they were not all murderers. I found out later what happened to teachers of mine who refused to join the party.

In 1939, my father got a job in California, and he, my mother, and my little brother left. Consequently, I didn't have enough money to eat sufficiently. I had no source of income except for what I was making at night and weekends at the New York Public Library. I had a dime for lunch, and as a special treat on weekends I got a Chinese dinner at restaurant for thirty cents. I was actually starving.

After Pearl Harbor, I tried enlisting in the navy but was denied because I was an Enemy Alien. When I ultimately went down to Whitehall Street for my army physical (I received a draft notice), I was frightened that the authorities would refuse me because I was a Jew or maybe too small. I still had this acute paranoia left over from Germany. But the army took me.

When I was inducted, I had my first solid meal at Camp Upton, and it was the first time I ate well in years; I loved the army right away. I fit right in with all of the guys and worked hard to become a good soldier. The world had opened up to me and I felt like I was born again.

After my basic training in Camp Croft, South Carolina, I trained as a radio operator and then was sent to the 309th Infantry Regiment of the 78th Division, where I became a sergeant and chief of a radio platoon. I was proud as hell. Then in December 1943, I was sitting in the orderly room, where I was in charge of quarters during the weekends, and a teletype came in: "We need eight radio operators for a special mission." It didn't say what mission it was, but I knew this was for me and I'd get out of there. So I shipped out with seven other radio operators from the division to an unknown destination. We had our papers to report to a camp near West Point and I was happy as a lark. I arrived at the outfit, the 293rd Joint Signal Assault Company, which was just about to go on the ships to go overseas. You cannot imagine my excitement and the thrill I felt when I heard that. I thought, "At last I'm going to go overseas; I'm going to see action and get into this war." Before I knew it, I was on a ship in the Atlantic in a big convoy. Eight days later we landed in England.

The outfit was composed of U.S. Army, Navy, and Air Corps platoons. Their mission was shore fire control; they had the radio operators communicate between the shore and the ships to direct naval gunfire, and between the ground and aircraft to direct air strikes. My platoon was to be the communications center for the beach master, who coordinated troop and equipment movement and commanded a beach during an invasion. We were taken to Torque in Devonshire, England, and were quartered in private homes.

During the day, we drilled pretty hard; we practiced with radio nets, waterproofed our equipment, had bayonet drills and hand grenade practice, and did the usual army stuff. In March and April, we were taken in trucks and jeeps—a company convoy—to Exeter, and then to Slapton Sands, which was an area similar to Omaha Beach. Then we were put on LSTs, taken out to sea, and were to make a combat landing for training purposes. This was a training ground for all of the units that were going to take part on D-Day and was under the direction of Brig. Gen. Norman Cota, one of the leading lights of the planning and the attack itself. We went through the entire training process with the communications platoon of the 116th Infantry, 29th Division. We got to know a lot of those guys, including their commanding officer.

Still we didn't know what was going to happen. Sure, we knew there was going to be an invasion, but we didn't know when or where. In the middle of May, we were taken to a camp on the south of England. This camp was gigantic; it had forty thousand troops concentrated in it and was surrounded by barbed wire and British Army Home Guards. That's when it got exciting because we felt that something was going to happen. There were artillery units, mortuary units, chemical units, amphibious and infantry units. Every morning, we were taken to one of the buildings where officers had posted aerial photos of the beach where we were going to land, and then we were given operational orders. Our lieutenant read us the field order: Omaha Beach, Easy Green sector, on the right flank of the beach near the Vierville exit—establish communication with the beach master and various command posts.

On June 1, we boarded an LCI (landing craft infantry). LCI 94 was one of a huge flotilla of LCIs, which were one-hundred-foot-long ships with three holds for troops. There was a tower in the center, and a bridge with ramps on both sides of the bow that would lower to discharge personnel. We were then briefed; we checked our equipment and were assigned to one of the holds. The mood was pure excitement, but this big event was overshadowed by concern of my fatigues and equipment and the job at hand.

We all had battery-operated radios and I listened to Radio Berlin propaganda, as well as different news stations; I listened to the German news discussing victories in the East with great interest. As a GI, I was not immune to the general tenor of American propaganda of that period. Like everyone else, I hated Hitler and called the Germans "Krauts." At any rate, the others relied on me to translate whatever we heard on the radio.

On the night of June 5, the boat finally starting vibrating, the engines started to hum, and we left at sunset with no fanfare from the harbor. This was no fishing trip! We were out in the English Channel in a fleet that included barrage balloons that prevented the Luftwaffe from attacking us, and the boat was rocking like hell. We latched down all of our equipment on deck, and I didn't get too much sleep that last night.

I remember thinking that since we were in the second wave, the first wave would be so far inland by the time I landed that I was going to miss out on everything and not see any action. I also figured that this was going to be a mop-up operation. I had the impression that the Germans were beaten. They had no air force to speak of, so I thought the first wave was going to be in Paris by the time I hit the beach. I was a stupid kid.

Just after dawn, we all went up on deck, and the LCI started moving toward the shore. We didn't really see the shore though; we saw a fog in the distance, and the coast was one big puff of smoke. The armada was overwhelming, with hundreds of ships. There were British E-boats speeding by us, with British skippers standing on the bows with bullhorns directing traffic and communicating with our captain as we went toward the shore. The scene was incredible. A battleship was firing inland, belching yellow smoke, and then we were told to go down in the hold.

Within minutes, I started to hear a pinging sound: "Ping! Ping! Ping! Ping!" It was almost like we were scraping something. Then there was a blinding flash in our hold. That flash changed my life. The ship had been hit and things started breaking from the wall—pipes and equipment—and the ship started listing. Our lieutenant shouted, "Line up, bayonet out! Cut the pack of the man in front of you and get out!"

One after another we made it out of the ship's hold. The ship was drifting, the conning tower was smoking, and there was a fire. As I got on deck, I saw sailors lying around as if they were sleeping. I said to the guy next to me, "What are these guys doing? These guys are sleeping!" I didn't realize they had been killed.

I climbed down the ladder and I started toward the shore, swimming on my back, doing backstrokes. As I got closer, I saw what looked like pebbles hitting the water around me, like someone was throwing little stones. They were machine-gun bursts.

I was carrying my rifle, helmet, and hand grenades. I just got to the beach with the last of my strength, half drowned and in horrible shape. When I crawled up the beach I saw nobody alive, just dead Americans. I crawled past the bodies of the communications platoon of the 116th, the same guys with whom I had trained the month before at Slapton Sands. They had landed completely unprotected and were wiped out. It was then when I started to have the greatest fear for my life.

I saw a tank that had been shot up right at the Vierville exit, on the crest of the beach. I had just crawled under it for protection when I heard someone scream, "You idiot! The Krauts got that tank in their sites! Get the fuck out of there!" I made it up to the sea wall where guys from the previous waves were cowering. Engineers, navy guys, some from my outfit, and infantrymen from the 29th were crawling every which way. The sea wall was probably an elevation of five feet, and we were all petrified and digging with whatever we had. Everyone looked the same to me. The guys who landed in the first and second waves all had yellow faces, probably from the adrenaline. They all had that skin color. Fear did that to you. I didn't think I was going to make it.

The shelling was terrifying. It went whining over our heads and into the water. We saw the tracers coming at us. I saw LCVP (landing craft, vehicle, personnel) boats being blown up and guys thrown up in the air. I saw this all happening as if it were a newsreel. Things were exploding all over the place, the noise was deafening, the smoke and the stink of burning oil was just overpowering. The tide was coming in—parts of dead GIs, boats, cargo, and all kinds of stuff was floating to shore. I can only describe this as a great train wreck.

A British ordnance unit landed in landing crafts with trucks in our sector by mistake. It was getting shelled badly, and it was just dreadful. Soldiers and trucks were getting hit, and most of these English guys were running around in flames. Corporal Kelly from our outfit left his foxhole and ran out and rolled this guy in the sand to extinguish the flames. He should have gotten the Silver Star.

That was how we spent the afternoon hours, just dodging the shells. I didn't have my radio because it was still on the ship, which was on fire and drifting toward the beach. Everybody was petrified and digging in, not knowing what to do. I wasn't an infantry man, and since my radio was nonexistent, I had no function and felt like I was a passenger on a sinking ship. But my platoon chief, Master Sergeant Coachy, went back and forth onto the LCI, despite all of the small arms fire and the exploding ammunition, and brought all of our equipment, including my radio, to the sea wall. Coachy was my hero. He could have been the model for Private Prewitt in *From Here to Eternity*. He had been through it all—the fall of the Philippines and Pearl Harbor. I found out later that he crawled onto the beach exit and started to kill Germans.

By noon, the fire was still very intense and it wasn't too healthy to stand up. Infantry officers from the 29th were constantly moving up the sea wall, picking out men by their insignia from their unit, and chasing them over the top shouting, "Get going, go over!" and began leading them inland. In the afternoon hours, I started to crawl back toward my exit where I had originally landed because it was getting a little better. I went behind a German bunker that hadn't been finished and there was a guy, an infantryman, lying there aiming his rifle. I wanted to talk to him and didn't see that he was dead.

Despite my fear, I was still functioning and was able to do my thing like an automaton, communicating with the others around me. I found my buddy Newman and we kept moving. All morning I kept passing this one corpse, which at some point I noticed was an officer with stars, a brigadier general. The last time I passed him, I saw that he had been pilfered—the stars were missing. If I had seen the son of a bitch who did that, I would have shot him.

Newman and I crawled back to where the LCI had been beached at the Vierville exit. We crawled a bit inland, went halfway up the bluffs, crossed the beach, and went onto the hills, still crouching. The artillery had diminished, but there were still snipers, so we couldn't walk around. I saw all of this German equipment, uniforms, hand grenades, and a German MG42, which was magnificent. I picked up a helmet and kept it as a souvenir for about five minutes, because shells started coming in and I had to run for it.

We gradually began to reorganize with guys from my unit, the 293rd. We started to dig in and stayed that night on the cliffs on the Vierville exit. I remember looking out at the horizon toward La Havre and thinking, "My God, if I survive this, won't I have some tale to tell." The beach looked like a train wreck: burning LCVPs, trucks, and dead bodies everywhere. I also remember thinking that if there was going to be a counterattack, I was going to defend myself; I was going to stay and die there. Thankfully, there was infantry ahead of us on the cliffs and troops had been coming ashore all day.

The next morning, a squad of us went onto the Vierville Road and to the bottom of the hill. The exit had two hills on each side, and there were two German bunkers. As we got closer, we heard talking and I shouted, "*Hande Hoch! Raus!*" About thirty Germans came out with their hands up. They were scared shitless. Their faces were white from all of the reverberations from the shelling of the cement in the bunker. We were terribly excited. My buddy, Wroblewski, a coal miner from Pennsylvania, was standing there with an M1 and a bayonet; he looked at me and said, "Fritz, just tell me, and I'll kill 'em."

I said, "Don't kill them."

Then I told the Germans to form a line and I marched them down to the beach. This later became famous in the company and was written up in our unit newspaper: "Weinschenk marched these Krauts down in military fashion." On the beach, there was an infantryman from the 116th in a rage, cocking his M1 rifle and saying, "These sons of bitches killed all my buddies, and I'm going to shoot them."

I said to the German noncom in German "*Los Veck, Hau ab!*" (Get out of here!) I wanted them to just march down and get on an LCVP. I turned to the GI and said, "Now wait a minute, hold it. Please don't do this." I prevented a war crime. I didn't want to see that happen.

That's what I remember about D-Day itself and the day after.

After that, we organized very rapidly and we set up the beach master communications as we were supposed to do on D-Day. I did duty on ship-to-shore through the beach master's office. It was a well organized operation. The job was to get the cargo out of the holds of these ships and onto the beach. While I was on these ships, I had the opportunity to listen to the big radio receivers in the radio rooms. On July 20, in the evening hours, I was listening to the Nuremberg Boys' Choir singing Bach's cantatas on Radio Berlin when suddenly the music stopped. A voice came on and said, "In twenty minutes, the führer will speak to the German people." I couldn't believe my ears, but sure enough, twenty minutes later there was an announcement and Hitler came on. He made that famous speech about "a small band of traitors" that had made an attempt on his life and that by divine providence he had escaped. Now he would take care of these traitors in the manner to which national socialists are used.

THE TRAFFIC OF ALL OF THE LIBERTY SHIPS coming into the harbor made it look like Grand Central Station. The black quartermaster outfits unloaded cargo, and I passed statistics about the unloading, requested more stevedores, and took care of whatever radio traffic that had to be handled by the ship's captain. We even used prisoners to work on ships as stevedores; the captured Germans worked like hell for the Allied war effort, and got paid in cigarettes and good food, which they loved.

I had an interesting talk with an *oberfeldwebel* (staff sergeant) who had the Iron Cross and the Narvik insignia and was in charge of some of the other "supermen." They were doing all the work, and he was doing nothing but gabbing with me while smoking those excellent *Amerikanische* cigarettes. Once in a while, he'd tell one of his men, *los,* and they'd jump too. We talked about everything from soup to nuts. He was from Constance and was a pretty good egg—I had to grant him that. It was funny to see all those *be-swastikad* blouses hanging side by side with American field jackets with T-4 and T-5 stripes on the wall. You'd think there was a drinking party of "Axis-Americano" someplace. I remember he looked out at all of the equipment coming to shore and he said, "If we had had this, we would've won." I replied, "Thank God you didn't have it."

One day in August 1944, we were told to leave all our equipment as it stood, except for our personal belongings, and were sent to the main assembly area of the company HQ located on the top of the bluffs. We were taken to the beach, put on an LCM (landing craft mechanized), and shipped out to a British troop transport. We were in Portsmouth the next morning and put on a sealed train. We went to Scotland, had a two-day pass in Glasgow, and boy, did we use it. Soon after that, we were taken to the *Queen Mary* and were one of the few outfits on that ship. After a few days of sitting on that ship, a barge appeared with Winton Churchill and a British marine contingent, who were off to meet with Franklin D. Roosevelt. They boarded our ship and we landed in Halifax, Nova Scotia, five days later. Churchill gave his infamous "V" sign and everybody was yelling and applauding.

In Camp Kilmer, New Jersey, we were told by a brigadier general that we had one week's leave and were then supposed to report to Camp Stoneman, California. Before I knew it, the outfit embarked on another transport and took a thirty-five to forty day cruise to New Guinea, where the army was staging for the invasion of the Philippines. We had our naval shore fire control and air liaison to coordinate air strikes and naval gunfire, as we had done in Normandy. When I landed, I saw my first Filipinos and fell in love with the people—I'm still in love with them. I saw Douglas Macarthur land, with all the press and the jeeps ready for him. He was cheerful and waving and I was very impressed. I also found some Jewish refugees in Manila who had come from Germany and had been given asylum in the Philippines. They had been in Manila for a while, and the Japanese didn't bother them because they did not make a distinction between Germans and Jews.

One of my biggest memories of that campaign was when the U.S. troops captured the airfields and one of the Japanese POW camps where they kept the survivors of the Bataan Death March. When I saw these prisoners coming out, it was one of the few times that I actually cried during the war. They were in their original uniforms—the blue denims that they had been captured in—and like the concentration camp survivors in Europe, they were emaciated skeletons. It was heart-wrenching to see them.

I was spared the large-scale invasion of Japan when the United States dropped the bomb on Hiroshima and was back in America in February 1946.

I was discharged from the army in December 1946, finished college from January to June 1946, and graduated with a Bachelor of Special Studies from City College of New York. I then applied and was accepted for a job (qualification: German speaker) with the War Department, and in July 1946 I was on the boat back to Bremerhaven, Germany.

I returned to Mainz (in the French zone of occupation) many times, also Gonsenheim where I was born. There were some old friends still there. Mainz had been bombed to pieces and was a desolate, unrecognizable place. My house in Gonsenheim was still standing, but I never went back inside.

I was at first assigned to the Civil Censorship Division, where I censored German mail and phone calls for evidence of subversive (Nazi) activities. I joined the Counter Intelligence Corps (CIC) in 1947; that's what I really wanted to do. My rank was a civilian with the War Department (GS-7), but then I moved up to GS-12 and also obtained a commission as second lieutenant in U.S. Intelligence Reserve.

It was mainly on-the-job training and directives and instructions from superiors. I had an intense (though not necessarily favorable) interest in the Germans and what was happening to them.

At first, I must confess, we of the occupation looked down on them for what they had done. In the CIC, I located and interrogated Nazi figures, including members of the Gestapo, and reported my findings to my superiors. I also sent some of them to the "special branch"—the Denazification branch of Military Government. I also investigated falsified questionnaires. In my view, the Denazification program was a total and colossal failure. I came in contact Gestapo figures during my CIC time and mainly dealt with Nazi bureaucrats, mostly questioning their Nazi affiliations, etc.—in other words, interrogations.

One incident I'll never forget: I questioned one guy who had gotten a job with the Americans by lying about his background. I had his photo in my drawer showing him in the uniform of an SA captain. I asked, "Were you ever in any national socialist formation?"

He replied, "Oh heavens no, never." I thought I had him there. I showed him the photo and said, "Who's that?"

He said, "Oh that? That was taken during Carnival in my costume." I had a hard time getting control over myself before I had him arrested. Most Germans admired my knowledge of the language, but never let on that they thought I was a Jewish refugee—at least not to my face.

My main contact with Nazi crimes really came after my admission to the bar when, from 1964 till about 1995, I acted as commissioner for German courts and a prosecutor in Nazi crimes cases pending in German courts. Germans could not act by themselves here in the United States because of international jurisdictional rules prohibiting one nation to perform judicial acts on the territory of another. Also, most witnesses were in America and refused to go to Germany, so the Germans needed a local "yokel." I got witnesses for them, interrogated these witnesses, recorded their testimony in affidavits (which, over the years, added up to more than a thousand), looked for evidence in Washington, and even presided over courts that came here. I did this in over two hundred proceedings, including the Majdanek, Auschwitz, and Josef Mengele cases.

I was, and still am, a member of the board of directors of the Claims Conference, as well as several committees. Furthermore, I am honorary legal advisor. I am also still president of the American Federation of Jews from Central Europe, which was founded before the war by German-speaking refugees. We have about four hundred members, but we are getting smaller day by day, since many members are joining that great refuge in the sky.

Looking back, I would say that I regarded some Germans as morally inferior people who had succumbed to the biggest criminal in their (and maybe human) history. I also regarded some as having been trapped in a totalitarian net. My feelings are mixed and hard to describe. I had relatives who were murdered; there were two old widows (Morgenthau) living in Paris with their son, Julius. These poor old souls, wonderful people, perished; their son as well.

In June 1950, after Korean War broke out, I returned to New York and went to law school at New York University to prevent my having to go to Korea. I'd had enough war. I chickened out.

I was admitted to the New York State Bar in 1953 and got involved in restitution problems almost immediately. In 1958 or 1959, I was hired by

Dr. Adolf Hamburger (formerly a lawyer in Berlin) and was busy with restitution and indemnification cases fulltime.

In my view, the Conference on Jewish Material Claims against Germany (Claims Conference) has been a huge success, supplying many thousands of Holocaust survivors with essentials and supporting Holocaust education and research. I have devoted a lot of time and energy to the Claims Conference since my "retirement." I'm satisfied with what I did, but also feel I didn't do enough or should have done more.

Weinschenk lives in Baldwin, Long Island, and continues to practice law in New York City.

Chapter 7
PETER TERRY

VIENNA, AUSTRIA

3 Troop, 10 Commando
Normandy Campaign

Peter Terry was born Peter Tischler in Vienna. Just after the German annexation of Austria, his family departed for England in 1938. After serving a brief stint in the Royal Pioneer Corps, he volunteered for the commandos and was assigned to 3 Troop, 10 Commando—X Troop—a top secret brigade of eighty-seven refugees from the Nazis. On D-Day, he landed with 47th Royal Marines as a frontline interrogator.

The Enemy I Knew

I had a happy youth, and in retrospect, and a very comfortable time until I was fourteen. Austria was a good country to grow up in, provided you weren't too politicized. But then again, thinking back, it really was a lousy country.

I grew up in Vienna. My parents had a house on the outskirts. My father, Maurice, was a surgeon who switched to dental surgery: restorative surgery on the face and on the mouth and jaw. He was quite prominent and well known. Vienna was relatively a small town back then. It was a life surrounded by servants, although I went to public school until I was ten, and then I was sent to a boarding school outside the city. It was a fairly classical education—Latin, Greek, etc.—compared to England, which was very continental, concentrating on learning things by heart and absolutely devoid of any creativity.

My father had been an officer in World War I and thus, as was usual in those days, there was a fossilized history for the Jew. My grandfather, who was born in Romania and moved to Vienna when he was a small child, was more consciously Jewish. There were occasions when I was consciously made to feel Jewish, but I never suffered from any outright anti-Semitism until my family had neighbors who were German diplomats; that was when I started to be conscious of it. I was ten years old and their daughter and I went to school together. One afternoon, I was invited over for tea and I noticed on their wall was a poster—"Down with the Jewish Press" with a swastika at the bottom. It was obvious I was invited over to their house for a reason. The following morning the two older brothers of this girl beat me up. Their father, the diplomat, came by our house and he and my father had a long talk. To make a long story short, the two boys were made to apologize to me.

THE ANSCHLUSS, THE GERMAN INVASION, came totally unexpectedly. I remember March 11, 1938, was a Friday. We were dismissed early from school and told to get home as soon as possible. On the trolley car, I noticed a large demonstration, an anti-Nazi demonstration, and I joined in—mostly for fun—chanting, "Red and white color until we're dead." Somewhere near the Opera, from our right, a Nazi demonstration was coming toward us, and we noticed they were protected by Austrian police wearing swastika armbands. They started running toward us, and I ran all the way home. I got home just in time to hear the final speech of the Austrian chancellor, Kurt von Schuschnigg, announcing that he was offering no resistance to the invading German forces. It was a very worrying night.

We had telephone calls from people telling us about nasty things that were happening. One very good friend of my parents told us that brown-shirted Nazis had already come within a few hours. A truck stood downstairs and they stole everything there was to steal and then dragged her husband away. When she asked about what would happen to him, they said, "You can collect his ashes tomorrow at Gestapo headquarters."

We also received several phone calls from people abroad urging us to get out immediately, including one from the Duke of Windsor (who was then staying at the Ephrussi de Rothschild Villa in Saint-Jean-Cap-Ferrat) asking if he could help. Vienna used to be an international medical center, and patients like the Duke came from all over Europe to be treated. The Duke visited Vienna yearly before and after his short reign as Edward VIII, partially to consult some physicians, including my father, with whom he became quite friendly. (On one of my birthdays, I received a present from him, the latest model of a Puch bicycle.) Back then, the Duke generally stayed as a guest of Alfons de Rothschild in the country and at the Bristol Hotel in Vienna, where a complete medical unit with X-ray and other equipment had to be installed because the Duke did not visit doctors' offices. At the time, my father declined his help, thinking that the League of Nations, or at least the British and French, would force the Germans to turn back.

Brownshirts, the SA, were the worst. When we looked out the window on the street, and we lived on the sixth floor, we saw horrible scenes—people, mostly Jews, being arrested, being forced to clean up the anti-Nazi slogans from the street.

At that point, somebody called from England and offered to help—which they eventually did—but at that point, my father said, "There's nothing that you can do." The next few days were pretty rough. German planes flew over the next morning and dropped leaflets. Right in front of our apartment was a park, which became an encampment for hundreds of German soldiers.

The German soldiers came into Vienna and I watched that. Unexpectedly, they were a very bedraggled group. The German Army broke down forty miles between Vienna and Linz because their supplies hadn't reached them, which was because they entered three days later. They were dirty, as if they had been through a war. Still, the Austrians greeted them with open arms and cheered and shouted, "Heil Hitler!" I remember distinctly that they didn't look like the German soldiers that I expected to march into town.

Everybody wore a swastika badge unless the person was a foreigner or a Jew. Therefore Jews were recognized for not wearing anything. These badges were sold on every street corner for a few cents and were available in all different sizes. Real anti-Nazis also wore the badge but a tiny one, so if you saw somebody with a small badge you knew they were anti-Nazi Austrians. The bigger the badge, the more support the wearer wanted to show.

On the second day, the concierge of the building came up with enormous Nazi flags and said he was told that each apartment had to fly one. Since we were Jewish, he said it was best to comply so as to not draw attention to ourselves. So, from our porch, there flew a Nazi flag and no one bothered us.

My parents didn't allow me to go out on the street, mainly because of the scenes we kept seeing and people who kept calling our house. The mother of the writer Stefan Zweig, who lived in England, was an old lady who, at that time, had a nurse. She was used to going for a walk every morning in this park. Literally within a day or two of the Anschluss, park benches were marked that Jews were forbidden to sit on them. She saw that, but sat down anyway. She wasn't asked to move, but the nurse refused to sit with her. When they got home, Mrs. Zweig was agitated and her doctor—a colleague of my father's—said that he wanted the nurse to stay overnight. The nurse said she couldn't stay overnight because she read in the papers that Aryan women were forbidden to stay in a Jewish house (unless they have been employed for a great deal of time) and especially if there was a male Jew was present. So, the doctor ended up staying with Mrs. Zweig, and she died shortly after.

The next few weeks, none of us Jews went out. We found out on the telephone that all schools were closed, mainly to weed out Jewish teachers.

I had one incident after school started. When I had to change trolley cars, I saw a department store and there were some Brownshirts with an Austrian woman carrying a poster that read, *"Ich bin Christian Schwien"* (I'm a Christian pig because I shop at a Jewish store).

My father and I were arrested in May. One Sunday morning my father said, "We should get fresh air and go to the park." There was a park called the Prater in Vienna. It was the first time my father and I went out for pleasure. We were suddenly surrounded by Brownshirts who had come out from behind a tree.

They asked my father, "Why aren't you wearing our badge?"

My father replied, "Because we are Jewish." He then produced a document which had been given to him at the instigation of Dr. Seyss-

Inquart, the new chancellor Hitler had installed (he was hanged as a war criminal at Nuremberg at the end of the war). We had known Seyss-Inquart very well from before the Anschluss. There had been chamber music at my house every Sunday afternoon, and one of the guests who often came was Seyss-Inquart, an attorney, but back then nobody knew he was an illegal member of the Nazi Party and also close to Hitler. About two or three weeks after the Germans entered Vienna, Seyss-Inquart made an appointment to see my father professionally. When he arrived he was already chancellor of Austria. He had seen somebody had scrawled "*Jude*" across my father's glass plaque downstairs at the entrance of the office, which he ordered removed. He gave my father this document, which said, "Herr Tischler is not to be arrested for the purpose of street scrubbing and other purposes."

The Brownshirts in the park took the document to a man sitting in a staff car, and they came back and said, "Seyss-Inquart is out of the country today, so it isn't valid, and anyway it doesn't apply to your son, so come with us."

We went down this big boulevard to the football stadium, and there were thousands of Jews being arrested that day. There were a couple of Austrian patriots looking on from the sidelines; one policeman threw his swastika badge to the ground in protest and was forced to march with the Jews, while one elderly woman yelled insults at the Nazis for being like animals, acting like it was the Middle Ages. She said, "I'm a good Catholic and I won't stand to see this."

We walked to this spot where people were screaming at us, throwing eggs—it was bad. I think the worst thing for me was to see my father, who was a dignified and well-known person, in that situation. When we were marching down the boulevard, we were told to undo our ties and mess up our hair, because some SS man thought we'd look more Jewish that way.

We were told to stand at the Danube Canal, facing the water right in front of us. We were told anyone who turned around would be shot. I remember my father put his arm around me and said, "If they throw us in, the first thing you do is take off your shoes." And then there was silence. Finally, I turned around and they were gone, and in their place were taxis. By the time we got home, my mother was frantic. I remember my father looking out the window for a long time, and he finally said, "Now we leave, we can't stay here." Until then, my father thought everything would pass.

The problem at that time was not leaving the country but finding the country that would take you in. The policy at that time was not killing Jews in Auschwitz but finding ways to send them out of the country. This was also the case in Germany. It was virtually impossible to get to the United States or Great Britain; there was a quota system and you needed a sponsor.

The worst thing was the paranoia of who you could trust.

Two months after the invasion, in May 1938, my father was arrested and imprisoned at the Gestapo HQ, which was formerly the Hotel Metropole in Vienna. The Hotel Metropole was a quite large, old hotel on the Danube Canal bank on the opposite bank from what had been, until the mid-nineteenth century, the Jewish Ghetto. The Gestapo took it over as a headquarters and a prison for some of the more prominent Austrians. Among them were Kurt von Schuschnigg, the now deposed chancellor of Austria, and Baron Alfons de Rothschild, the head of the Austrian Branch. Both Rothschild and Schuschnigg were made to clean the Gestapo latrines.

My father was taken there after a former employee at his office denounced him for having dismissed him when he was found out to be a then-illegal member of the Nazi Party. My father was kept in a single, quite comfortable but locked, former guest room and taken for interrogation every day by an Austrian Gestapo official named Dr. Schmidt, who greeted him each time with the question, *"Sind Sie dret Jude Dr. Tischler?"* (Are you the Jew Dr. Tischler?)

Meanwhile, my mother contacted the Duke of Windsor and asked him if he could now help us get to England. One day, Dr. Schmidt suddenly rose from his desk, apologized to my father for the past "inconvenience" and personally took him down to a waiting car displaying the British Union Jack flag. It had been provided by the British Embassy through the intercession from the duke. Who, after all, could refuse a request from a former king?

That scoundrel Schmidt also got in the car, and they were driven to our house, where my father's unexpected appearance sparked a joyous reception from my mother and the servants. She thought Dr. Schmidt, who was in civilian clothes, was responsible for his rescue, and greeted him and thanked him profusely, to which that bastard replied that he would be happy to help us in any way he could. The surprising thing was that he actually did, and he facilitated our departure for Switzerland five weeks later.

It was a very moving scene on the plane. In those days, a three-engined aircraft was used and the flight to Zurich took three hours. At one point, there was an announcement from the captain that we had just crossed the border into Switzerland. There were several other Jewish families onboard and they all got up and embraced each other. One very old Jewish lady grabbed a Swiss Air flight attendant's hand and kissed her. There were also some German businessmen, Nazis, sitting silently. No smiles there.

We arrived in Zurich that afternoon. It was incredible for me to not see swastikas everywhere and one really felt free. We took a night train to Paris and then stayed there for many months. My father went to England, where he treated many members of the royal family and tried to decide whether he should practice medicine there or in Paris. He decided on England and we followed.

Despite the nasty things said about the duke and his domineering wife, Mrs. Simpson, regarding their apparent admiration for Hitler, it was he who had got us out of occupied Austria and had his former equerry Sir Geoffrey Thomas to meet us at Victoria station in London. Among my father's patients was Sigmund Freud, who was already in England at the time, and he had arranged for us to stay temporarily in the house next door to his in Hampstead. This place was a boarding house for retired colonels of the Indian Army, and it smelled like boiled cabbage. We ate awful food compared to Vienna.

Former patients of my father started to shower money on him. Subsequently, we moved into a newly acquired house in St. John's Wood (near Abbey Road). When the Germans first penetrated the London defenses, we watched a dogfight over Regent's Park, and that night we were bombed out of our house. My parents were then offered a small house belonging to Lord Victor Rothschild in Buckinghamshire, outside of London.

IN 1940, I WAS SENT TO BOARDING SCHOOL and England became my home. I had already spoke English when I arrived, and I soon became more British than Austrian. I immediately began writing letters in English because it was easier to converse than in German. To the other kids, I was this colorful personality because I was from someplace else, and was immediately accepted.

On my eighteenth birthday, I enlisted into this awful Pioneer Corps. It was an unarmed British regiment that was a glorified Labour Corps for men unfit for military service and Enemy Aliens like me.

Yet there was a tremendous class difference; the unfit British couldn't read or write. That first night, I thought I was in a place where all of the British jails were open, and the escapees had the better jobs. I spent a month rolling tar barrels over uneven ground that were unloaded by English pioneers, and another Enemy Alien had to roll tar barrels across the field to unload onto a train. I always suspected it came back every day just to keep us busy.

From the moment I got in, I wanted to do something. I made a nuisance of myself and kept on going to the colonel every day and telling him, "I have to join a fighting unit. I'm fit and speak several languages and there's got to be a better way." Finally, they got somebody to interview me. That's how I ended up in this funny German-speaking English unit.

We had to go to Bradford in Yorkshire, which was the original induction center when I joined the Pioneer Corps. We were told to get rid of our uniforms or anything with our names in it. We didn't know why, but anything we wanted replaced, we just put our names in it. Then we were told to follow somebody to a train station. That somebody turned out to be our future sergeant major, who wore a funny uniform. We got onto the train. In England all signs of towns were removed during the war, so in case German parachutists were dropped, they wouldn't know where they were. But somebody who knew the area said that we were going to Wales.

When we arrived at our destination, I remember seeing men in commando uniforms and green berets and suddenly recognizing someone who had mysteriously disappeared from the Pioneer Corps. Then we started to recognize more people whom we knew. The lorry driver taking us to camp was Private Tennant, formerly Von Troyan, a non-Jewish Austrian from the province of Styria.

I asked him, "What is this place? Where are you taking us?"

He said, "There will be no return ticket; once you're here, you're here. You're lucky if you come out alive." It wasn't much of a welcome.

We reached a house and saw the man who interviewed me in London. He would be known to us as "the Skipper." He had the London phonebook out and gave me a few minutes to choose a name; I chose Terry. Now I had to let my parents know how to contact me. It was up to us to find a mail drop—someone with an English name who lived nearby and knew my parents. To this person we would address the letter so that the local Welsh postmaster in Aberdovey wouldn't suddenly start seeing letters to people called "Tischler," or other German names and ultimately get suspicious as to who we really were.

The Skipper was Brian Hilton Jones, a smallish fellow with a baby face. He looked like a fifteen-year-old. He was a Cambridge graduate who majored in German but very few of us knew this. In fact, he never let on that he knew German probably because he wanted to know what we said to each other. He was a somewhat remote person but a superman. Having come from North Wales, he was a rock climber.

It was pretty horrendous in the beginning what he made us do. He told us to go down into the village to the jetty and, in full uniform jump, into the sea. Then he would scream at us because we got our weapons wet and make us do the whole thing again.

I remember a ridge almost at the top of a mountain, where we were in single file following the Skipper, who hailed from these parts and had probably done this many times before. The ridge was sometimes just a foot or so wide, with almost vertical drops on either side, and there was a howling wind. Ahead, the Skipper walked with hands in his pockets as if this was just a stroll along Regent Street in London, while we, laden with fifty-pound gear, negotiated the ledge by sitting atop and moving ourselves along on our bottoms, trying not to look down on either side. I felt rather foolish doing this, especially when I saw the Skipper come to the end, turn around, and look at us in those embarrassing positions, slowly shaking his head in apparent disbelief at that sight of his commandos being scared stiff. I have forgotten what he said after we reached him. We all sat or lay down and lit our mess kits to prepare some warm rations. Finally, after a rest he ordered us to get up and descend the mountain, so we did, re-negotiating the ridge in the opposite direction, this time standing upright. Hours later we reached Harlech, the town from which we had started. There was never a bad word said about this man.

In addition to this, we were taught demolition and house breaking—there was a former burglar they let out of prison to teach us. I can still get into anyplace you'd want me to. I know how to break in.

During a survival course, there was a man who joined us called the Duke of Rutland, a frightfully aristocratic fellow. He was training with us because he was going to join the Long Range Desert Group. During the course, we were told by some man in the catering corps how to fend for ourselves when we were nowhere. This idiot started off by saying, "Well, if you are out in the middle of the jungle or somewhere, if you want to cook, the first thing you have to find is a frying pan. Now you can always find a frying pan."

And there was the Duke of Rutland leaning on a stick, who said, "Oh *can* you?"

I had a German Army course taught by a former sergeant who was in the Afrika Corps and captured by the Eighth Army. From this course, I learned every rank, the whole order of battle, names of German cleaning materials for jackboots, brass work, and glassware. We even learned German songs.

There were some very colorful characters. One of my best friends was Julian Sayers—a Hungarian Jew named "Sauer," who had been an art student in Paris. When war was declared, he was afraid that France would be invaded and went south to Marseille, where he joined the French Foreign Legion and was sent to Morocco. When the Germans invaded the first countries, Denmark and Norway, the French Foreign Legion was sent to Norway to fight the Germans. When the British and Free French withdrew, he got on a British destroyer, which was sunk. Julian was now swimming and was somehow saved. He was picked up by another British battleship. When the British realized he was Free French, they dropped him off in Calais, France, instead of taking him to England. He was sent to an army hospital in northern France to recover from his wounds. When the Germans invaded northern France, he walked out of the hospital and managed to get to Dunkirk and then to England.

We called him "the old man" because he was thirty. We all thought he looked like the French actor Charles Boyer and considered him like a papa. He had been on the Dieppe Raid in 1942, which was a compete disaster and in which he was shot in the right arm. When he landed on D-Day, he was shot in the same arm again. He eventually became a very successful fashion designer.

There was George Saunders—whose name was Saluschin—from Munich, where his family owned and ran a well-known magazine similar to *Life*. They were a prominent family, non-Jewish and anti-Nazi. A friend, who was in the SS, told them that the SS had orders to arrest the whole family and managed to get them out to England, with a number of SS men actually packing up their belongings! Georgie went to school at Gordonstoun, founded by a famous German educator named Kurt Hahn (not Jewish) at which Prince Philip, later Duke of Edinburgh, was a pupil. Later the royal children, including Prince Charles, were educated there. Somehow, George inherited a title from his mother's family several years ago and is now a count.

Eight of us were sent to Officers Selection Board in Winchester and were told D-Day was about to happen. If we stayed, we would be sent to Officer Training School for three months and we would miss the invasion. We decided to rejoin our unit, admittedly after we were told that in all likelihood we would get field commissions if we behaved ourselves. All of us left except for three people.

The biggest fear was hearing the letters "RTU" (returned to unit), if a soldier couldn't handle the training. That would mean he would be sent back to a non-fighting unit, and for us that was not acceptable. We were looking forward to killing, I'm afraid.

At that time, however, we didn't know that we would not all go into action together. When it finally came to it, we were all divided among other units. This was Mountbatten's idea, the reason being if we all went in together as a unit and if the Germans should capture all of us, they would soon learn that we were all either Jews or deserters and they would be legally allowed to shoot us. So, we were sent in groups of four or five to serve as German Army experts in different commando groups—to interrogate right on the forward line.

After we left Wales, we were together with the Free French and Dutch Commandos, and there was a pre D-Day exercise, just to embark and go close to the German-occupied French coast. We were just ten miles away where I could actually make out houses, but none of us knew that it was just an exercise. Why the Germans didn't start firing I will never know, but I shall never forget the French men shaking their fists at the coast and cursing the Germans.

We were in quarantine in Portsmouth with 47 Royal Marine Commando a few weeks before D-Day. I was sent there with another colorful character, a Viennese chap called Didi Fuller, or Eugen von Kagerer-Stein. What was unique about that unit was that we were the first ones to land on D-Day.

We were on a boat for three days anchored off the Isle of Wight. Then we transferred into these small LCA boats, about thirty men to each. What is not generally known is that we were in the water for four hours in that landing craft, because we had to line up in the correct order and circle around in very heavy seas. The last half hour, being seasick and mortared, along with small arms fire, was certainly without a doubt the worst time I've ever had in my life. It was absolutely dreadful.

I had managed to stand up and saw the boat in front of us being hit with my friend in it from 3 Troop named Webster (Weinberg). I got glimpses of Webster in the water and another boat throwing him a rope, but it missed him and he died.

As we neared the beachhead, it became obvious that the Devonshire Regiment had not taken Le Hamel and there seemed to be heavy fighting. The Devonshire Regiment (part of 50th Division) was to have established a beachhead to allow us to get through. Then, hopefully avoiding German units farther inland, it was to swing west parallel to the coast and cover twelve miles of gap between the British beaches and Omaha in order to attack Port-en-Bessin from the rear. It could not be taken from the sea, as there were these two ominous German "features" on the hills either side of the port.

Our LCAs were manned by two naval personnel steering them, and they received radio orders from HQ to find some other place. Thus we went along the coast to find map reference "Jig Green" at the end of Gold Beach, where it became Juno and Sword beaches, awaiting Canadian armor. We came under heavy fire from guns at Longes and lost five LCAs along with their men and equipment. On those was most of our equipment, including all except one three-inch mortars, and all working radios. Out of the original fourteen landing craft, we were now only nine, and the fire was all concentrated on our remaining craft, the only ones in that area. Absolute hell!

Nobody believes this happened, but it is absolutely true. When the ramp went down, I was on dry land. We ran on this enormous beach there, and it looked like least a half a mile until we could find some cover. People were falling left, right, and center—it was really dreadful. When I saw the Spielberg movie, *Saving Private Ryan*, I had heart palpitations, not only from what I saw, but also because of the sound effects, the noise. It all came back.

We didn't see any Germans, just their constant fire. After we recovered, we were lying in the dunes and I saw more men landing and being mowed down. After a while some of the medical chaps picked up the dead, covered them in blankets and put them in a very neat row on the beach. Then suddenly the tide came in and these corpses were bobbing up and down.

We happened to be with a very good man named Major Walton, who said, "We've got to do something, we can't stay here." So Didi Fuller and I, being the German Army experts attached to that unit, were sent to find out where we were. We decided to go beyond the dunes where there was this road parallel to the coast and we saw German vehicles going up and down it. So we went back and came to a pillbox which had fire coming out of it. I was armed to the teeth and I had a row of phosphorous grenades and all kinds of weapons I could find. Suddenly a German came running out of the pillbox and toward me. Somehow in my mind, I don't know whether he had his hands up or not—he probably didn't—but I fired and he fell. I don't know whether I killed him, but I think he might have been the first guy I killed. By the time I got there, Didi Fuller had opened the German's tunic and took his pay book out, and it turned out he was a Pole in the German Army.

FULLER AND I HAD BEEN TRAINED in German military radio usage, and our mission was to detach ourselves from 47 Royal Marine Commando before reaching Point 72 overlooking Port-en-Bessin and find German divisional HQ in Caen. None of us expected that we would have to fight Germans units on the way, which held us up. I was constantly being called to the front whenever they saw a German. Occasionally, we had to fight through villages, including a battle near La Rosiere. Later I found out that 47 Royal Marine had only 180 odd men left out of a total of 345 who should have landed in the morning.

The most extraordinary story happened when somebody was looking through binoculars and saw a German riding a bicycle coming toward us on the road. I was called up front, and I looked and he appeared to be a high ranking officer. We had blackened faces and I was lying in a ditch. When he passed by us, I jumped out and said, "*Halt Hande Hoch.*"

Slowly he got off his bicycle, put it down, and said, "*Ich bin Regimentsstabsfeldwebel und erwarte dass ich im Sinne der Genfer Konvention behandelt werde.*" (I am regimental staff sergeant major and I have to be treated according to the Geneva Convention.)

When he told me he was regimental staff sergeant major, I remembered something. In training, we learned it was a rank that didn't exist anymore. It was highly unlikely that I would ever find somebody like that, and I was very proud of myself.

He was an interesting guy. He had been on the Russian front, got frostbite and had his toes amputated, and got a medical discharge. When things were going bad for the Germans, he was drafted and sent to Normandy. It was considered a cushy job. At any rate, he had decided to give himself up because he had had enough of the war. But before doing that, he wanted to go to a brothel. He called it a "poof." At that point, Didi Fuller pulled out a notepad and asked the German for directions to it.

The German told me that when he first saw me, he had a shock for a minute because he thought we were British Indian Army. They had been told never surrender to British Indian Army because their soldiers cut out the tongues of their prisoners. I assured him I wouldn't do that.

I had a Viennese accent and could call to Austrians to give up. Surprisingly, whenever we took prisoners, all of the Germans wanted to go to Canada, which for some reason they thought was ideal. So I shouted that if they gave themselves up, they would go to Canada. It worked a few times.

I thought the prisoners would be surprised to see me, a British soldier speaking perfect German. Their reaction was most extraordinary. One of them said, "Of course all of you British speak perfect German." None of them ever asked me how. I used their language and their terms. Some actually thought that I had been in the German Wehrmacht, surrendered, and gotten into the British Army. Often they were so scared that in spite of all the revenge feelings that so many of us had, the first thing I did was to offer them cigarettes.

I had hoped to get some lousy SS guy and we did catch some from Panzer Lehr Division. I caught an officer who was an absolute bastard and treated him accordingly.

He was very arrogant and wasn't like the others who had been with me. They had all stood at attention when they spoke to me. We were really supposed to keep prisoners under constant tension, and I yelled at him to stand at attention and salute. I did things I should not have done.

We detached ourselves from the unit in mid-afternoon—by which time we should have not only reached Port-en-Bessin, but also assaulted and taken it! German divisional HQ was in a chateau in Caen, the biggest town in the area. The wires from the chateau were supposedly just lying above ground and then connected to the pylons of the French postal telephone service. We were to plug into the wires and provide confusing information to the HQ.

Fuller and I lay up in the high grass, observing the chateau from about two hundred yards. I had a wonderful pair of large Zeiss binoculars I had earlier taken from a German officer prisoner. We saw no activity, until we heard the voices of women walking along a lane crossing our field of vision. To my surprise, they were speaking Spanish.

Fuller and I stood up to show ourselves and received the most fantastic welcome imaginable. The girls were mostly in their twenties, many of them quite pretty, and were all refugees from the Spanish Civil War and interned by the French at the chateau. They had been in their early teens when they had fled to France with their families in the late 1930s and had been interned ever since. The French Milice and police, and a few German guards, had disappeared that morning when they observed the Allied fleets on the horizon. We were, of course, the first Allied soldiers they had seen. They told us that one part of the chateau had been occupied by a few Germans with a lot of telephone or radio antennas, but they had all had disappeared a week earlier, with only a skeleton crew left behind.

In retrospect, the hour or two we spent with the girls represented the only really good time I had on D-Day, and regrettably we had to leave them to rejoin the 47 at Mont Cavalier before nightfall. The 47 had taken it without a fight. Before that, however, Fuller and I looked for and found the above-ground wires, which had been cut. Quite a lot of equipment had been left in one room of the chateau, so I threw a grenade through the window in case the Germans decided to return.

When we got to the bottom of the hill, we reported to Colonel Phillips and were shown a dugout with about a dozen German naval personnel. They had been wounded by our naval bombardment and were under the care of a German doctor from Munich named Dr. Grunwald, with whom I got along quite well. He gave me some very important information, including the names of the commanders of the German garrison in that town. This was important to know because when we shouted across at the Germans, we could call them by name, or call to the troops: "Hauptman, so and so is leading you to surrender and you will die unless you give up."

I told that German doctor to ride his bicycle into Port-en-Bessin, which we could see from the top of Point 72, with a pillow case we found to be used as a white flag and a letter I had written to the German commander. The letter explained that they were surrounded, exaggerating our strength, and that the entire garrison should surrender. We never did see the doctor again, and they never did surrender, so the place had to be taken.

I did not take part in the assault on Port-en-Bessin because I had been shot in the leg by a sniper. I was helped by French farmers who hid me overnight me on their farm. When I woke up, suddenly a whole German company was coming into that courtyard and started eating. I had my Tommy gun, which I instinctively grabbed, and then the French woman there put her arm on my shoulder and said, "We have children here, don't fire."

Port-en-Bessin was taken that day, and in the morning I had forty-odd prisoners locked up in the barn. The same Germans who were in the courtyard were absolutely quiet because they did not want to be found out by the Germans that they had given up. The prisoners found a cart and wheeled me into town and I was evacuated to England. D-Day was on a Tuesday, and by Saturday, I was in my parent's house.

THREE WEEKS LATER, following my recuperation from the leg wound in England, I was on an American destroyer heading for Gold Beach, which had been secured. After I arrived back in Normandy on June 25, I got a jeep to find 47 Commando holding a line just above the village of Salnelles, which was still in German hands—that is, at the extreme eastern end of the beachhead overlooking the French town of Cabourg. To get there, I drove over the now-famous Pegasus Bridge, and along some stretches of the road, there were large handwritten signs with arrows pointing in one direction saying, in English, "Danger! Next three hundred yards covered by enemy sniper in village on your right. Increase speed and do not stop under any circumstances."

The 47 Commando was actually entrenched in individual foxholes at a place called Le Hauger, consisting of what had been three small hotels, in one of which we had established our HQ. Before it was taken, one of those buildings had been a brothel for German officers, with the second floor furnished with nothing but beds divided by curtains on rails fixed to the ceiling. That was now where Colonel Phillips and his officers slept.

The road from Hauger then curved downhill for a short distance, at the bottom of which was the village of Salnelles. (When driving down during the 1994 fiftieth D-Day anniversary, it took me less than a minute.) To the right of Salnelles, there was an unpaved lane leading to a large farm called La Grande Ferme du Buisson.

Then there came a terrible patrol. The reason for it was madness: General Dempsey, Montgomery's second in command (similar to Omar Bradley in the

U.S. forces), had arranged to visit us at Hauger. So Colonel Phillips planned a "fighting patrol" for that night to ascertain the nature of some vehicle noises we had heard from the German lines and the road they used for supplies, to determine if they were armored or just lorries. We were also to capture and bring back a German officer.

The latter was almost a daily occurrence, mostly deserters who were Poles and Ukrainians serving in the German forces. Lately, however, we had captured no officers except for one lieutenant I had caught some days before. I was particularly leery, after some Poles, who were brought to me a couple of hours before we were to start the patrol, said they had been laying mines along the very path we were to take along the hedge to the famous T-Junction.

Of the fourteen of us, I was the only one who had patrolled that same area along the hedge, where I had been several times before, though not beyond it, as the Germans were dug-in there. So I was chosen to lead up to there, and when we got there, the rest could decide what would happen next. So we were lying there, whispering. A South African captain, who had joined the unit from England a day before, wanted to be up front. So when we moved forward, I was roughly in the middle. Ahead of me, there was an explosion and a flash, and then there was silence. This was at 2 a.m. The captain had stepped on a mine and then MG34 machine guns opened up on us. Then our mortars started shooting but fell short.

I don't really know what exactly happened, but I was thrown forward and felt something on my back—no real pain, but I couldn't breathe properly. I just remember calling out, "I'm hit!" Somehow in this pandemonium, I found myself in a ditch inside one of the hedges and passed out. When I came to, I saw some Germans with Red Cross and an ambulance. I called out to them as I had been taught to do: "I am a wounded British soldier and I need help."

They either didn't hear me or didn't want to hear me; I'm lucky they didn't. I decided if I stayed there I was going to die, so I made my way back inside the hedge, which was very difficult because it was filled with roots and water. At one point I didn't think I could make it anymore, so I climbed out of the hedge because I figured I was closer to our lines, but then I got shot in the arm—a 9mm bullet from our own chaps who saw someone (me) coming from the wrong direction. Ian Harris (who wasn't part of that patrol) from 3 Troop heard I was missing and decided to come look for me.

When he got to the hedge, he shouted, "Is anyone down there?" I made some noises, and when he found me, I was in a pool of blood. He carried me back, got the help of a brigade major halfway, and got me to a first aid station.

I spent seven months in the hospital. I still think that patrol was all for show, and it ended with 100 percent casualties on our side. Every one of the fourteen men I led was wounded or killed. That was the end of my war.

Peter Terry was a principal of the British manufacturing company, Sericol, specializing in chemicals needed for the manufacture of the then newly invented printed circuits. He and his family moved to the United States to start subsidiaries in New York, Chicago, and Singapore. He retired in 1994 at age seventy and moved to Bridgehampton, New York.

Chapter 8
WILLIAM KATZENSTEIN

SCHENKLENGSFELD, GERMANY

505th Parachute Infantry Regiment, 82nd Airborne Division
Normandy and Holland

*William Katzenstein left Germany in 1937 and settled in
New York. He was sent to the Military Intelligence School
at Camp Ritchie, Maryland, and soon volunteered to join the
paratroopers. After jump school at Fort Benning, Georgia, he
was sent to England and joined the 82nd Airborne Division,
505th Parachute Infantry Regiment (PIR) regimental
headquarters company, Intelligence Section, S-2 Section. He
is pictured above in 1945.*

I was born on May 5, 1924, in Schenklengsfeld (county Bad Hersfeld) in Central Germany. My father was Isfried Katzenstein, whose grandfather came from a town named Katzenstein near Fulda, Germany. My mother, Lina (nee Weinberg), could trace her family roots to Spain.

In 1929 my family moved to Bad Langensalza, about 18 kilometers northeast of Eisenach-Thoringia, Germany. My father was a successful dairy cattle dealer and had built up a great business in Langensalza from 1929 on. He lost his business in 1937.

As a child in Germany, I played soccer and other games with other children in my town. I had a normal childhood in the late 1920s and early 1930s. By the mid-1930s, things started to change in Germany. I remember that things really started to change when most of my friends began joining the Hitler Youth. At that time, they started calling me a "dirty Jew." The insults soon escalated into violence that included beatings. I remember many trips home from school that included bloody noses and broken glasses. Only ten to twelve Jewish families lived in the Bad Langensalza, and almost everyone in town ostracized us. I began to find different ways to go home, but that did not work.

My father asked me if I wanted to take some boxing or wrestling lessons so I could defend myself; I wanted both. A day or so later, my father found a man named Georg Ehrlich, who was not Jewish. Ehrlich means "honest" in German. He had been a professional boxer and wrestler. He was about thirty-five years old and a socialist [of the left, not a National Socialist], and the Nazis banned him from all professional sports. To make a living, he taught wrestling and boxing. In the basement of his house was the gym where he gave his lessons.

Ehrlich taught me boxing, wrestling, and judo. His lessons included stuff both in the book and not in the book. I trained three afternoons a week for six months. Finally, he told me, "You're ready."

One afternoon shortly after my last lesson, the same Hitler Youth gang that regularly assaulted me on the trip home from school confronted me again. That day I felt prepared and confident. Recalling my lessons with Ehrlich, I was able to maneuver the fight to the ground of my choosing. I chose a building that had a large brick wall and had my back to the wall to eliminate the possibility of being jumped from behind. That day, there were five or six boys taunting me.

When they confronted me, I turned around but didn't cringe or plead with them to let me go, as I had in the past. They were surprised and shocked at my reaction. I then pointed at the largest boy and said, "Who's the first Fatherland's fighter to beat up on the dirty little Jew?" I told the largest boy to step forward and fight me one on one. As he moved forward, I kicked him as hard as I could in the groin. He crumpled forward in a great deal of pain. I grabbed him by the hair and swiftly and forcefully raised my knee to his face. As I pushed him back, I gave him a kick in the belly and he landed flat on his back. I then said to the other boys, "Who's the next Fatherland's fighter to beat up on the dirty little Jew"? At that, the boys fled and left me alone thereafter.

About a year later, we immigrated to New York. Our family had several relatives in America who sponsored us. My mother visited in 1936 and returned with visas (good for one year), so we came to the United States in 1937. Before that, my mother had arranged for a tutor in English in addition to my three and one-half years in school. I was very anxious to go to the United States and experience freedom for the first time. We went by train to Holland, stayed for a few days with friends in Hoofdoorp, and then came to United States via the SS *Staatendam*. We landed in Hoboken, New Jersey, in October.

First of all, everything was bigger; we lived in Manhattan in the Washington Heights neighborhood, so populated with German refugees it was jokingly called, "the Fourth Reich." There we knew many people and were constantly visiting back and forth. I delivered groceries and laundry packages, shined shoes, delivered newspapers, and so forth. My father, a businessman who didn't speak English, had a terrible time, but we eventually moved to Middletown, New York, in October of 1939, where he bought a farm with big barn and an eleven-bedroom house. He started in the cattle business again, my mother opened a summer resort, and things were looking up. After I graduated from Middletown High School, I went to Baltimore, Maryland, where I worked in a dental lab and took pre-dental at Johns Hopkins University at night.

We still had family members trapped in Germany. My second cousin Rosel, my great aunt Minnie, and other distant relatives remained behind. My father "bought" my aunt Minnie out of a concentration camp, but could not get Rosel out. Prior to the big roundup in 1940 and 1941, he got visas for forty-eight people. He accomplished that by having $20,000 in a bank; to sponsor each person, you had to guarantee you had $5,000 by getting an affidavit from the bank and then you got four visas. He would then move the money to another bank, get an affidavit from that bank, and bring over more people, etc.

My father anticipated the war. When the United States started sending convoys to Britain, he said, "Sooner or later, we will have to get in." I wanted my revenge, so I volunteered at the draft board.

In March 1943, I was inducted into the U.S. Army. I went to Camp Pickett, Virginia, for my basic training. Solicitation boards arrived on base and I signed up for the Military Intelligence School at Camp Ritchie, Maryland. At that school, I learned numerous ways to think on my feet. For example, I learned everything from how to drive a train to flying a Piper Cub plane. I even learned how to make a crude map with just a pencil, a piece of string, a clipboard, and a piece of paper.

Following Military Intelligence School, I volunteered for airborne training because of what I had been through, and what the Nazis were doing to my people. I figured that Uncle Sam was doing me a great favor by training me and providing me with transportation and weapons to help me get my revenge. It was strictly voluntary and more dangerous. To my thinking, it was well worth putting my life on the line. Most of the guys I trained with were okay, but there were always a few anti-Semites. Since I had good hand-to-hand training, I usually challenged the biggest one and quickly put him on his behind; as a rule, the rest wanted to be friends with me after that. Every once in a while, I had dealings with a few refugees and we helped each other.

In May 1944, a few months after I graduated from the Parachute Training School at Fort Benning, Georgia, I was shipped to England and assigned to the 82nd Airborne Division, and subsequently to the 505th PIR regimental headquarters company, Intelligence Section, S-2 Section, as a translator/interpreter/interrogator. My unit went from Boston to Southampton, England, via the *Queen Mary*. It only took three and one-half days, since the *Queen* could outrun the U-boats.

My first action was on D-Day, the night before the beach landings on June 5. Before my jump, my heart was beating like crazy and my guts were churning, but I got used to it. I was a "pathfinder" and part of the first unit to hit the ground and liberate the French town, St. Mere-Eglise. My primary job was to be in charge of observation posts from which we went on night patrols to take prisoners alive (if possible) for interrogation. We were aware of impending attacks and laid ambushes. On one occasion, we annihilated about thirty Krauts and took prisoners. With prisoners, I usually asked questions about family, their hometowns, etc., and then led into pertinent questions. Out of 150 interrogations, I had only 2 who refused to answer.

We then invaded Holland—Groesbeek and Nijmegen. In Normandy, there was constant movement, but Holland was different. We had taken it and the Germans were constantly attacking. A few days after our initial jump into Holland, at about ten in the morning, I was "requested" to go to a U-shaped hill outside the small town of Reithorst. I was to interrogate and bring back a captured German captain and two enlisted men. I traveled to the hill with a lieutenant in a small staff car we had liberated. As we approached the hill, there was no activity, not even small arms fire. There was a windmill on top of the hill, as well as a small building that resembled a log cabin. The prisoners were inside the building guarded by one of our men, who left after I arrived.

Suddenly, all hell broke loose. It was the beginning of another German attack on the hill. The building had a sliding door with a latch on it, which I closed. I had my Tommy gun with me and went down the hill to join the fighting. As I made my way toward the men, the Germans were coming out of the woods attempting to overrun our position. This was my first eye-to-eye contact with the enemy. It was different from Normandy, where I had fired a few shots, but because of the tremendous hedgerows, I could not tell if I hit anybody, although sometimes I heard someone cry out.

A German soldier charged out of the woods in my direction, less than thirty yards away, and my finger froze on my trigger. I let the whole thirty rounds of ammo go into this man, ripping his waist open. I was pretty scared and also out of ammo. Another German lunged at me with a bayonet. I called to the guy next to me to throw me another magazine of ammunition, but he wasn't able to get the ammo to me quickly enough. So I reached for my knife, which I held in my right hand, while deflecting his bayonet with my left. Although he ran his bayonet over the knuckle of my index finger (the scar is still faintly visible), I managed to shove all seven inches of my knife into his belly, just above his beltline.

I often reflect on this encounter and realize that if it were not for my training, I would not be here to tell this story. Moreover, most of us young Panthers thought we were invincible and I was an agnostic; however, at that moment I became a believer. While the military hand-to-hand combat training was excellent, I felt that there must have been someone "up there" looking out for me. My old trainer, Georg Ehrlich, must be looking down on me smiling from ear to ear.

At any rate, the German attack was repulsed within about ten minutes after my encounter; however, during that short period of time, one of our lieutenants was in the top of the windmill directing mortar fire while the Germans were firing mortars on our position. I called up to the lieutenant, "Sir, you better get out of there quickly." A moment later, a shell sheared off the top of the windmill, not more than two seconds after he left the premises.

The lieutenant then directed me to get the prisoners out of the area. I found a jeep and driver and piled the Germans in the jeep. There was no more room, so I jogged along the right side of the jeep with another trooper on the left. About one to two hundred yards from where we started, we were fired upon. I yelled out, "You sons of bitches, stop firing!" thinking it was likely that it was our own men were firing on us after seeing Germans in the jeep. A few seconds later the firing stopped, but not before our right rear tire was blown out. The driver asked me whether we should change the tire. I responded, "To hell with the tire, let's get out of here." We then proceeded to regimental headquarters on the double.

My next action was the Battle of the Bulge where we were trucked in. I was only in the Bulge one day and was wounded. I caught shrapnel above the left knee and, the next morning, was evacuated and sent to recover. Although I left to rejoin my unit in March on French 40 and 8s (trains from World War I), we were constantly sidetracked to other places, so I didn't get back until May 13, after the war had ended. I was more than overjoyed, if not totally ecstatic, that I had been a conquering soldier. I felt that I got my revenge for my second cousin, Rosel Faist, many cousins more removed, and murdered friends. I did not have the opportunity to return to my hometown until 1995.

I was awarded the Purple Heart, Bronze Star with four clusters, Combat Infantry Badge, ETO Ribbon, French and Belgian Croix, and Fleur De Guerre. I even got a good conduct ribbon and more. For the last sixty some odd years, I have often reflected on my war experience; I told my friends and grandchildren war stories. The latter fought over my medals.

As a civilian, William Katzenstein continued to work in U.S. Army Intelligence for many years in Washington, D.C. He lives in Virginia and remains active in the 82nd Airborne Association.

Chapter 9
KARL GOLDSMITH

ESCHWEIGE, GERMANY

142 Interrogation of Prisoner of War (IPW), U.S. Army
European Theater of Operations

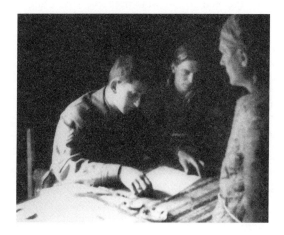

Karl Goldsmith was born Karl Goldschmidt in 1921 in the Hesse region of Germany in a town called Eschwege. After Kristallnacht, he immigrated to the United States in 1938 where he finished high school in Upstate New York. Upon graduation, he was accepted to Cornell University, where he studied agriculture until being drafted into the U.S. Army in 1942. Goldsmith trained at Camp Ritchie, Maryland, as an interrogator of prisoners of war and landed in France with his small unit, 142 IPW, in September 1944. After VE Day, he was appointed military governor of his hometown of Eschwege. The photograph above (Goldsmith at left) is during his service in the American Military Government, Germany, 1946.

To understand what went on in Germany in the 1930s, history books are of very little use somehow. They cannot grasp the reality of a single life or that of a family. William L. Shirer's book, *The Rise and Fall of the Third Reich*, is about as accurate of a chronicle as I have read. However, to tell a personal story is different. Not as earth-shaking perhaps, but probably a bit sadder. In retrospect everyone's vision is 20:20, but it seemed utter nonsense to my father to leave Germany in 1933–1938—after all we were all Germans. He and my male relatives had served with distinction in the German Army in World War I.

We were Germans first and Jews second. Was this the reason why, in our myopic stupor, we could not see the handwriting on the wall?

Hitler must have seemed unreal to my father. He thought that this must pass. After all, anti-Semitism had been in Germany before. We lived with it. Epithets had been shouted at us occasionally and I had been hit, but somehow it was not so terrible. I felt secure at home with my family.

As soon as Hitler came to power, things got worse. My friend from across the street, Wolfran "Dieko" Schaefer, called to me out of his basement window. I went down and he was polishing his shoes. We were both twelve years old, and his birthday was July 24, a month and four days after mine. He said, "Karl, I can't play with you anymore. If I play with you, none of the others will play with me." After that, he would only occasionally acknowledge me with a nod when no one would see us.

In 1934, it was constant harassment. I was in the third class of the Gymnasium [high school] and it became brutal. During recess, we Jewish boys stood together so as not to be so vulnerable to physical attack, but no luck. My friend, Kurt Frankel, was beaten unconscious over the head with gym sneakers, was hospitalized with a brain concussion, and was never the same again. He survived, but was a very sad man throughout his life.

My teacher, Mr. Almerodt, one day simply ordered me in front of the class and caned me with the words to the class: *"So verfrugelt han einen Jude"* (This is the way you beat up a Jew). For this episode, which I never forgot, I ordered him to pull weeds in the Jewish cemetery in 1946, when I was back in Eschwege in charge of Denazification for the U.S. Army.

Practically daily on my way to and from school, I was stopped and had to fight. But when you're one guy against ten, you're not going anywhere.

It was a hellhole for us in 1935 and 1936, but we lived a fairly normal life. We had a beautiful home with a lovely garden. It became obvious that us Jewish youngsters would not be working in their father's businesses (most of which had been seized by the Nazis), but rather would have to learn a practical trade that could be put to use wherever we would find ourselves—hopefully abroad. I wanted to be a gardener, which in Germany meant fruits and vegetables, as well as flowers.

The Jewish community in Hanover had set up the Israelische Gartenbauschule-Ahlem for homeless Jewish boys, or those who had been in trouble and were sent there to learn a trade or enter a business career, rather than go to jail. The school had developed over the years into an outstanding model of a training center for a gardening career. The director was Mr. Rosenblatt, a wonderful man crippled from French bullets when fighting for the German Fatherland in World War I. The master gardener was not Jewish and, to top it off, was a Nazi Stormtrooper. It was interesting to see him in his brown uniform going off to his meetings. He was the only Nazi I have ever met who was not anti-Semitic. It was to his credit that during the infamous Kristallnacht (Crystal Night), in November 1938 when the synagogues were sacked and hoodlums invaded all Jewish homes, Ahlem was not touched. We could still see the glow of the burning synagogue in Hanover, and during that night, two of our teachers killed themselves.

The Nazis came looking for my father, and my mother said, "Lutz [Ludwig], run. Don't come home for two days and then you can still help me clean up afterwards." So, he ran up to the attic and lay on the crossbeams. As the Nazis stormed in the house, he opened an attic window, let himself to the ground by the drain pipe, jumped in the car, and left.

Closets crashed around my mother as they ransacked the house. Telephones were ripped out. Paintings were slashed. Crystal and china were broken, and then they left.

Thank heavens my uncle Walter in New York had given us affidavits. We were called to the American consulate in Stuttgart to be interviewed and examined. Here was to be more horror.

The consulate employed Germans and never before had I been treated like cattle. This was degradation at its worst. My father, who had had cancer two years before I was born and had surgery to remove it, was told by the vice council that he could not go to America because of his medical history. You cannot imagine the absolute fear, horror, and terror this produced in my family. It was a horrible experience for me, a seventeen-year-old boy to see my proud, sixty-year-old father degraded, insulted, pushed around, and treated like dirt. He actually broke down and cried. And so, my parents insisted that I take the visa and go to the United States with the hope that I could send for them later after they had gone to Palestine. I never saw him again. He died two and one-half years later.

So I received a visa for the United States stamped into my passport. The passport itself was another form of degradation. Unless a Jewish person in those days had an obvious Jewish first name, he had to add "Israel" as a second name. My father's name was Ludwig Goldschmidt, so the name in his passport read "Ludwig Israel Goldschmidt." Then, to make sure, a large red "J" for Jew was stamped on the passport.

So, it was destined that I was to go to the United States and my parents to Palestine. We went to the railway station, and the train took us to Holland. At the border inspection came a final Nazi guard admonishment not to ever come back. Soon the train was over the border and we were free at last. The clock had turned back maybe 500–1,000 years, and my family was wandering the world and looking for a home.

When you are young, however, you look at the world maybe with rose-colored glasses. To me, it was an adventure. I was all alone on the damn *Queen Mary*. I was a top-notch ping-pong player at that time, and I won the ping-pong championship on the ship. That to me was important.

I stepped off the boat with $3.50, or something like that, in my pocket, and that's how I started out in America. The first impression I had of the United States was that all the girls wore hats that were shaped like bird nests. And I saw children who didn't beat each other. I also didn't have to look around the corner to see if someone was going to beat the daylights out of me. All of this provided a tremendous sense of relief.

My first job was as a landscaper in Lake Mahopac, New York. After I left there, I ended up in Bedford Hills at a tuberculosis sanitarium as a pot washer and an onion peeler; every day I peeled twenty-five pounds of onions. During all this time, my correspondence was regular with my parents in Palestine. By 1941, the world situation got more serious, and I was ever more concerned about the war. My father died in June of that year.

The Japanese did a miserable thing at Pearl Harbor, and it was a matter of course that the Germans would follow, collaborating with them, and there was a declaration of war. I listened on the radio to the president, and I knew I had a job to do. That job was to help America win the war.

Karl Goldsmith

On December 8, war was declared and I found myself as being classified an Enemy Alien. I wanted to get in the army to fight for America, but enlistment at that time was the privilege of citizens only. It took me a while to convince someone to let me in the army, so I wrote a letter to the then Governor Herbert Lehman, and I received permission in 1942 to volunteer for the draft.

It took till September 1942 for me to report to active duty after obtaining a leave of absence from the university. At the induction center in Syracuse, I hoped no one would notice my flat feet. Thank God they didn't, and I was in. Next stop was Fort Niagara, where I was sure they would assign me to either the field artillery since Cornell University's ROTC training had prepared me for that, or engineering to take advantage of my camouflage training special courses I had taken to supplement my knowledge of plants. I was also positive that I would be placed in military intelligence to take advantage of my knowledge of German or somewhat poor French and Dutch.

Instead it was dress parades, VD films, and watching AWOL prisoners smash rocks so we would learn by example, and then off to Camp Wheeler for thirteen weeks of infantry basic training. I attacked basic training with everything I had. I was a good shot and great with a bayonet. Following this glorious time with all its episodes of rifle, machine gun, and bayonet training, I thought I would be chosen for Officer Candidate School because of my "superior intellect" as a college student, but it was not to be. Again, I was still an Enemy Alien by definition and not yet a citizen, so it was back to the barracks and to St. Augustine, Florida, to become a valued member of the 254th Military Police Company for riot control.

Before leaving Camp Wheeler, however, I was to taste my first Americanized form of anti-Semitism. We were on a field exercise and it was close to the time when selections were to be made to determine our next assignment. I wanted infantry, specifically a heavy weapons platoon. It seemed the quickest way to get into active combat. It may sound childish, but I had this feeling that I was going to be able to do something. You take this for granted that you can make a difference. Being a European boy, especially having gone through the Hitler period the way I had, I was so gung-ho it was absolutely a riot. I had a grudge to settle.

The officer in charge came by and I asked if it was possible to request this assignment. He answered, "Why not join the Jewish Army?" This was the derisive term for the Medical Corps.

I became livid and impulsively shot back at the captain: "I don't have to take that kind of shit from anyone!"

The captain walked off. This kind of language was a court martial offense in 1942. So, we all marched back to the barracks, and pretty soon a sergeant summoned me to the company HQ. I was ushered into the captain's office, who closed the door, and I was alone with him. This man, my company commander, a captain of the U.S. Army in the year 1942, turned to the private in his fatigues, who only three years before came from Nazi Germany, and said, "In regard to this afternoon I want to apologize to you for what I said."

I thanked him and left the room. I stepped out in the Camp Wheeler sunshine, head held high and deeply grateful that my belief in the justice of the American system had again been confirmed. This episode, so very significant to me at that time, can probably be only understood if the reader places him or herself in those times. Somehow, it seems that throughout my life at crucial moments there always appeared the right person, remark, or action that reinforced my evermore deeply felt belief that America was great because of its people. It's a bungling country, maybe crude and rude, but always searching to be better. I felt, and feel, lucky that my father's foresight sent me here.

So it was not the infantry but a new "elite" MP force, not like in the past of having just simple soldiers on police patrol, but a special unit of well-trained MPs trained in riot control for future problems to be faced in captured enemy lands.

In the U.S. Army on February 5, 1943, in the district court in Jacksonville, Florida, I became an American citizen almost exactly four years after coming here. It was a wonderful moment on a great day. In our group, I was the only German and by definition the only Enemy Alien.

In June our training finished, and we shipped out to the Yukon Territory in Canada to protect the new Alcan Highway, which extended from the railhead in Dawson Creek, British Columbia, to Fairbanks, Alaska. This part of my war experience was strange, boring, and in some ways maturing. I was reduced in grade from private first class to private because I shot a hole in the barracks floor with my .45.

I felt strange; I wanted to get into the real war and not just sit it out in the Yukon directing traffic, patrolling highways and streets, and guarding gasoline dumps, no matter how essential they were. One day, I saw on the company bulletin board that anyone having foreign language skills could apply directly without going through channels to the War Department in Washington, D.C. Needless to say, I saw a way to get out of there and wrote immediately.

Soon, I was sent to Military Government School at Fort Custer, Michigan. This was a great experience. Many of the nation's finest historians and international law experts taught us what to expect in occupied territories. I was then told to report to Camp Ritchie, Maryland, to train as an interrogator of prisoners of war. At Camp Ritchie, the washout rate was very high, but I made it and with luck I met John Slade. He was born Hans Schlessinger in Frankfurt and was thirteen years my senior—highly intelligent, honest, and decent, and as good of a man as one could wish to be with. When he arrived in New York, he started out as a foot messenger for a very small investment banking firm called Bear Stearns, and he made such an impression on the head of the firm, Joseph Bear, that he kept getting promoted.

After he made enough money, John was able bring his entire family over to the States. When the war started, John, who was already thirty-four at the time, really wanted to serve in the army, but since he was the sole provider for his parents he wasn't sure whether he should go. Joseph Bear, who absolutely loved John, told him, "You go into the army; I will take care of your parents, and when you come back your job will be waiting for you." What employer would do that today? Anyway, John Slade was probably the finest interrogator in the European Theater of Operations. I held the rank of staff sergeant and John was a technician third grade, which was just half a grade below mine. We were a successful team.

We left Camp Ritchie and were in Camp Kilmer, New Jersey, awaiting our ship. We soon boarded our transport in New York and started our convoy trip to Europe. The quarters were cramped, the food was so-so, but what the heck, we were in good spirits. By the third day out, I had lost all my money playing poker—I have stayed away from gambling ever since that sobering occasion. Basically, the trip went smoothly; there were some U-boat alerts but no attacks, and we landed in a "camp," which was actually a group of row houses evacuated for our use, near Manchester. There I was exposed to true hunger. We Americans had plenty of food, which was dispensed to us out of large containers directly in our mess kit. When we finished, we put the scraps in a refuse barrel. There were always children, English kids, with buckets asking for our scraps. No scraps ever went in the scrap barrel. This was a sad sight.

John, nicknamed "Pop" because his being older than all of us, and I decided to go out on the town and eat in a good restaurant. What followed was almost like a scene from the Marx Brothers. The waiters brought a beautiful silver-topped cart, ceremoniously lifted the cover, and, lo and behold, there appeared the tiniest morsel of meat, looking totally lost on this silver serving tray. It was comical.

London was being bombed at that time by V-2 bombs. V-1 could be seen because they looked like miniature airplanes; their motors sounded like a motorcycle, so as long as you heard the motor you were safe. When the motor cut out—look out below, down comes the bomb. Much more sinister was the V-2, because no one could hear it. It just came. It happened all around, but I didn't get a scratch.

Soon our orders came to go. I couldn't begin to tell you how excited I was. I was a very proud American by that time, and I was doing something that it was high time we were all doing it together. I was surrounded by people with whom I already had a lot of experiences, and this camaraderie that we had, I guess it's what only happens in wartime. I felt that I was going to show those German sons of bitches what we could do—we, that motley crew from America, that nobody believed could do a damn thing except build automobiles. I wanted to stand on top of my jeep and shout, "Hooray!"

Somehow I was the driver of our jeep. Our team consisted of two complete units made up of six people: 1st Lt. Rudy Freier, 2nd Lt. Michaels, Sgt. Karl Smith (AKA Karl Goldschmidt), Tech. Sgt. John Slade, Sgt. Wilder, and Cpl. Jancowitz. Freier, Slade, and I were always teamed together. The jeep had a trailer that held all our work material including desk, typewriter, etc. Our weapons consisted of one Thompson submachine gun for each jeep, and each of us carried a Smith and Wesson .45-caliber automatic pistol. With these, we drove onto an LST to go to France.

On the first day out in the channel, it was Rosh Hashanah and I made up my mind that we were going to have Jewish services. We had our army- issued prayer books and the word spread. It was unbelievable. It seemed as if the whole LST became Jewish. I suppose when in danger, we all pray to the same God, but I am sure half or three-quarters of my "congregation" were Christians.

When we got to the beach, we were unloaded and we drove into the water. When we came into shallow water, we had been told, "Whatever you do, gun the damn thing and go like hell and don't stop." A special tailpipe was fitted, which was about four feet above us, so we could drive through the surf. About five guys with baseball bats stood there waiting and the moment your tailpipe was out of the water at a certain level, they'd hit the damn thing, out flew that extension and we were on our way.

There were MPs all along the way who directed us. There was a red line and a blue line, one going east and one going west. It was unimaginable to see the vast stream of vehicles and equipment. The Germans had never seen anything like this, nor had the world. Americans production lines back in Detroit trained Americans well. Within moments, if a truck got a flat, or something, there were wreckers, always at the side of the road, that hooked up and pulled the truck off so that the line would never stop. Funny I've never seen that in a movie.

Then we had to establish immediately a POW camp.

Naturally, we moved with the advance and were attached to different units. At first we were with the Ninth Army, and for a short period, because they were short on interrogators, we were attached to the British 5th Armored Division. When we were at the German–Dutch border in a town called Eschweiler, we were with Terry Allen's Timberwolf 104th Infantry Division. Depending on where we were, we interrogated mainly German prisoners who were generally captured only hours or even minutes beforehand. Usually, we would know 50 percent or more of what the picture in front of us presented, since the prisoner did not know what we knew. It was not difficult to ascertain when they were not telling the truth. The fact was that practically all of them talked most willingly. The movies often depict the interrogators as villains, using threats, even force. All I can say is that we got more information with friendly talk and a cup of good hot coffee than shown in all the movie versions.

Once when we were all the way at the Mosel River facing a very tough SS outfit, my IPW was attached to Patton's Third Army. We were at division HQ when Patton had a meeting of his noncoms. He stood on top of a tank, and among other things, he said to pep the guys up over there: "And as far as those damn interrogators are concerned, don't take prisoners! Shoot the bastards!" I'll never forget that. It was typical Patton.

For the most part, prisoners were in shock. One moment they were surrounded by their buddies, the next moment, they would be hit in the head, or stabbed, or a bullet would strike them in the leg and they'd fall down. Now what?

One story that never leaves me is when I knelt down to a POW who had a piece of shrapnel in his partially shattered leg. It must have been horrendously painful for him, and he muttered a few words to me: "*Comerade, gib mir Deine Hand*" (Give me your hand, comrade). I gave him my hand, he did his best to muster a grin and I could just feel that by holding his hand I had helped. And that was wonderful in itself. He did his duty. He tried to fight for Adolf Hitler, and it didn't quite work out.

For the most part, I was very gratified to see captured Germans. I've always said there is no one who rules as harshly and no one who crawls so low as the Germans in victory and defeat. But I didn't have rage. I just felt that they had stolen my country away from me, they forced my father to go to some crazy place called Palestine, and I knew we couldn't let these people run the world, that's for damn sure.

One day Freier and I were going in the jeep through an area that had been infiltrated at night by Germans and *bang*—a bazooka shell whizzed by us and hit an embankment we were passing. It was luck. Freier couldn't hear out of his right ear after that, and to this day he collects disability from Uncle Sam for this souvenir. Only one of us became a causality. One day, Jancowitz drove his jeep over a mine and it killed him. He had just gotten married before we went overseas.

As the war came to a close, we were in Tann, Germany, near the Alpine region where Hitler's troops were supposedly making their last desperate stand. When we were advancing, the front lines were rather fluid and I was bored and wanted some excitement. Freier and I went south and saw a German soldier with a pistol. I stopped the jeep, disarmed him, and asked him where the American tanks were. He said we were the first *Ammies* he had seen. The next town was Landshut, so I asked him if Landshut was in a defensive position. He said there were no troops there. So I said, "The hell with it, let's capture a town." After all, we had a submachine gun and two .45s. Freier thought I was nuts, and was probably thinking of his wife. But I prevailed—maybe he had a little spirit in him after all—and we took off.

At the beginning of town, we stopped some rather frightened Germans, who told us that there were no German troops in town. So we sped to the town square for reassurance; I held the submachine gun—not much help against a good sniper. Out of the bakery came a bunch of French slave laborers. We were their first liberators. Our fun seemed short-lived, though. From the other side of the square appeared four German soldiers with rain ponchos over their shoulders. I could not see their hands, so I took out my automatic. Our liberated Frenchmen scattered, but our luck held. Up went the four Krauts' hands. I relieved their sergeant of his Lugar. (I gave it to my son later on.) As we left town, we had one Kraut on each fender and one in the rear, to discourage snipers. The streets and windows were festooned with white flags made of bed sheets.

Landshut had surrendered to the U.S. Army. When we got back to intelligence HQ, I looked at the map and told them they could move the pins twelve miles farther south to Landshut.

This episode is not glorious, but like many things war is no fun, and when I hear about "atrocities," we committed our share. Those who condemn others, just remember that no matter for what reason, man's inhumanity to man is never justified. Half of our team—Freier, Slade, and I—was running a POW camp of thirteen thousand for which we had the responsibility to weed out SS and other criminal types, and then send the regular POWs to their home as expeditiously as possible. Usually this was by army truck to about thirty or fifty miles from their home, at which point they had to walk or hitchhike the rest of the way, since there were no trains yet and there was no gas for civilian vehicles like buses or cars.

The other half of our team—Michaels, Jancowitz, and Wilder—was in charge of a collection place about thirty miles farther south. They were to send any POWs as quickly as possible by truck for processing. The reason for all the rush was simple: food. The U.S. Army never realized that within a few short weeks, hundreds of thousands of Germans would give up. Obviously, they had to be fed prior to processing. We, in our camp, had a simple solution: one to three horses had to be delivered daily to the camp to be butchered. Obviously that, in combination with whatever flour and vegetables could be acquired, was the POW diet. So, unless we wanted a bunch of wild POWs, we had to process quickly. It all went well, and everyone was moderately content. One day, a fairly high-ranking Nazi was brought to me. After asking him a couple of questions, all of the sudden he popped something in his mouth, fell to the ground, and in an incredibly short time—probably less than a minute—was dead. He had a cyanide capsule, which many of these people were provided, just like Goering who took the same route.

One day, we were expecting a truck load of about fifty POWs from Lieutenant Michaels' group. More than an hour later, there was no truck and no prisoners. I took one of the CIC fellows with me in the jeep to trace the route. About halfway, two hundred or so feet from the road, I saw an awful sight—fifteen dead POWs obviously all shot with submachine guns. Some of them were even some stray civilians. That happened sometimes when soldiers rounded up POWs and suspected that certain young types had thrown away their uniforms and picked up civilian clothes. Unless we cleared them, they were treated as prisoners. But what on earth happened here?

Apparently a bunch of new soldiers who had never seen combat were to guard the POWs on their route from the collection point to our camp. Apparently they "borrowed" the submachine guns from our three guys down there and just decided to kill these Germans. In the pocket of one of the dead men, I found a letter to his wife about how happy he was that this mess is over and soon he would be home. My God, what horror that was. That was not war, it was murder. We decided something should be done. We had the names of the soldiers who did it and the guns, and we forwarded a full report. In short, the judgment came through as case dismissed because of insufficient evidence. What they were really saying was that the 13th Armored Division was ready to go home and this would unnecessarily delay their departure.

I just want my feelings on record that Germans, Japanese, Arabs, or whatever are not the only humans who have acted inhumanely, even though I doubt whether anyone would be able to do what the Germans did in World War II. Six million people—men, women, children—shot and gassed because of some people's crazed racial superiority complex over others just because they were Jews. My mother's sister Anne, her husband Emil, and their daughter Lore are part of this statistic.

When the war finished, I immediately put in a request to be involved with the Denazification of my hometown. I wanted to do that so badly. They kicked the shit out of me so much as a kid. I had earned some brownie points with a whole bunch of bigshot officers, because I had done them favors in my team's capacity as interpreters and interrogators. I got the transfer, and as far as I know, I was the only one of the interrogators who ever succeeded doing that.

The first thing I was concerned about was get the dammed Nazi teachers out of the schools. I worked bitterly hard to get things straightened out.

This was my town, Eschwege, the birthplace of the Goldschmidt and Plaut families—the gardens, woods, trails, hills, friends, enemies, Bar Mitzvahs, parties, frightful beatings, Nazi torch parades, Kristallnacht, and the end of the town's Jewish population in 1942 after more than six hundred years of settlement.

As the military governor, I really think I was a pragmatist. I believed in law and order, and I was a presence in that town. Yes, I found the Nazi perpetrators and they wound up in jail. Aside from that, we cleaned the town up. Everyone knew me, and naturally, people came and asked me for this and that—and I did nothing. I wasn't going to treat this one better than that one. Old acquaintances would come to me and say things like, "Oh, you remember Analee?" Of course, I remembered Analee, she lived four houses away from us. "Well, she's expecting a baby anytime and she is in a third floor walkup. Can you help us?"

My answer was always: "I'm sorry, I cannot do anything about it." What was I supposed to do, inconvenience one miserable German for another miserable German? I was flabbergasted that these people had the temerity to face me and say these things to me, when they knew what they themselves had done to me and my family. Forget about all the other people who got burnt up in concentration camps.

One of the old neighbors called me *Der Ungerkronte Konig*, the "uncrowned king." I lived well and had a great social life. I doubt if my father would have approved, but I did not compromise or bring dishonor on my adopted country or family.

About two years later, after I'd come back to America, my mother had gone to Eschwege to take care of our properties there. When she came back, she said, "Karl, you can never go back to Eschwege; they'll kill you." So, I didn't have a good reputation.

One day I was told that thirty Hungarian Jewish girls had come across the border. It turned out they were the remnants of Hungarian ultra-Orthodox families that the Germans used as a labor force in concentration camps, but if any German touched them they would commit suicide. The youngest was thirteen, and the oldest, their leader, was twenty-one. I immediately got them a house and requisitioned from the Germans clothes and food. The most beautiful moments in my memory will always be when I was permitted by them to come to their home and sit in the dark with only the Shabbat candles burning, while they sang the beautiful songs sung on Friday evenings (Sabbath). I understand that shortly after I left to go back to the States in

January 1946, they found enough families and mates of their background and by now are probably all grandmothers either in the States or in Israel.

When I eventually left to go home to America, I believe I was on the noisiest ship that ever existed. It was wonderful. When we pulled into New York Harbor and saw the Statue of Liberty, the ship listed to one side because everyone was going to the side to see it.

Then there was some kind of welcoming ship, that was small but had huge loudspeakers, and they played "God Bless America." Saying I wanted to kiss the ground is putting it mildly, because it was only at the time when we really did know how lucky we were that we went through that war and survived. We returned as vets and were a different breed. Our innocence was gone. We were all better students because we had a greater sense of purpose. I was an ex-GI, had the GI Bill money in my pocket, and I bought a 1930 Chevy for $125. I had wheels and returned to Cornell University to finish my studies.

I really think I tried very hard to do what I consider as fulfilling the debt. I think I paid back a little bit to the good old country, and what I was given was a new life and future. My reward for going to war was a free country.

Karl Goldsmith entered the insurance industry in 1957 and worked until his death in February 2002. There is a bench named for him in the Cornell Plantations botanical gardens at Cornell University, from which he graduated.

Chapter 10
HENRY KISSINGER

FÜRTH, GERMANY

335th Infantry Regiment, 84th Infantry Division
Division Headquarters, G2, Intelligence

*Heinz "Henry" Kissinger (left) was born in 1923 in the town
of Fürth, located on the outskirts of Nuremberg in Bavaria. His
father, Louis Kissinger, a highly educated teacher, earned the
prominent role of schoolmaster at three different private schools
in Fürth and was a proud member of the town's middle class.
The Kissingers were observant Jews, and Heinz, the older of
the two sons, was eventually sent to the Israelitische Realschule
with other Jewish children from Fürth who could not attend the
state-run schools after 1933. Finally, with help from a cousin in
New York, the family obtained visas in the spring of 1938 and
fled to the United States via England.*

*In New York, the Kissingers lived in the Washington
Heights neighborhood. Kissinger was drafted in February 1943*

and became a private in the U.S. Army. He was assigned to G Company of the 335th Infantry Regiment of the 84th Infantry Division and returned to Germany in November 1944, initially as a rifleman. Upon reaching the frontlines, Kissinger was reassigned to the Counter Intelligence Corps (CIC), where he served until the occupation of Germany, when he became the military governor of Krefeld. In the photograph on the previous page, Kissinger stands with Fritz G. A. Kraemer, an early mentor while in the Counter Intelligence Corps, in Germany, 1945.

One didn't need a huge amount of foresight to leave. The policy of segregation for Jewish people was created so it would become increasingly uncomfortable to stay. When we left, it had not yet reached the killing stage, so we were fortunate in that respect. Also my mother had an uncle in America who had left a tiny amount of money when he died. All of this induced my parents to leave.

I came to New York in December 1938. We settled in Washington Heights where there were many other German Jewish refugees, a lot of whom came from my hometown. Of course it was a totally new experience. I had never seen any African Americans before; the architecture was very foreign to me as well, and I thought the fire escapes were balconies.

We didn't have any money. My mother's inheritance was negligible, so I had to go to work when I was sixteen in a shaving brush factory and go to high school at night. I did not have the normal teenage existence, but then again, all the people that I grew up with, most of whom were German Jewish refugees themselves, all worked during the day, went to school at night, and helped their families. That was the normal way to live for us.

I must say, however, I did not think I was having a hard time. Now I don't know how we lived that way. My brother and I slept in the living room. We had no privacy and no rooms of our own, but I did not feel that I was suffering. I felt like we were accomplishing things, and now I look back to this time period with great satisfaction.

Above all, I didn't realize how discriminated against we had been until I came to the United States, and so it was a tremendous sense of relief and freedom. Those of us who grew up in a dictatorship always appreciated America more than some of those who were native born. It's one reason why, during the Vietnam protests, I never joined any of the people who were saying that America was a dictatorship and spelled America with a "K." I had seen a real dictatorship; to me, these people didn't know what the hell they were talking about.

I wanted to be inducted after Pearl Harbor, but I was seventeen when the war broke out. I had to wait until I was drafted at nineteen. I made no effort to defer, or delay being drafted, or get a special position. Our formal induction took place in Fort Dix, New Jersey. We got our uniforms there and stayed for a couple of weeks.

I remember that my father took me to the train station where we were put on the trains for Camp Croft, South Carolina, near Spartanburg. I did my basic training there and became a citizen about a month after I arrived. They took all foreign-born GIs in my basic training unit; there must have been about fifty boys that were sworn in together. We had to go to court in Spartanburg and take the oath. It was one of the proudest moments of my life.

Before I got into the army, I had never met any really native-born Americans, so being in the army was a way of Americanizing me. In New York I only knew either German refugees or the Italian immigrants with whom I worked in the shaving brush factory. When I was in the army I met real Americans, and these soldiers, mainly people from the Midwest, were very tolerant and friendly—so much so that I thought I'd lost my accent because they never referred to it.

At the end of basic training, especially qualified people were sent to college. I was sent to Clemson University and Lafayette College to the Army Specialized Training Program until Congress closed it down and sent us all back to the infantry. I wound up in the 84th Infantry Division in Louisiana as a private. That meant I had to undergo additional infantry training in the summer months, which were unbearably hot in Louisiana.

I went overseas with the 84th Infantry Division, first to England and then to France, where we landed at Omaha Beach in early September, after the breakout of Normandy. We then went to the front on the border of Germany and Belgium in November, and our regiment was assigned to the 30th Infantry Division for combat experience.

Combat is usually an ordinary experience of extreme boredom, followed by moments of intense danger, but the period of intense danger is very short. I initially came to the front as a rifleman. Then one day, while I was on latrine duty, an encounter happened that changed things. The man in charge of latrine duty had to keep the situation map, which was in the dayroom, of where the front was. Our general came by for inspection, and said, "Soldier, come over here and explain this map to me." I translated it and he said, "What are you doing in a rifle company?" I must have said, "I don't know. I was assigned here." So, while we were still on the frontlines, he gave an order to pull me back to his headquarters, but this wasn't executed for a while, so I remained at the front.

After we had left the 30th Division, I reported to division headquarters for the G2 Section, which was Intelligence. My job was to recapture documents and help interrogate prisoners. However, my primary task was to look after security, catch spies, and prevent our documents from falling into enemy hands.

Once I was more or less assigned to the CIC, I was then sent down from division headquarters to regimental headquarters, which was even closer to the front, and I worked on counterintelligence there.

After that combat phase was over, I was assigned to regional Germany, a county in the American zone of occupation near Frankfurt with a population of about two thousand. My job was to maintain the security of that area and arrest all Nazis above a certain level. I had the right to arrest anybody I wanted for security reasons, which was a strange reversal of roles. Of course, no German ever claimed to have been a Nazi.

Everything had broken down in Germany; there was no postal service, there was no telephone, there was no communication—a total catastrophe. We in the military had our own telephones to other military posts, but no one could call a German on the telephone. There was a food shortage and a terrible black market. It's hard to imagine today how a society could break down that completely. At that time, if anyone had shown me a picture of what German cities look like today, I would have said, "You're insane. It would take thirty years just to clear away the rubble."

At some level, being back in Germany as a conquering soldier gave me some degree of satisfaction when I saw the people who had been so swaggering now on the other side. But on the whole, I felt that I had a job to do, which incidentally I found very interesting. I had always been interested in foreign policy, but I tried to keep my own personal experiences as much out of it as I could.

After the surrender, the first thing I did was look for members of my family to see whether any of them had survived, but they hadn't. I went back to my hometown, the place where my grandparents had lived, and that was somewhat of an emotional experience. Having lost many members of my family to the Nazis, I had considerable animosity toward them, but even with this, arresting people and seeing crying wives and children, was no fun. At least it wasn't fun for me. It gave me some abstract sense of satisfaction, but no personal satisfaction.

For us German refugees, going to war was something that we felt needed to be done, but that we might not particularly enjoy once it happened. For me, however, I now think that it was the most important experience of my life.

Henry Kissinger was the national security advisor and later secretary of state in the Nixon administration.

Julius Hamberg, father of Eric Hamberg, and his brothers serving in the German Army in World War I. *Eric Hamberg*

Jews forced to scrub anti–Nazi Party slogans off the sidewalks of Vienna after the Anschluss. *United States Holocaust Museum*

SA men block the doorway of a Jewish business in Berlin, April 1, 1933. The signs read: "Germans, defend yourselves against the Jewish atrocity propaganda, buy only at German shops!" and "Germans, defend yourselves, don't buy from Jews!" *United States Holocaust Museum*

Karl Goldsmith's German passport, stamped with a red *J* for *Juden*. *Karl Goldsmith*

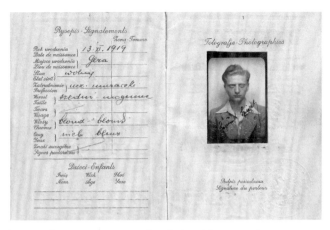

Siegmund Spiegel's passport, issued in Poland because his parents were born in Galicia, a province of the Austrian Empire that became part of Poland after World War I. In 1938 his parents were among thousands of Polish Jews the Nazis deported. *Siegmund Spiegel*

A German Jew at the Mutual Aid Society for German Jews desperately seeks help for his family. *Marc Vishniac Kohn*

Jewish refugees, London, 1940. *Eric Hamberg*

Jewish refugees gather below deck on the SS *St. Louis,* 1939. *United States Holocaust Museum*

Karl Goldsmith (top row, middle) with an interrogator prisoner of war (IPW) team; John Slade (Hans Schlessinger) first row far left. *Karl Goldsmith*

Bernard Fridberg (standing fourth from left) and flight crew. *Bernard Fridberg*

A Jewish chaplain conducts services for Jewish soldiers in the "dragon's teeth" of the Siegfried Line, 1945. *Author's Collection*

Left: Kurt Klein on a mountaintop near Oberammergau, Bavaria, in 1933; Right: Kurt Klein sits in the same spot twelve years later as an American soldier during the occupation. *Kurt Klein*

Friday, January 7, 1944

OUR GIRLS

Von links nach rechts: Pvt. Lillian Zwikler (WAC, U.S.); Corp. Marianne Hirsch (British Army, ATS); Otti Berg, International Fire Service, London.

AND OUR BOYS IN THE ARMY

Von links nach rechts: Siegmar Lachman, Henry Steinhardt, G. W. Leopold.

German refugee newspaper *Aufbau* regularly posted the names and photos of refugee men and women serving in the military.

Manfred Gans standing in front of his family's home in Borken, Germany; during the war, it was Gestapo headquarters and ultimately Headquarters for British Occupational Forces. *Manfred Gans*

Siegmund Spiegel (at podium) speaks on Holocaust Remembrance Day, Long Island, New York, May 1993. *Siegmund Spiegel*

Ralph Baer is awarded the National Medal of Technology, February 13, 2006, by President George W. Bush in recognition of his pioneering work in the field of interactive video games. *White House photo by Eric Draper*

Chapter 11

JOHN STERN

GILSERBERG, GERMANY

100th Infantry Division, 397th Battalion

John Stern was born in Marburg, September 14, 1923. His father was a businessman and owned a general store. When the Nazis came to power, his father sold his business for pennies on the Mark to a local German businessman, and the Stern family was forced to move to Frankfurt am Main. He left Germany on the Kindertransport in June 1939 and stayed in England until May 1940. Upon reaching the United States, he settled in Oklahoma where he completed high school before going into the service. He is pictured above in 1945.

I lived in Gilserberg until I was nine years old; at that time I was no longer allowed to attend school because of Nazi intervention. After that I lived with my mother's sister in Marburg, Germany (about an hour away from Gilserberg), where I attended the Jewish school until age thirteen when I graduated. At age thirteen I returned to my family in Gilserberg for my Bar Mitzvah, but my father was arrested by the Nazis the day before and incarcerated for approximately eight weeks. My father had made a comment to a little boy that he should clean his yard because the German Army was going to be marching in the next day. The Gestapo heard it and said my father was slandering "the glory of the army." It was just an excuse to arrest him. When the SS came, they looked at me (I was very little at the time) and said, "You're too small. We'll come back in a year and get you." When my father came back, he was a broken man.

All I can say is that country treated our family so incredibly bad. I saw my mother and father being beaten by a blacksmith who owed them money. My father asked him for some money and he came in and beat them. We then moved to Frankfurt am Main, where he died on November 3, 1938, five days before Kristallnacht.

I was not allowed to go to high school. Instead I took a job as clerk in a fabric wholesale company and was able to attend a private trade school to learn more about this business. When my Jewish employer had to turn his business over into Aryan hands, my job was terminated.

While I was in Frankfurt, a cousin of mine was arrested and sent to a camp. They hung him upside down and put a water hose up his rear end and killed him. Within two days, his body came home. Thank God my father died before all of this happened.

IN EARLY 1939, we made a serious attempt to leave Germany. We applied for visas and were told there was a long waiting list. Luckily, my brother Gunther had been able to leave Germany for Anadarko, Oklahoma, in 1936 due to the affidavits issued by our cousins who had resided in Oklahoma since the late 1800s. Due to the efforts of some friends in England, an arrangement was made for me to leave Germany through Holland to Harwich, England, via a Kindertransport on June 6, 1939. My mother was left behind in Germany.

In England, I was privileged to live with a wonderful Jewish family in the East London suburb of Forest Lane. This family had three retail stores, and I was fortunate to find employment in one of them until leaving for the

United States. During my stay in London, systematic bombing on the part of the Germans started, and we were all in bomb shelters when this happened.

In May 1940, I left from Liverpool on a Kindertransport for New York. I arrived on May 16, 1940, and was greeted by a cousin who already lived on Long Island. As I recall, I had three English pounds when I arrived (which amounted to approximately ten dollars at that time). Another distant cousin sent me off to Oklahoma on a Greyhound bus with a twenty dollar bill, which I thought was a fortune at that time. I stopped briefly in St. Louis to visit my father's brother and his family who had arrived there shortly before I did. I then went on to Anadarko, Oklahoma, where I was greeted by my brother and my mother, who had finally gotten out of Germany by fleeing into Holland and had arrived in Anadarko shortly before me.

I loved the United States immediately and assimilated myself really fast. The American kids were so accommodating. They were so very curious about my background and would ask me all sorts of questions. I would go from high school to high school explaining what I had gone through and how I came to the United States. I used to fill auditoriums even though I wasn't much of a speaker. I even lectured at the teacher's institute in Weatherford, Oklahoma. People hadn't seen too many Jewish refugees in that area of Oklahoma. Our high school principal (a good friend of ours) was pushing it also, and I was glad to oblige.

After high school graduation, I attended the University of Oklahoma at Norman, Oklahoma, for approximately one and a half years until I was drafted into the army on November 12, 1943. I was quite pleased because it offered me a chance to do something for the country that adopted me. Naturally, what I had experienced in Germany made a serious impact on me and gave me the extra incentive to be a good soldier.

Initially, I was inducted at Fort Sill, Oklahoma, and subsequently transferred to the combat engineering training camp at Camp Abbott near Bend, Oregon, for basic training for demolition and building of bridges. We were shifted as a replacement company to Camp Beale, California; we thought we were going to be in the Air Corps because it was an Air Corps base, but they took us to Camp Reynolds, Pennsylvania. Then we thought that we were going to fight Japan, but we were sent east to Camp Shanks, New York. Thereafter, we boarded the original *Queen Mary* (now docked in Long Beach) for a four-day trip across the Atlantic to Greenock, Scotland. We were all transferred to Oulton Park near Chester, Wales. Before crossing the English Channel, we spent some time in the Salisbury barracks in southern England for more training. Since there was no need for combat engineers, I was sent to the infantry. Not being completely trained as an infantryman, I was a little afraid but I adapted quite easily.

We crossed the English Channel at night in a transport boat on June 22, 1944, and arrived north of Utah Beach near Le Havre, France. Our assignment was to guard the costal guns, which were aimed toward England, around Le Havre, a town recently liberated from the Germans. I remember all of the coastal batteries had already been blown up. That was at the end of June 1944, and yet there were still some snipers shooting at us. After La Havre, we slowly went south to Paris (already liberated), and then joined the 100th Infantry Division, 397th Infantry Battalion, in Nancy, east of Paris.

We subsequently went through little towns and then went up into the Vosges Mountains to our first combat assignment at Raon l'Etape. Within a few hours of being there, we were hit by a tremendous German artillery barrage by the terrifying German 88 guns, which after awhile seemed to be around us most of the time. This was my first time in combat, so I was terrified to hear and see all of the shells landing around us and had this sickly feeling in my stomach.

When that stopped, we moved toward the east and took part in capturing the fortress of Bitche. The 399th Regiment took the brunt of the fighting, and both our regiments had some casualties. We continued east toward the town of Rimling in the Alsace region of France. I am an honorary member of the "Sons of Bitche" (100th Infantry Division). We dug in and held a defensive position.

In the infantry I was a scout, right up front, and in some cases, I was a platoon guide, but under most circumstances I was on the line. My primary function was to kill Germans, plain and simple. For some reason I got very used to seeing dead Germans and GIs. I was young and foolish and didn't think about these things. It's a terrible sight, but you get hardened to it.

AFTER WE CROSSED THE RHINE and the Saar rivers, we went into a city called Hilebraum, where we had a hell of a fight. My glasses were blown off my face. I didn't have glasses for a day or two, even though they replaced them as soon as they could. I couldn't see very well, but I did my job anyhow.

On Christmas Day 1944, the weather was dreadful, sleeting, snowing, ice all of the time, and it was freezing out. We were eating turkey on paper plates when our officers suddenly told us to pack it up and get out of there. The Germans were shooting at us from our left flank, and a bullet grazed my helmet, taking off a chunk of it. There was artillery and German infantry trying to encircle us from behind, so we ran for our lives. Then they put us on trucks, and after twenty-four to forty-eight hours we were back on the front. We were on the southern edge of the bulge when we heard that nearly 50 percent of the 106th Division (a "virgin" division) had been wiped out—that scared us.

We regrouped and Patton's tanks came up around Bastogne—twenty to thirty kilometers due north of us—and rescued us. The worst day was when we were dug in near the Rhine and some American planes came over—and started bombing and strafing us. They were actually captured planes being manned by German pilots.

I would say the majority of us were trained in such a way that we were able to take it, but there were one or two in every platoon who couldn't. Some would roll around and cry under fire. They could be in the back as support, but they shouldn't have been up front, because they weren't temperamentally suited to be combat soldiers. The army didn't make a distinction in those days. I was a combat engineer, but I never built a single bridge. When the Bulge happened, we were *all* in the infantry: medical people, surplus, drivers. Some of the GIs didn't want to take prisoners back, so they shot them. Some of the prisoners were never heard from again. In the passions of war, these things come up and no one can help that. We didn't ask any questions.

We were always advancing, so that's what I did. If I didn't get home, then so be it. Being disabled was the only thing that really scared me.

There was another city called Wiesloch in Baden, near Stuttgart, where we had terrible problems and lost a lot of people there. One instance in the Vosges, some Germans were hiding in the bushes. We went after them with bayonets, but ended up shooting them, and captured a lieutenant. I took off his ribbons and his pistol.

The gratification was that there was retribution being heaped upon the Germans and it made me glad, but on the other hand, I didn't particularly cherish this too much, because I was restrained from taking individual action. It had to be a group action. If we saw a German soldier, we were supposed to shoot him and often we did, but generally there was no individual gratification so to speak. It was something we trained to do and we did it. We would shoot first and ask questions later.

On January 7, 1945, early in the morning I was in a foxhole with another soldier, Nick Herres from Chicago. While observing the area, a German sniper sent a bullet through upper fleshy part of my right shoulder, barely missing the jugular vein. Luckily, I had a first aid kit with me and could apply a bandage immediately. Our lieutenant witnessed this and had the first aid medic take me to a medical facility approximately one mile behind our front. The wound required a few stitches, and within four hours I was sent back to the front.

I had a feeling of elation the first time I stepped on German soil when we crossed the Rhine to Mannheim and Ludwigshafen. I was not a victim but a captor and the feeling was unbelievable.

Within a few days, we were sent to the Neckar River in Germany. We went across in an assault boat under sporadic German artillery fire and advanced toward the city of Heilbronn, Germany, where we encountered stiff resistance from the Nazi SS. We lost several men and the battalion was demoralized.

Once we advanced through Heilbronn, we encountered our first German jet fighter plane. We all took cover and had no casualties. We then advanced toward the city of Stuttgart, which had been evacuated by the German army that had been patrolling the city and the surrounding areas for a month or so. Some of us were transferred to Ulm on the Danube, where we encountered some Russian soldiers who had escaped from German prisons. While in Ulm, I was walking with an Italian friend and a British friend when a woman came out of a house and said, "*Sindehoch alle Juden*" (They're all Jews). I guess we all looked Jewish. I ran up to her and said in German, "Don't ever say that again, otherwise we'll make it very rough on you." I added, "*Nicht Ale Juden* (They're not all Jewish). We're conducting a war here against the Nazis." This incident upset me quite a bit.

While in the Stuttgart area, we had found and liberated two displaced persons camps.

Around that time, I was able to requisition a jeep and a Polish lieutenant from the labor supervision company (a Polish company) went with me for protection while I visited my birthplace, Marburg on the River Lahn. I also went to Battenberg, my mother's birthplace, and Gilserberg, where my parents lived before moving to Frankfurt. In most places, the Germans had innumerable requests for cigarettes and cigars, but I wouldn't give them any. In Gilserberg, I met some of my earlier acquaintances who went to school with me before 1933 and it was interesting because quite a few people welcomed me. My grandfather's name was Gutkind—they used to call me Gutkind's Hans.

It was clear that they were astounded that I was an American soldier and back there. Some woman said, "You never looked like a Jew. You were always so nice." All of the others were stoic. They thought we were going to take all of their property back.

I looked for family in Marburg. I had two cousins who were deported with their mother to Theresianstadt. Nobody wanted to tell me anything. We know an uncle, aunt, cousin, and a baby cousin were transported to Theresianstadt and ultimately perished there. During the Holocaust, the Stern family lost twenty-six close and distant family relatives.

This, in itself, dampened my spirit at homecoming. We stayed there overnight with a family that was close to my father; one of the sons was killed in Russia.

After returning to Stuttgart, the 397th Infantry became part of the army of occupation in Stuttgart and the surrounding area for several months. We had been on the line 192 days, with small breaks in between.

The captain and lieutenant of our unit had arranged that I act as an interpreter when questioning of German officials, such as mayors of towns, police chiefs, and German military people, took place. I interpreted for several months. I also taught a forty-hour German course to about fifty of our soldiers. I was promoted to sergeant before all this occurred.

I liked the fact that members of the Wehrmacht were being captured. I interrogated many Germans, and there were plenty to interrogate. If we asked them if they were members of the Nazi party, they were scared because they knew we were after them. Whenever the *burgermeisters* (mayors) were pulled into the headquarters and asked a lot of questions, I was involved. On different occasions, they often said to me, "I think you were already in Germany," but I didn't answer them. Whenever we captured SS, we stripped them (to see tattoos) and put them in a different camp than the Wehrmacht. There was little German pride left when we were through with Germany. I think the general populace was glad it was all over.

We were assigned to an artillery regiment for return to the United States. On March 10, 1946, we were transferred to Bremerhaven to board the *Lehigh Victory Ship*. After we arrived in the United States, we were trucked to Camp Kilmer, New Jersey, and then boarded a train to Camp McCoy, Wisconsin, for discharge, which took place on March 26, 1946.

I returned to Chicago by train to join my mother and various other relatives. My mother had moved to Chicago once I had left for the army. My brother Gunther had been inducted in early 1942 and served in the U.S. Air Corps as first sergeant at Warner Robbins Air Force Base in Georgia.

Fortunately, due the enactment of the GI Bill, I was able to go to Illinois Institute of Technology from June 1946 through June 1948 to study industrial and mechanical engineering. This helped me find employment in the plastic industry and eventually led to the establishment of my own business, Jomar Industries, Inc., in Gardena, California.

In early 1947, I met my wonderful future wife, Margaret. We tied the knot on June 19, 1949, and moved to California in 1954, where we raised our two sons, Larry and Jeffrey. We now have five grandchildren and three great grandchildren.

John Stern started Jomar Industries, a plastics packaging business, in 1959. This year the company will celebrate its fiftieth year in operations. He and his wife live in Orange County, California.

Chapter 12

RALPH BAER

PIRMASENS, GERMANY

Military Intelligence

Rudolph "Ralph" Baer was born in 1922 in the town of Pirmasens, Germany, a small city in the Rhine-Palatinate region of southwestern Germany, near Strasbourg on the French Alsace-Lorraine border. After arriving in New York, he taught himself electronics through a National Radio Institute correspondence course and then took over two radio repair shops on the East Side of New York City. Three years later, he was drafted into the army and trained as an order of battle specialist at Camp Ritchie before shipping out to France. He became an expert on both Allied and German weaponry and lectured to thousands of GIs. He is pictured above in Tidworth, England.

I was beginning to wonder whether I would ever get that letter from President Roosevelt telling me to make an appearance at the local draft board or at some induction center. It was early 1943 and I was certainly overdue. While I waited, I continued to work at Parkay Radio, the idea of getting out of the rut of servicing radios and TVs being uppermost in my mind.

My dilemma was resolved in March 1943 when I finally got that long-expected official notice. By this time the United States was building up troop concentrations in Great Britain. Anybody and everybody who was male, breathing, and unattached was being called up.

I was proud to be finally part of the action. Despite having lived in the United States for barely more than four and one-half years, I was well on my way to feeling at home here. Furthermore, if there was one war that seemed to have the support of most of the American public, it was World War II. It was hard not to be swept along with the spirit of the times. Having had my life turned upside down by Hitler was another piece of the picture. Time to get even . . .

A WEEK AFTER MY INDUCTION, I said goodbye to my folks, packed a small bag of things, and reported back to the induction center in the cavernous Grand Central Terminal building. I was assigned to a group of several hundred new draftees and promptly shipped off to Fort Dix in New Jersey.

After a four-hour ride in the back of an army truck, we arrived in Fort Dix in the midst of an early-March downpour. Once there, we ate our first army meal in the mess hall; then we lined up in the stockroom, where we were outfitted with GI clothing from top to bottom. "Civvies" (our civilian clothes) were shipped home. Underwear, socks, shoes and boots, overcoats, fatigues, and dress uniforms loaded us down as we dragged them to our assigned bunks in a large barrack.

Daily close-order drill in the company street started the next morning. It took a while before it sank in: we were going to be bullied and yelled at and generally treated like some subspecies barely worthy of the drill sergeant's attention. As we got better at close-order drill, we no longer stumbled around like drunken sailors.

Little by little we began to feel and act like soldiers in "this man's army," as the phrase goes then. The weather was frigid and wet. I caught a bad cold the first day I was there and so did everybody else. We slept in barracks that were about as cold as the outdoors.

Finally, three weeks later, orders arrived and a number of us were shipped off to a place I had never heard of before—Fort Belvoir in Virginia. I wasn't too sure exactly where Virginia was, never mind Fort Belvoir. Based on what little I knew about the job of the combat engineers, it sounded to me like I was going to be trained to become prime cannon fodder, preparing roads and bridges for infantry grunts and armored troops. I had been dreaming of becoming an engineer, but this was not exactly what I had in mind.

It was early April 1943 when I started my combat engineers training, along with all those other raw recruits from the Big City and a fair number of six-foot-plus Texans, Georgians, and Tennessee hillbillies. This was also my first encounter with southern drawls and anti-Semitism in the ranks.

True to my nature, I kept much to myself, did what I was told to do, and took the training seriously. If anything, I took it too seriously. I was certainly uptight about my performance. My German upbringing and the martial discipline of that school system were part of it.

Even in April, it was hot and humid in Virginia; we drilled and worked hard, building roads, assembling sectional Bailey bridges and erecting pre-cut wooden barracks; we also laid and removed lots of mines and booby traps, both our own and several German models.

There was, of course, the usual contingent of twenty-mile hikes. We would lug full field packs, wear our heavy helmets, and carry the even heavier M1 rifles slung over our shoulders. I held my own; even my feet didn't bother me. Hiking, walking, and all other forms of physical exercise had not exactly been my thing, but I was surprised to note how many of the young, athletic-looking guys in my platoon had difficulty during the forced marches, while I just plowed on.

Several men in the platoon were well over thirty years old; they had a hard time coping with the strenuous regimen, what with their bum knees and bad backs. I wondered why they would draft some of these guys and felt sorry for them. There was definitely a war on!

We were taught how to fire both the army's standard M1 rifle and the much smaller carbine. Out on the firing range, I turned into a good marksman with the M1 rifle. Actually, I enjoyed firing weapons, a sign of things to come.

During one of our firing exercises, it was my bad luck to wind up next to the platoon fuck-up. Every small organization seems to have one of them. He would do stupid things while laying prone on the firing line. One time, he pretended to have a misfire, whereupon he would turn the rifle around and look down the barrel. I didn't particularly care whether he might blow himself away, but naturally I didn't like having a loaded rifle swing by me in the process. When I complained to our noncom about this, I got my just desserts and wound up getting assigned to cleaning that man's rifle.

I MISSED MY RADIO WORK most of all during those first weeks in basic training and took every opportunity to fix odd radios that were kicking around and needing attention. I tinkered with radios even if they didn't need attention. In my spare time I wrote my first technical paper: "Converting Radios from AC to AC/DC Operation." It described the theory and practice of the art form that I had practiced so often in my Lexington Avenue repair shop.

After four weeks of basic combat engineers' training in the 2nd Platoon, we got a week's leave of absence. My folks were glad to see me. I was in great physical shape and was tanned a deep brown from the exposure to the strong Virginia sun. While I was home, I moved into my new bedroom-cum-lab. I hurriedly installed all my test equipment and wired up the heavy desk that served as my bench, ready for work. In the short time before my pass expired, I designed and built a tiny battery-operated covert listening device. It consisted of a small microphone, a battery-operated amplifier, and earphones for listening in on conversations through walls and the like.

My naive assumption was that the U.S. Army would really appreciate my compact design. At Fort Belvoir I had seen and operated the crude, oversized, vintage gear that the service was using at the time. My experience with battery-operated portable radios had taught me how to build amplifiers using the latest tubes. The army's covert listening gear was a generation behind those radios, a situation typical of operational equipment in the military back then.

I took my little battery-operated amplifier by train to Fort Monmouth in New Jersey. Monmouth was the U.S. Army Signal Corps' headquarters during Word War II. I hoped to get transferred there and get an assignment as a radio operator. After all, I was a radioman with almost five years of technical experience.

At Monmouth, I demonstrated my amplifier to an officer, but nothing came of it. It was naive of me to think that an unauthorized private currently undergoing basic training in the combat engineers could simply walk into Fort Monmouth and get himself transferred on the basis of some prior professional ability. The army didn't do business that way. In the first place, nothing short of a pile of documents obtained through the "right" connections could affect such a transfer.

During service, my major connection with my previous electronics experience was converting German mine detectors into radios that would tune in the American Forces Network in Europe so we could listen to Glenn Miller. What else is an electronics education good for in the army? Cooks and bakers' school?

When my leave was up, I left New York and took the train back to Fort Belvoir for the last four of our eight weeks of basic training. By now it was early summer. As usual, the Virginia weather was extremely hot and sticky, yet the daily grind of marching went on. We went back to building bridges, erecting barracks or shooting our M1s or carbines on the firing range.

On several other occasions, we were ordered to shed our green fatigues, dress up in formal khaki uniforms, and march in formation around the camp's parade ground. There, we stood at attention in the hot sun for review by some higher brass. It wasn't long before we would hear a rifle hit the dirt, followed by the thump of its owner dropping to the ground seconds later. Pretty soon, two or three other guys would pass out with a similar bang and whoosh.

The moral of the story is this: When you're in the army going through training exercises, you follow orders, oftentimes suspending your belief and common sense—until you get into combat, where you may have to do exactly the opposite.

One day in July we were up to our necks in the Patuxent River working on a Bailey bridge. It was a relief considering the heat. Soon after I got to work in the water, fatigues and all, I was called out again to report to the orderly room. I got into the back of a jeep, still sopping wet and dripping all over the place. The driver drove me back to camp and told me to report to the first sergeant's office. That was more than a little peculiar—what had I done this time? Nothing, it turned out; they had received orders to ship me off to Camp Ritchie, then a Military Intelligence (MI) training camp near Hagerstown in Maryland, wherever that was!

Camp Ritchie was a unique place among U.S. Army training facilities. There were perhaps two to three thousand GIs stationed there at any one time, and not one of these guys was a U.S. national—Ritchie comprised a bunch of foreigners! What we all had in common was the ability to speak a foreign language fluently. In particular, men whose native tongues were German, Italian, or French might wind up in Camp Ritchie. Most of us were there to become interrogators of prisoners of war.

We spent the next six months studying intelligence subjects such as the order of battle for every European army then in existence. The order of battle is the organizational structure of an army starting with the smallest unit, the squad, and moving up through the platoon and company level to the battalion, regiment, division, corps, and finally the army—as in Eighth Army. Of course, there are dozens of variations on that theme in various regular foreign armies and also their specialized organizations, such as their armored groups, mechanized groups, or paratroops.

Now, one cannot properly interrogate an uncooperative prisoner unless one can immediately determine such basic things as his rank and organization by looking at his uniform or by observing other telltale signs. An interrogator would have a hard time getting useful information out of his prisoner unless he had the experience to figure out these basics, even in the absence of any insignia, which many prisoners remove and toss away during capture if given a chance. Those were the tricks of the trade, we learned at Ritchie.

Three months into our training, we graduated from classroom instructions and started doing special intelligence field exercises. We often used maps of the area printed in German or in French, or worse yet, in Russian—as if it wasn't hard enough to get oriented using only a map and compass in some godforsaken part of the Maryland woods. Some GI truck drivers would drop us off there, often after nightfall on some moonless night, and tell us to find the trucks by a specific deadline. The trucks would then be waiting for us at a destination marked on our doctored maps.

BEFORE THEY COULD SEND the non-U.S. citizens overseas, we had to be sworn in. That was the law, or least, it was back then. So, they had piled groups of us into trucks and took us to a courthouse in Hagerstown on October 5, 1943. Once we were inside, we lined up in front of the Maryland judge, raised our right hands, and pledged allegiance to the flag. The ceremony was short and sweet. We were sworn in within five minutes. Then they handed us our citizenship papers. This qualified us to become legal cannon fodder.

When finally our training was complete, I found myself standing outside on a sunny day, one man in a long line of GIs, duffel bag at hand, waiting forever to get onto the trucks that would take us who knew where on our way overseas to the war.

We shipped out in early February on the *Mataroa*, a British freighter no bigger than about twelve thousand tons. Altogether, there were about sixty MIs onboard, including me, plus a much larger number of GIs from various other organizations. At night the MIs slept together in a hold below deck, using hammocks slung over the wooden tables and benches where we ate and sat during the day. Antiaircraft guns went off frequently above us on deck, but nobody told us what was going on. We never knew whether the gunfire was for real or simply a training exercise. We also did not know initially where we were headed. It turned out we were part of a large convoy of ships that zigzagged across the Atlantic toward England, in the hopes of avoiding German submarines.

For the duration of the ocean crossing, about ten days, I lived on imitation Coca-Cola and boiled potatoes. I couldn't stomach the limey mutton that they served us down below. It was forever stinking up the mess room and our hold. I haven't eaten lamb since, except when it's been prepared as shish kebab and that basic lamb taste is conspicuous by its absence.

While onboard the *Mataroa*, a pecking order among the MIs began to develop. Hans Otto Mauksch became our virtual leader by dint of his strong personality. Hans—who was a private first class in this man's army, but had been an officer candidate in the Austrian Army in the 1930s—gradually became our recognized leader. Hans was about twenty-six—old compared to most of us—fairly tall and imposing, and light-years ahead of most of us in maturity, with guts and leadership qualities. He was abundantly equipped with the chutzpah needed for coping with unusual situations.

He was a guy with a mission and he had a vision of what we could do for the troops with our MI training once we got to England. Wisely, he kept the details to himself.

Heavy betting on assorted card games went on amongst the other troops all the way across the ocean, but not by the MIs; somewhere along the line the first mate was reputed to have been heaved overboard during a game—tough crowd!

WE ARRIVED AT THE PORT OF Liverpool on the east coast of England on a sunny afternoon. Leaning over the railing topside, I watched our deckhands and the British dock workers secure the vessel while we looked out at our first sight of old Britannia. She was already well past the major portion of the clobbering by the Luftwaffe, but the scene looked serene and completely normal that day. Liverpool was too far north to be accessible to German bombers or V-2 rockets.

We spent our first cold February night at Miller's Orphanage in Liverpool, sleeping in a cavernous place that had once been a gym where we were quartered alongside troops who had arrived before us. Late at night, we promptly got called out of that huge barn to hit the trenches outdoors because of an air raid alert. The tail end of the Blitz—what was left of the intensive bombing of English cities by the Germans by aircraft and V-2 rockets—almost reached us.

After morning of marching and doing close-order drill as a unit, our group of about sixty MIs got orders to report to the 19th Replacement Depot. On our way there by train, we stopped over in Manchester. While hanging around the station's elevated platform for a couple of hours, waiting for the train that was to take us to Chester, we got a glimpse of Manchester. I remember looking out onto the street from the open platform that was one level above and seeing that old, grimy textile mill town full of ancient brick factory buildings.

After we arrived in Swindon, we were quartered with other troops in a large barracks. We were assigned a new course of basic MI training, the so-called combat intelligence refresher course given at the American School Center, located in Bristol. It was déjà vu all over again!

In Bristol, we were quartered in a large barracks and would soon become an active MI training cadre group for the first time. We would be charged with running classes and lectures for GIs on such esoteric subjects as recognizing German uniforms, ranks, organizational affiliation, and the handling of German weapons and prisoners. Before this, however, most of the group did several weeks of the usual infantry drill stuff, to say nothing of day and night KP.

The major subject headings of various syllabus summaries were:

- German infantry weapons—a detailed discussion and a demonstration of German small arms that we had collected for this purpose
- Identification of aircraft—a two-hour lecture on recognition of U.S. and foreign aircraft in daylight or at night

- Reading foreign maps—a four-hour lecture series covering the reading of German maps and an hour each on French and British map reading in comparison with our own
- Military sketching—a quickie course in the art of making stride scales and planometric sketches for practical field use
- Reconnaissance—a two-hour lecture on day and night reconnaissance methods and procedures
- Aerial photography—a one-hour lecture on definitions and uses of aerial photos, making photo maps, obtaining stereoscopic images from photo pairs, and so on
- Staff duty procedures—a lecture explaining the procedure used by intelligence personnel in handling information from collection to evaluation to interpretation and, finally, dissemination

Additional MI training subjects included a series of lectures on German Army identification, for which I drew several sketches showing the many insignia, patches, head dress, boots, and uniform styles worn by the German Army ground forces and those used by the tank, air force, and paratroop units.

I also reworked a lot of Camp Ritchie material into a series of lectures on German history, with details about the most prominent military and political leadership persons. Abstracts from that lesson material came in handy during our next assignment, when I had to lecture on this subject to large numbers of troops then being staged for the imminent invasion of the mainland. Part of that lecture was an overview of what the German male can expect from life. I made a sketch showing the conscription duties of every German boy and man.

In a matter of a couple of weeks, I was done with the syllabus. Our highest-ranking noncom, Corporal Massimi, became our clerk-typist and helped crank out the lecture notes. Mauksch assigned various members of our group to study my notes and begin teaching classes. The group, now down to fifty-five MIs, was organized into an orientation section, a terrain intelligence section, a German Army section, an aircraft team, an armored vehicle team, a security team, and a training aids department. Our courses covered map reading, identification of enemy personnel, safeguarding military information, German Army, handling prisoners of war, identification of armored vehicles, identification of French, German, and English aircraft, and French and German phrases. "Zip your Lip" also stayed on the program.

As for me, I was soon far more interested in concentrating on our new weapons collection than teaching classes. To that end, I started to pick up whatever training manuals were available on German handguns, rifles, submachine guns, and light machine guns. Although I certainly had no notion of planning it that way, this activity started me on the long road of mastering all manner of detail about European weapons. Almost imperceptibly, I slid into a pursuit that occupied much of my waking hours for the next two years and more.

We packed our duffel bags, left Bristol behind on May 1, 1944, and took a train to Warminster. Our destination was a former British horse-artillery camp located outside of the town of Tidworth. The camp was part of the Salisbury Plain, which was—and still is—basically a very large British Army reservation. It had been used as a training area, where artillery, tanks, and other weaponry had been exercised indoors and outdoors since long before World War II.

The U.S. Army had taken over most of the Salisbury Plain by 1942 and used it as a staging area. The army stationed and trained large numbers of our troops there in preparation for the invasion of the European mainland. There would soon be several hundred thousand U.S. servicemen in the general area. Our common home for an undetermined time would be Tidworth.

We went through our now standard speech of how our group of MIs would serve as instructors for intelligence subjects.

I sat on my bunk in our barrack and updated the lecture notes that I had first generated for the Bristol MI school. They covered the same material of message-handling and recognition of German uniforms, insignia, and weapons, but also some new instructions on the training and psychology of German soldiers, whom the troops would soon encounter.

In short order, we rounded up additional German weapons. In this, we were aided by a ground forces training inspector who saw what we were planning and procured some German small arms for us. The idea was to introduce our troops to the handling of these weapons when needed in a pinch.

I have no idea how all these weapons got to the British Isles. Most likely, they were captured during the North African campaigns and brought back for training purposes. In the weeks that followed, we took advantage of that situation and started hunting for additional German light and heavy weapons, uniforms, rifles, handguns, machine guns, mortars, mines, and booby traps. Lucky for us, that stuff seemed to be everywhere in the Salisbury Plain and places beyond.

After we had acquired a collection of German arms suitable for a teaching display, Mauksch persuaded the camp administration to give us sole access to a huge, empty brick building. It had an arched, corrugated sheetmetal roof, perhaps forty feet high along the crown. Before we Yanks moved in, this building had been used by British horse-artillery troops for indoor exercises, thus it was big enough to allow drilling horses pulling howitzers inside the hall across a dusty dirt floor. Anything would do to keep out of the British weather and the all-pervading muck outside, particularly heavy artillery weapons!

One of the major pieces of heavy German weaponry was the 88mm antiaircraft and antitank gun. We acquired an early "88" that had been used in the Spanish Civil War and did not yet sport the recoil-reducing muzzle-break of the later models.

We focused our collection on German weapons, of course, since the job of our Military Intelligence training centered on the immediate enemy. Specimens from other European countries would come into our collection over the course of the next year, before we established a second Military Intelligence school and museum in Normandy.

Somewhere in Tidworth, we also found a working model of a German Army Volkswagen. It was open on top, its canvas roof was missing, and it had a two-cylinder, air-cooled rear engine. That early version of the civilian VW was a real piece of junk and no competition for our jeeps by any stretch of the imagination. Our specimen was working and we tooled around in it for a bit. Someone was brave enough to try and give me driving lessons in that crate. After I nearly drove it off a small, wooden, banister-less bridge over a shallow gully, my instructor decided to cut my lesson short.

On several occasions I taught visiting British artillery troops how to disassemble and reassemble the German quad antiaircraft gun and the 47mm antiaircraft gun. The antiaircraft gun barrel was about six feet long, so the gunner sat on a perforated metal seat and traversed and elevated the gun with two rotary hand cranks.

It was recoil-operated like an ordinary machine gun and could be disassembled without the need for tools—exactly like the German MG38 and MG42 light machine guns, except that every part was oversized by comparison. As precision machinery goes, it was a good-looking piece of hardware. I got really fast at taking it apart and reassembling it.

In exchange for taking the time to instruct them in the details of these guns, the British invited me to their artillery range in another part of the Salisbury Plain. They offered to let me fire a German 105mm field gun, lobbing shells from one hillside into another across one of those British villages that had been abandoned ages ago when the plain first became a military installation. Of course, I didn't know that little detail. I saw them shooting across a village in the valley below and thought "What a callous bunch!" Nobody set me straight at the time.

A big, burly noncom with a Scottish brogue called out to me and said something I couldn't understand. I thought he'd said, "Fire!" so I pulled the lanyard of the 105 that was assigned to me and off went the shell. It impacted a couple of seconds later on the opposite ridge of the valley and exploded. Echoes of the sounds rang through the valley for several more seconds, whereupon the noncom sauntered over and asked me whether I was in the habit of ignoring commands. Embarrassing moment! Good thing those guns were laid in properly, so no harm done.

I also gave speeches on German arms and psychology to very large groups of soldiers from the 3rd Armored Division, including their general staff. That was something of an anomaly, for I was still only a lowly private. The armored troops were on their way through Tidworth to other staging areas.

At one of these lectures I read from those notes that I had already made in Bristol. I faced about three hundred GIs assembled in a huge barn of a building, one similar in size to our "museum." Halfway into my talk, my microphone went dead; I also dropped my prepared notes. Since they weren't stapled together, they flew all over the stage and were instantly useless. I had to extemporize from there on, but I got a standing ovation by finishing up my talk by yelling something like "Let's go get the bastards!" Throughout it all, my knees were fairly knocking.

Our weapons exhibit kept growing and its reputation began to spread. Eventually, we wouldn't allow anybody into the building after hours to see the weapons collection if they were below the rank of major. We couldn't be bothered to unlock the front door unless they were serious brass—office hours are office hours. Hubris had already set in.

Those weapons soon became entirely my responsibility. Before long I was caught up in the details of their fascinating history and of the technology of European small arms in particular. I started studying whatever descriptive material I could lay my hands on, which were mostly German and British military manuals. It had taken us several weeks of hard work to get the museum in shape for classes and casual visitors. After we opened the doors, over four thousand GIs wandered through our place on their own time.

Our training course was so successful that word got around. The press showed up one day and interviewed us. A story, almost exclusively about Mauksch, eventually appeared in the November 3, 1944, issue of *Yank* magazine, the Sunday edition of the army newspaper. Mauksch was shown demonstrating a heavy machine gun to Colonel Moore, the station commandant. Next to that photo was a great view of the museum as it was late that year. A very complimentary story appeared inside.

After that article appeared, MI headquarters in London—located at Eisenhower's European Theater HQ on Grosvenor Square—duly noted what we were doing.

All had gone well except for a detour late in May 1944, when I was accidentally separated from my MI group. Some orders got screwed up and even Hans Mauksch couldn't get them countermanded in time to keep me from being shipped off. Suddenly I found myself among a bunch of other GIs on the way to another replacement depot somewhere else in the south of England. It was not a great place to be. I was unassigned, had no recent combat training of any kind—including no U.S. weapons firing—and I seemed destined to become a prime candidate for combat of some sort in the near future. The invasion of Normandy was just a month off, though of course no one in the ranks knew that.

The weather was abominable. It rained constantly. There was foot-deep mud all over the place. Duckboards were laid out in the company streets so people wouldn't sink in past their ankles. Everyone was cold, damp, and mostly miserable all the time.

We were housed in old, single-story British Army barracks that had a dirt floor and a single, little potbelly coal-fired stove at its center. In the morning we would wake up covered with soot. Our GI blankets were black with coal dust and so were our nostrils, mouths, faces, and hands.

I wasn't happy. I had left a secure and interesting job behind in exchange for waiting to be shipped to the Continent along with other, basically undertrained replacement troops. Meanwhile, here I was, pulling night KP, or guard duty. Once, I "walked a post" around a water tower on top of some godforsaken hill in the middle of the night, with my M1 at right-shoulder arms, in pitch darkness! Around midnight, the officer of the guard appeared from nowhere and made me jump.

Like everyone else around me, I looked ahead to an uncertain future amongst troops I did not know. Rumors about the impending invasion of France set the scene.

Probably the worst duty I had during those weeks at the replacement depot was night KP, during which I scoured the inside and the carbon-black outside of GI garbage cans from the canteen, working outdoors in nearly total darkness in the dead of night. I came back to my barracks looking like a chimney sweep.

When I wasn't sleeping off guard duty or night KP, or wasn't washing my clothes, underwear, socks, or my heavy GI overcoat in cold water, I sat outdoors during every available daylight hour studying my algebra correspondence course. My feet were constantly caked with mud, and my leggings and socks were soaking wet, like everybody else's. We still had canvass leggings at that time. Paratrooper boots with leather bindings a third of the way up the calf from the ankles hadn't been issued yet—at least not to the regular ground troops; that came later. Naturally, and as if I had planned it so I could leave that miserable place, I caught pneumonia.

The next thing I knew, it was morning, I was on a stretcher, blood was trickling from my nose once again. I was feverish and I was being carried—along with my duffel bag—into an ambulance. I was taken to a field hospital occupied by the U.S. Army, somewhere to the north. During my hospital stay, I sat in bed between clean, dry, white sheets. Meanwhile, the replacement troops I had left behind were on alert. Shortly after I had left them, they were shipped off to the Normandy beaches on D-Day, June 6, 1944.

A couple of weeks later, now Lt. Hans Mauksch managed to get me reassigned to Tidworth and I was reunited with my MI group. Who knows how he pulled off that one. Fortunately, Mauksch appreciated my contribution to the group and wanted me back there—needed me, in fact. By now, I was the only member of the group who intimately knew every aspect of each of the many weapons that we toted around with us. They were our most prominent calling card. That suited me fine.

While the battles in France raged on, we remained in Tidworth, training troops on their way over to the mainland. The war was next door, but it seemed far away. How fortunate we were! We had no idea, of course, how long our present situation would go on.

Meanwhile, we were definitely earning our keep. During our stay in Tidworth, over 120,000 American and 5,000 British soldiers received training in important subjects from us. We worked all kinds of hours, and all that before we were even "officially recognized" and attached to Military Intelligence Service (MIS) in London. It was all highly irregular, but it worked.

TWICE DURING MY PROLONGED STAY at Tidworth, I got an opportunity to go on leave and visit my uncle, Heinz (now Henry) Kirschbaum, my mother's youngest brother. Even before I had met Heinz and his brother Fritz in Berlin in May 1938 during my brief vacation there and in Guben, Heinz had already briefly wound up in a concentration camp, ostensibly for "fooling around" with an "Aryan" girl. By the time I met him in Berlin, he was starting to keep company with Lea Goldhammer. I met Lea several times in Berlin during my last late spring vacation in Germany and liked her instantly.

Both Heinz and Lea were fortunate to get to England in 1939. Heinz managed to join a rescue program for German Jews run by a Jewish aid organization in Berlin. That got him out of Germany and into England, where he first spent some time interned at a Kitchener Camp for displaced persons. Lea had also been lucky. She had a cousin in Wales who provided an affidavit for her so that she could immigrate to the United Kingdom. Later that year, this same cousin got Heinz out of the Kitchener Camp. Heinz married Lea and went to work in her cousin's factory. They moved into a small house in Tufts Wells, a town near Cardiff in southeast Wales.

Winter had finally ended, and with it went the miserable English weather. In the spring of 1945, everybody else had been sent off to France. We stayed behind and waited for orders or a new assignment. Finally, a decision was made at MIS and we were told to report to MI HQ in London.

We took a train to London. Once there, we moved into the Red Cross building at Charing Cross, not too far from Eisenhower's headquarters on Grosvenor Square. A few buzz-bombs were still coming into London at night. I heard one of them hit one morning while I was standing in front of a mirror and shaving at our Red Cross quarters. The mirror blurred my image for a second, but that was all. The worst of the Blitz had passed by then. British and American air forces had taken over the skies, and German bombers now rarely ventured into English airspace. Normandy was also a much safer place now than it had been nine months earlier, particularly on D-Day.

Our new assignment from MIS was to move our training activities to a new camp in Normandy, near the small town of Dreux, sixty miles southwest of Paris. The army engineers had built barracks for a Military Intelligence School there.

To get over to France, we boarded an Army Air Force "Gooney Bird," Douglas C-47, the military equivalent of a commercial DC-3.

We had an uneventful flight that November 30, 1944—just a short hop—to an airfield near Paris. Once there, we boarded a decrepit French passenger train. We rode along for about an hour and finally passed through Dreux and the small French village of Saint George-Motel that bordered our new camp. It was a warm and sunny that early spring day; I saw daisies everywhere as we passed through the village with its ancient stucco houses and cobblestone streets.

Much to our amazement, our "camp" turned out to be located on what we were told had been a former Vanderbilt Estate. Driving through the gates of the estate, we entered what once must have been very beautiful, sculptured gardens. A few hundred feet farther, a French château came into view, complete with steeply gabled twin wings. All that was missing was the drawbridge over the moat. The grounds were in bad shape, but the castle seemed untouched by the ravages of the war and the occupation. A Luftwaffe contingent had cleared out of there months earlier, we were told upon our arrival.

Soon our small group got ready to teach again. We were scheduled to conduct our standard curriculum of training courses—basically the program that we had offered the troops in England, but adapted to a new contingent of GIs, mostly officers and noncoms. Everybody quickly settled into a routine. Their work was not particularly strenuous. There was plenty of free time for most of our crew. It was also definitely safe.

SEVERAL WEEKS AFTER OUR ARRIVAL in Normandy, we finally succeeded in having all of our small arms shipped over from England; they were our teaching tools and we needed them urgently. The heavy weapons had to stay behind, much to my regret. In no way were we going to be able to cart the 88, the mountain howitzer, those antiaircraft guns, and other heavy equipment across the English Channel. We had enough for a new small-arms display; now we needed a proper venue in which to display our goodies.

I had small group of guys assigned to me for a few days. Together, we planned how to build a really good-looking and functional weapons exhibit. We settled on having one display case for each major machine gun family in our collection. Handguns would be displayed on tables throughout the large open floor area.

We kept an eye out for additional small arms, and over the course of several months, we assembled and displayed quite an impressive collection of European small arms, as well as a few Japanese guns. Those display cases around the three walls were very professional looking. The Smithsonian would have been proud to have them, we thought. Tables located on the floor throughout the large arboretum displayed additional small arms, mostly our large collection of automatic pistols and revolvers, all appropriately labeled. We also acquired a sizable number of German uniforms, several German mines and booby traps, and a motley collection of other gear including some mortars and light antitank guns. These were displayed on the floor against one of the two short end walls.

I was beginning to think of myself as a small arms expert and was busy writing my manual whenever there was a free moment to communicate my insights to the rest of the world. I also studied my collection of small German antipersonnel mines and booby traps, some of which were of doubtful safety. On one occasion, I tried to determine whether they were really disarmed. I tied them in place behind a large rock near my museum and pulled their releases via a hundred-foot-long string. Nothing happened; that I didn't blow myself up goes without saying.

THERE WAS A LARGE GERMAN AMMUNITION DUMP on top of a hill adjacent to our camp; it was located in a wooded area half a mile behind and two or three hundred feet above the estate. The dump was filled with a great variety of stuff. We had been up there repeatedly to take a rough inventory. Various types of ammunition and rockets lay piled up in stacks throughout the dump. After we had been up there to inspect the place, Mauksch made an offer to an interested ordnance officer of letting him have him at least one sample of each of the different types of ammo we had found up there. Hans also offered to transport these selected items to a designated ordnance depot located elsewhere in Normandy. I didn't comment on the wisdom of this offer, although my intuition told me it wasn't a great idea.

That German ammo dump occupied several thousand square feet of wooded terrain. Everything that was ever fired out of a barrel or otherwise launched into a suborbital trajectory seemed to be stored there. We found Polish mountain howitzer rounds, German rockets in their wooden launch crates, Italian, French, and Spanish artillery shells, and mortar rounds of many types and calibers. Cases of small arms ammunition were piled everywhere in no apparent order. It was our guess that the Germans had hoarded this stuff for emergency use with captured weapons, or perhaps it was stored there just to keep it out of the hands of the underground army. There was no sign of matching weapons anywhere, however.

Our job was to deliver as many different samples to that ordnance depot as we could manage to squeeze into a two-and-a-half-ton truck. Our route was a drive of about seventy-five miles over bumpy French country roads that sported large potholes left over from World War I, never mind the current one.

Throughout this trip, I was in the back of the truck, sitting on the wooden launching crate of a German rocket. Assorted pieces of ammo were bouncing up and down on the floor of the truck during the entire trip. Mortar rounds and artillery shells were clanking and banging into one another—but what the hell, there was a war on! Those rounds weren't designed to go off by merely bouncing around. All the same, we were not too unhappy to unload the stuff at our destination.

I wondered what the recipient was going to do with that motley collection of bullets, shells, and rockets. Possibly, he was an ambitious, self-elected collector of foreign arms, like myself, who would eventually make them his ticket to go home, bound for some appropriate U.S. destination ordered up by the War Department. A kindred spirit—good luck to him!

The following month, on April 20—Hitler's birthday—someone sabotaged the ammo dump, and it went up in flames. The bushes and other combustibles burned for the next week until the fire spent itself. At the height of the heat up there, stuff would cook off and come flying through the air. Those projectiles didn't actually explode on arrival, thank heaven! After all, they were not armed, but some of the pieces weighed several hundred pounds.

SUMMER OF 1945: The war in Europe was finally over. The Allied armies were in parts of Eastern Germany, but we were still in Normandy. Plans for redeploying troops to the Pacific were being put into action, so I was ordered to start training U.S. artillery officers in the recognition and handling of Japanese heavy weapons, just in case these officers were redeployed to the Japanese front. Of course, those transfers never happened. We dropped atomic bombs on Nagasaki and Hiroshima, and that ended the war over there before any of my student officers had to make that move.

In January 1946, I boarded a Liberty ship and our vessel began to plow through an Atlantic winter storm.

When I returned to New York, I went through the discharge process; I was handed a Bronze Star for meritorious service and they gave me a "ruptured duck," the embroidered eagle emblem of the discharged World War II vet, which was sewn onto the Eisenhower jacket I was wearing. Overseas, I had already received a Bronze Star, a Marksmanship Medal, a Good Conduct Medal, an ETO medal, and four overseas stripes for the left sleeve of my jacket—one for each six-month period of overseas service. And so I came to the end of my army career—being unceremoniously tossed out into the streets and on my own now!

It was April 2, 1946. More than three years had passed since I was inducted, three unforgettable years.

After the war, Ralph Baer pursued his interest in electronics, graduating from the American Television Institute of Technology in Chicago in 1949 with a bachelor of science degree in television engineering. He went on to pioneer the development of console video games and other electronic peripherals and games such as the handheld game Simon. In 2006, President George W. Bush awarded Ralph Baer the National Medal of Technology and Innovation for his "groundbreaking and pioneering creation, development, and commercialization of interactive video games."

Chapter 13

BERNARD BAUM

GIESSEN, GERMANY

66th Infantry Division

Bernard Baum was born in Giessen, Germany, and spent the first eight years of his life there before his mother, an American citizen by birth, was able to arrange exit visas for the family to emigrate in 1934. He grew up on the North Side of Chicago and attended Senn High School. After graduating at seventeen, Bernard enlisted in the army and was sent to Lawrence, Kansas, for the Army Specialized Training Program until he was sent to combat in France as an infantry replacement. He is pictured above in France, 1945.

My father was reared in a small town, Hessen, Germany. His father was a cattle beater, which was a common occupation for Jews at the time. My father was the first university educated member of his family. I was born in 1926 in Giessen, Germany.

My family was German by nationality and Jewish by religion. My father's military service in World War I left him very German. He fought for the Fatherland and carried shrapnel in his back for the rest of his life. At the same time, he was aware that Judaism made a difference to being a full-fledged integrated German.

I remember a couple of incidents of anti-Semitism in childhood, prior to September 1933 when we left. When I was on my scooter in a park across the street from our residence, I had been given a little swastika flag, which I tied to my scooter. One of the older women came up to me and said, "You can't fly that flag! What are you crazy?" I think she probably was Jewish. She took it away from me. She said, "You don't want this flag."

When I was in second grade, the teacher wore a swastika button on his lapel. He became a Nazi very early on. My older brother was tossed into a garbage can by his classmates or some other children at his school. They all chanted, "*Jude, Jude*." There was a parade of brown-shirted Nazis on the street right outside of our building. My father had an enameled sign that said, "Dr. Theodore Baum, Dentist" outside our door. Some ruffians came along, ripped it off, and threw it in the river. One night the police came to get my father and kept him all night. My mother was terrified. They released him, however, because it was sufficiently early in that regime so that they couldn't do much other than scaring the hell out of him.

My father was a reader and liberal by orientation and politically. He read *Mein Kampf* in about 1929 or 1930. As the story goes, when he finished that book, he turned to my mother and said, "If this man Hitler comes to power, we're leaving Germany." That was about 1930. In January 1933, when Hitler became chancellor, my father got the papers.

He said, "We've got to leave because these Nazis are bad for us." It wasn't a very sophisticated statement, but clearly we three brothers wanted to understand why this was happening. To this day, I have the occasion to say to my students, "Sometimes there's a payoff for reading a book," and I repeat the story that my father read that book and believed it. There is another factor that I think is significant: my father was a World War I hero, he got the Iron

Cross. People would ask him, "Why are you leaving? You've got a successful dental practice. You're living well." My father would say, "I've got three sons." The final irony in that regard was when in 1936 or 1937 Hitler sent my father a medal in honor of his service in World War I. I very much regret that my father didn't keep it, but he was a principled man. He sent it back. It must be documented that Hitler gave these medals out. There were many cases like my father, but clearly not the majority. My father was farsighted, for which I'm eternally grateful.

By September 1933 we were on a boat, the *Albert Belling*. I cite the name because it was named after a big Jewish industrialist and ship owner from Hamburg, Germany. At that point the ship was still named after him, but of course, it was erased soon after.

I remember dreaming we were going to cross the ocean in a rowboat because I didn't know anything about big ships. I thought to myself, "My gosh, how can we cross a vast body like that?" It was more like a nightmare.

My mother had family in Chicago and was, in fact, born on North and LaSalle in the city, so, it was a relatively easy decision. My mother's father was a widower, and he went back to Germany to get a bride in about 1890.

My uncle owned a clothing store that had decorators, so when we got to Chicago, they had made a big red, white, and blue sign with stars that said, "Welcome to the USA." I was very impressed that this sign was for us, and we did feel welcomed. We moved into a small apartment, and then we began to integrate. It was difficult to learn English. I remember asking a classmate of mine, "What does 'a few' mean?" She said, "Well, this is one, this is two, and three is 'a few,' but four might be a few and five might be a few." That kind of confused me. Now I understand it's a relative term, but I remember the difficulty of absorbing that kind of concept. It was not fun.

We grew up in a family that distinctly didn't want to live in a Jewish neighborhood. Americanization really put the emphasis on becoming an integrated—not assimilated, but integrated—American. Whereas some of the other German-Jews tended to congregate in their own German-Jewish communities, such as Hyde Park, or Washington Heights in New York, my father was in line with FDR. He put a national recovery act poster in the window. He was always kind of a political activist. Those two kinds of Americanization processes are really distinguishable—the ones who stayed very solidly German-Jewish, in their own communities, and those of us who branched out into other neighborhoods. I think those of us who grew up, who were immigrants, as I was perfectly glad to give up an upper middle-class life for something less secure for freedom.

My father predicted the war. Once again he was farsighted, and he didn't see any escape from war. I remember how vehement he was about Neville Chamberlain saying "peace in our time" and capitulating to Hitler for Czechoslovakia. He figured it would be another world war. Even though he had those experiences in World War I, he never for a moment thought that my brother Werner or I should not go into the armed forces; that would be unthinkable. I was an American and there was a war with a clear-cut enemy.

The year 1941 was a thoroughgoing shock with regard to the Japanese attack, but it was no shock to my father when we finally said, "We're with you." Of course we were interested, we had family over there. My mother's mother went back to Germany after she had become a widow and when my mother was only five years old. My mother went back to take care of her mother in Germany, so she grew up as a German. My father got two of my aunts and uncles out and my grandmother in 1937. However, my father's sister and her husband, and my cousin, her husband, and their baby were killed in concentration camps.

As for what was happening in Europe in the 1930s, my parents' attitudes were unambiguous about Hitler. We all thought that we needed to get rid of this son of a bitch. I think my father would have enlisted if he hadn't been too old. I was a high school senior and turned seventeen in April. I was to graduate in June, so it was just a couple of months. When I enlisted after graduation, I think my parents had to sign because I wasn't eighteen yet.

I became a citizen in 1934 by virtue of the fact that my mother never renounced her U.S. citizenship. So I was granted what was called a derivative citizenship, though the army, in 1943 or 1944, processed me again and gave me my own citizenship.

THINKING BACK ON WHEN I WAS SEVENTEEN is a bit difficult. I was nervous about being inducted, but I had a high respect for the armed forces. When I swore to uphold the constitution, I took that very seriously—perhaps more seriously than people who hadn't thought about it. I thought a great deal of it. I realized that this was a major decision of life. Without ambiguity I had some nervousness. I remember walking to 226 W. Jackson, which was a government building at the time, and going up there to be inducted, thinking, "My God, what am I doing?" At that time I didn't give it much more thought afterward. The decision had a considerable influence on me. I think I felt some sense of pride too. My brother was in the navy at that time.

I enlisted in June. The army sent me home for about eight weeks, then it ordered me to report to the University of Kansas for the ASTP (Army Specialized Training Program) in August. I went there, got fitted for a uniform, and got a duffel bag, toothbrush, and a razor, even though I didn't need one. I think there was more emphasis on leaving home for the first time than there was on the fact that I was going off to fight the Germans. Who knows, they could have sent me off to Japan.

I don't remember what my parents' reaction was the first time they saw me in uniform, but I think they were proud.

IN KANSAS, THEY WERE GOING TO TRAIN ME as an engineer. I took mechanical drawing and geography. Of course we also had discipline formations, marching and so on.

I had a distinct preference that I wanted to go to Europe, but I had no control over this. I was eighteen in April and in May the program was closed in Kansas. I went off to Fort Sheridan, got re-outfitted, and went on active duty. Then I went to basic training and was a member of an infantry cannon company, learning about cannons and mostly about how to fight. After basic training, I was sent to Alabama to join the 66th Infantry Division. While there, I went to the first sergeant of my company and said, "I want to join the paratroopers."

He said, "It's too late. We've been ordered to ship out."

At that point we shipped out to New York. I had one visit with my brother Werner who was stationed at Norfolk. My mother and I got together in Philadelphia. I have a picture of that. That was it. Her baby boy was going off to combat. I was a private in the 1st Platoon, the 66th Division, Company A, 262nd Regiment. I learned how to stand up straight at attention, live in a foxhole, and pull guard duty. We were being shipped over from the East Coast, so we knew we were going to Europe.

We really didn't know where we were going in Europe. We shipped out somewhere in England on Christmas Eve 1944, and the Battle of the Bulge was on. Our 66th Division was aboard two ships, the *Leopoldville* and the *Cheshire*. The *Leopoldville* was torpedoed, and we lost eight hundred lives as a result. We were out on a deck in life jackets and I watched, in horror, our buddies drowning and freezing to death. That was no way to spend Christmas Eve. Then we landed and ended up on an airstrip that night. I had gotten so close to a fire that my overcoat was burned. We went straight to France. We relieved the 94th Division that was holding the pockets of St. Nazair and Lorient, in France, when it moved out to fight the Battle of the Bulge.

In combat you're scared. You don't think as much of the enemy as saving your ass. There's no other situation like it. Yes, you cross the street and you run the risk of getting run over. But when you enter a combat zone, you dig a hole in the ground to survive. It's terrifying. I remember one particular scary moment. We were having lunch out of mess kits and the Germans started bombing us right where we were. All I remember was that I flew to the ground and my lunch went somewhere in the air. That was one nasty scary thing. I didn't think much about that the enemies were the Germans. I just thought, I'm here, I'm doing my job, and I'm going to dig the hole deep enough to accommodate me.

The 66th Division's main task was to contain and probe the German garrison and attack selected enemy installations in the port cities of St. Nazair and Lorient. It was essentially limited warfare. These were relatively fixed positions. It wasn't like the Battle of the Bulge, which was moving all the time. At the same time, we were very well entrenched. They shelled us, and we shelled them back.

One night I went out on patrol, as I did many times. We came under attack and I began to shoot. It was scary; that is the overriding, overpowering emotion. What else can you possibly think about in that situation? I did not think grand thoughts about "This will help to overcome Hitler's regime," or "This will put Germany in its place." Then, when we had victory on VE day, I think most of us thought: "Now they'll ship us to Japan."

I'm no hero and I don't have that much of a fighting spirit, but I think we have to be prepared to defend our liberty. We can't take them for granted. I have strong feelings about that. For me, it was also a feeling of wanting to get revenge with a tinge of remorse for fighting citizens of the country of my birth. It was the right thing to do. By the time I got there, there was no doubt: they had to be done away with. I never thought about killing as a crime in that sense. I don't know that I ever killed anybody. I never saw a body fall as the result of my shooting, but there would be no regret if I had. This was, if not revenge, at least justice.

After I had served in combat, I volunteered in the Military Intelligence Corps because I thought I'd be of more value to it since I spoke, read, and wrote German. So I went to the chief of the intelligence in Vienna when I was in the army of occupation and said, "I am standing guard at a little-used railway yard and that's all right. That's what infantry men are for, I guess, but think I can be of more help."

The colonel who interviewed me said, "I'll request your transfer of course."

When he requested my transfer, my company commander said, "Baum, you stupid idiot." He was out for me because I had broken the chain of command. I had gone from being a private to a full colonel, so my life was going to be a misery. Fortunately, I received an order that was signed by Gen. Mark W. Clark that said, "PFC Bernard Baum is hereby transferred."

So I got out and I encountered all kind of experiences, which made me feel like I did the right thing. For example, I was on a train in Austria and the conductor said something like, "At least Hitler had one great idea about getting rid of the Jews." Another night when I was at the opera in Salzburg, I heard the couple behind me, talking about "damn Jews." So I called the MP. I said, "Arrest those people. We'll talk about charges later."

In 1946 when I was discharged at Fort McCoy, I was asked if I wanted to join the reserves or the Army National Guard, but I said, essentially, "Up yours." Then the 1948 National Guard was offering second lieutenant commissions to people with a college degree and who passed a written exam. I had come out of the war a corporal. I decided that all things considered, I was twenty-two years old, I was healthy, and I was single. I said to myself: "They're going to get you again. Next time, I'd rather go as an officer and a gentlemen rather than creeping and crawling in the mud." So I accepted a second lieutenancy in the Army National Guard. Once I get into something, I tend to stay committed to it. The whiter my hair got, the more they promoted me. I retired a brigadier general.

I HAVE ALWAYS THOUGHT it was ideal to have good defense establishment. I feel strongly that the civilians are in the army reserve of the National Guard because we tend to keep the professional soldiers honest. I can tell you that I was opposed to the war in Vietnam. There were many of us reserve officers who were opposed to the war, and we marched (in uniform) during some peace demonstrations. I'm essentially afraid of the basic military type.

At twenty-seven I got married and we had four children. My wife died after forty-seven years of marriage, but life goes on and I've had a rich, full, colorful life, all these things considered: the Holocaust, wartime, and combat duty, my chance to get some revenge and have some pride about my career. My brothers and I all ended up becoming professors.

My thoughts about the Jewish experience in the Holocaust and World War II are that we've survived. I survived combat, but also Judaism survived. I have strong feelings about the survival of Judaism, but that in no way contradicts my loyalty to the United States, a country that has given freedom. The country is based on that. It's a wonderful thing.

I've taken the liberty, which many Jews before me have done, and I've edited the Passover Haggadah (prayer book for Passover). When I get to the part where it says, "Next year in Jerusalem," I suggest that the United States is our Jerusalem. Next year, in this blessed country again.

Dr. Bernard Baum sat on the faculty of the School of Public Health at the University of Illinois, Chicago, for forty years until his death on June 6, 2008. Baum was the chairman of the American Council for Judaism and the author of As If People Mattered: Dignity in Organizations.

Chapter 14

HAROLD BAUM

BERLIN, GERMANY

97th Infantry Division, 386th Regiment, L Company

Harold Baum grew up in Berlin. His family left Germany in February 1940 for Lisbon where they boarded a boat for the United States. After working a variety of menial jobs in New York City, his family moved to Cincinnati, Ohio, where he attended high school at night before being inducted. After basic training, he was sent to the 97th Infantry Division, where he became a frontline radio operator. He is pictured above in 1945.

I felt there should be some justice. As it is written in the book of Deuteronomy, Chapter 16: "An eye for an eye, tooth for a tooth, a life for a life." This actually came to fruition when I was a GI.

I was born in 1923. In 1934 I started in the Gymnasium in Berlin of which I was able to attend until the end of 1938. At that point, a regulation was set forth in the Nuremberg Laws that Jewish children could not attend German schools any longer. So, I transferred to a Jewish school. In 1936 we had the Olympic Games in Berlin, and it was a tremendous, spectacular event. Down the street, they put up a little news box for *Der Stuermer*, the anti-Semitic newspaper put out by Julius Streicher. After my mother saw it, she went to the American consulate in August 1936 and obtained a quota number for our exit.

In the meantime, I quit school in 1938 because my academic accomplishments were, as my mother said, not up to par. I started a training program for a machine shop operator, done under the auspices of the Jewish community in Berlin. I remember the Kristallnacht in November 1938, when we received a telephone call early in the morning from a friend in one of the outlying districts, telling us that all Jews were being arrested. At that point my father and I decided to take to the streets. I started riding my bicycle at six o'clock in the morning throughout Berlin, and I saw the red sky and watched the burning synagogues. My father started riding the subways, and fortunately neither one of us was arrested. After that I vividly remember when we were compelled to turn over all silverware that was in our family's possession. My mother and I went to the police station, surrendered the silverware, and we received a receipt as if we were going to get it back someday. Our quota number was to be called on August 15, 1939.

There was, however, a rumor circulating among Jews in Berlin that an anti-Semitic American official was in charge of the immigrants at the consulate, and whoever appeared there was turned down. My father was not going to take a chance, so we waited in line anyway. On the first of September 1939, the war broke out and all immigration came to a sudden standstill. I remember Polish prisoners of war that winter cleaning the streets of Berlin and being treated as sub-humans. I will never forget that as long as I live.

Jews had a curfew. We couldn't be out in the street between five o'clock in the morning to eight o'clock at night. We were put on restricted rations of approximately eight hundred calories a day—no meat, potatoes, turnips, etc. We were forced to carry a Jewish identity card called a Kennkarte at all times, to further identify and humiliate us. It was a very meager existence.

We lived in an apartment house on the third floor, and on the first floor lived a German air force major in the Luftwaffe. On Christmas 1939, there was a knock on the door, and there was Major Mueller with a big package. He asked, "Is your father home?" My father came to the door. "Herr Baum," said Mueller, "I have a goose for you for Christmas." This was a very kind gesture. So, there were some decent people amongst them. Then a change occurred at the American embassy because that same official in charge, a man named Breckenridge, fell out of favor and was relieved, and immigration again was allowed to occur, albeit on a limited scale.

We obtained our American visa on December 4, 1940. My mother was fortunate in obtaining a release from her place of employment and she was allowed to leave. The Jewish community in Berlin organized a transport destined to go to Lisbon, Portugal. We left Berlin on February 26 and were put in a regular railroad car. We had to bring enough food and water along for three days. The doors were locked and we were first taken to Cologne, then Paris, , and finally to freedom across the Spanish border.

Our first stop was San Sebastian. When we woke up in the morning, we were shocked to see that the whole town was flooded with German military personnel. It was really a nightmare. Apparently, there was a German submarine base there, but we were left alone. From there, we went on to Lisbon, boarded a freighter called the *Salpa Pinto*, and set off for New York. There were approximately five hundred passengers on the boat; the sleeping quarters were five bunks in the cargo hold, and two days out, all sanitary facilities broke down. We had no fresh water and no toilets, so we found some buckets and took turns to relieve our physical needs in that particular manner. So, it was a miserable experience. However, we were intercepted by the British Navy, hauled into Hamilton, Bermuda, and quarantined for about a week because they suspected that German spies were on the boat. Then the British set us free, I arrived in New York, and that is where the next chapter begins, although my experience with the Nazis remained vivid, and I would never forgive them.

I arrived in Staten Island, and a friend of my father's was there and advanced us ten dollars. "Well, get change," he said. "Get a nickel, and take the ferry over to Battery Park." I arrived on West 92nd Street, between Amsterdam and Columbus Avenues. Within five days I had a job as a janitor at a factory in New Jersey. I swept the floor and kept the tool room and machines clean. One day, I told the boss that I knew how to run the machines. He said, "Tool it up and show me what you can do." So I set it up, did a good job, and got my first promotion in America.

When my father could not find a job, we traveled on to Cincinnati, Ohio, where a second cousin of my mother lived. Within a short period of time, I was able to find a job in a machine shop where I worked the night shift from six o'clock in the evening to six o'clock in the morning. Then I found out that Cincinnati had a night high school, so I switched to the day shift, 6 a.m. to 7 p.m. and went to night school from 7 p.m. to 10 p.m. My first assignment in the English class was an oral summary of a *Reader's Digest* article. My way of speaking was considerably different then what it is now, and I was hesitant to open my mouth—ah, the embarrassment. But, I overcame it, gave the report, got a standing ovation, and had a great first experience in public speaking.

After Pearl Harbor, the Germans declared war on the United States, and we had to register as resident Enemy Aliens and surrendered our cameras and shortwave radio. In 1942 I had wanted to volunteer for the navy, but I was turned down at the recruiting office because I was not a citizen. I was finally drafted in May 1943 and made a citizen in December 1943, just prior to going overseas.

I started out in the combat engineers in Fort Leonard Wood, Missouri, and from there I was transferred to the Army Specialized Training Program at Kansas State University in Manhattan, Kansas. I spent two semesters there, but the need for troops became greater for the coming invasion, so I was transferred to the 97th Infantry Division. I was attached to the headquarters company in an infantry line unit. There were several platoons and a headquarters platoon that directed the action of each unit. I was with the company executive officer, relaying whatever communication I was given to the next echelon, the battalion headquarters. If we had to direct artillery fire, it went through me.

I came on a convoy and landed in Le Havre, the artificial harbor on the French coast. From there, we went to a staging area called Camp Old Gold. I saw my first real action near Dusseldorf and participated in the Ruhr

Pocket Campaign for which we crossed the famous Remagen Bridge—
terrible. Our first action was in Nois, where my company was selected to
send a patrol with assault boats over to Dusseldorf. There were six GIs to
a boat, and we were in a permanent state of diarrhea and fright during
the entire attack. I kept my head low, trying to reconnoiter the area while
under fire, and I made it back. We were coming from the west bank of
the Rhine, and Germans were on the east bank viciously firing at us. The
most frightening thing during combat, in which I spent sixty consecutive
days, was the uncertainty of where they were shelling us. That of course
was followed by a frenzied attempt to identify from where the shells were
coming and direct mortar fire in that direction.

Fortunately, in our company we had a light machine gun section, a heavy
machine gun section, and a mortar section. These people did a marvelous
job once we identified a target. We once overran a flak position of German
88s; our scout spotted them at dawn and called in mortar rounds on their
position. They were slaughtered. The 88s were terrifying German weapons
because they were used pointblank on us, instead of on airplanes. Seeing a
kid next to you fall, wounded, or killed was terrifying experience. I cannot
begin to explain the rage I had when seeing German soldiers come out with
white flags after an ambush. Needless to say, there were times when we did
not take prisoners.

We encountered fanatical German resistance in the Ruhr Pocket,
primarily from the young boys who were fourteen and fifteen years old and
willing to die for fuhrer and Fatherland. At times we saw people dangling
from trees, strung up by the SS, with signs around there neck reading, "*Ich
Bin Ein Fikling*" (I am a coward). That only intensified things for me. I
had a unique experience in Solingen where a German lady came to our
command post and told us that a German general was hiding out. The
captain said, "Lieutenant Winsam, Sergeant Miller, Baum, go and get him."
We surrounded the house. There was this middle-aged man, and I started
questioning him. In an almost defiant, arrogant manner, without getting
up, he said, "*Ich bin General Gustav Von Zongen.*"

Without undue delay I told him, "*Hande Hoch*," pointed my rifle at
the son of a bitch, and he turned ashen white. Then I told him, "*Ich bin ein
Deutcher Jude*" (I'm a German Jew), and this man was in an absolute state
of terror. He could not believe that one little *yid* should get him out of five

million GIs. A rifle pointed at an arrogant officer becomes a powerful persuader. It was a good feeling. Gustav Adolph Von Zangen was a lieutenant general, commander of the Fifteenth Army Group. His last command was in the Ruhr Pocket. I escorted him with the lieutenant to division headquarters where he surrendered in a customary procedure, like a soldier, which nauseated me—to me he was a Nazi, not a soldier. General Halsey, commander of the 97th Division, interrogated him while I was the interpreter.

After we occupied Solingen, there were Russian forced laborers who after being liberated went after the Germans, and the Germans wanted protection from the Russians. As you can imagine, we refused and justice was swift.

After completion of the Ruhr campaign, we were sent to southern Germany and started moving in the direction of Czechoslovakia. On the western border of Czechoslovakia and Germany, we encountered a concentration camp called Flossenberg and liberated one of the smaller camps of that facility. We saw scores of dying, starving prisoners. It was terrible, and the stench and odor of death, I will never forget.

There were also well-fed prisoners who had on the same inmate uniforms. I unsuccessfully tried to communicate with them in German; one kid in my company spoke Russian and Polish to them and they did not understand that either. We could not figure it out. My captain decided to strip them down and discovered that they had their blood type tattooed under their arm, which was customary practice among SS troops. They went into the mass graves and helped to dispose of all the corpses, but they did not last to face a war criminal trial. The justification for their demise was that they switched uniforms, which under the Geneva Convention is a punishable offense. They remained in the pits with the corpses.

From there, we advanced fifty kilometers short of Prague, but were pulled back into Germany. When the war in Europe ended in May, I was sent home. There I had a four-week furlough and was then shipped out to the Pacific on an attack transport to participate in the invasion of Japan. Fortunately, the United States dropped the atomic bomb and saved my life. I was on occupation duty in Japan for six months.

While I had a yearning to seek retribution, I felt such gratification for being accepted as a worthy citizen of the greatest country. It was my duty and obligation to serve. My goal was to be treated as an American, and when I had an opportunity to demonstrate my loyalty I did. I hoped that I would have the opportunity to get a certain amount of revenge, and I was privileged that I had that experience.

I was, and still am, eternally grateful to America. After the war, I was able to receive help under the GI Bill of Rights. I went to college, medical school, and made the grade. I delivered babies for over forty years. I have a beautiful wife and four children.

Dr. Harold Baum is a retired obstetrician living in Marco Island, Florida.

Chapter 15
EDMUND SCHLOSS

JESBERG, GERMANY

3rd Armored Division

Edmund Schloss arrived in Chicago with his family in 1938 and resumed his schooling. After graduating from Hyde Park High School, he was soon inducted into the U.S. Army in 1943. After basic training in Texas, Schloss received specialized training, learned some basic interrogation techniques, and was then shipped to England as a replacement. He joined the 3rd Armored Division in St. Lo, France. He is pictured above in 1945.

We lived in Jesberg, Germany, a town of about three thousand with about twenty-five Jewish families. In the beginning of the Hitler period, it wasn't bad. When we were little kids, we would go to the parades and give the "Heil Hitler" sign, but things changed considerably once they started clamping down on us. I remember one time when Hitler himself came to our town; they decorated it with flags, put trees up in front of homes, and everything was fine until an hour before he came. They came and removed all of the decorations from the Jewish homes—there were about fifteen to eighteen of them on the main streets—and painted Mogen Dovid on each house. That was a major blow.

In the early 1930s, there were about twenty people who owned cars in Jesberg; five were owned by Jews. The first car my father, Rudolf Schloss, owned was made in France, and in 1931 he bought a Ford Model A made in Cologne, Germany. Our auto mechanic was a very good friend of my father's. He joined the SS for business reasons; however, he remained a good friend until we moved to Frankfurt. My father, my brother, and I were never taken to a concentration camp because of this man. He always advised us before Jewish men and boys were being picked up.

One time he could not get word to my dad early enough, so at the last minute he told my dad to take us into the field outside of town, where we stayed overnight until he signaled us to come home the next day. Three times they came to our house that night and tried to break the door down. My mother was frightened. The Nazis used the Jewish-owned cars for transportation to the camps. I remember at least three occasions when the friend disabled our car so the Nazis couldn't use it.

We had Hebrew school every Sunday. As a matter of fact, the teacher was retired from the Jewish school in Borken, where my mother was from. We were brought up conservative. My father owned a department store that sold clothing, shoes, furniture, and anything needed in a home except food. It was a very good business until early 1934 when the Nazis started boycotting Jewish businesses. For a short period of time, customers would enter through the warehouse area, but the Nazis stopped that. Big items were sold on credit, and many of our customers continued to make payments even though they could not continue to come to the store.

Before we emigrated from Germany, my dad turned the accounts over to a German lawyer who made arrangements to continue the collections to support my father's mother, who died in Theresianstadt in 1942.

My older brother, Erwin, and I both went to public school and had a lot of gentile friends until the kids were recruited into the Hitler Youth. There were about twenty-two Jewish children our age and they became the only playmates we had after mid 1934. We had problems on the way to and from school, as the kids who used to be our friends beat us up.

One of our teachers made it a point at least once a week to find a reason to give us a penalty assignment, which kept us up to midnight to complete.

In late 1934 my father and one of my uncles were investigating the possibility of driving to Palestine. When this became unfeasible, my parents applied for a quota number to immigrate to the United States. By the end of 1937, my parents made the decision to move to Frankfurt, for my brother and I could not go to school anymore without sustaining bodily harm and my father's business was closed. It would make it easier to prepare for emigration since there was an American consulate in Frankfurt. There also were Jewish schools.

My mother's brother and his family, including my grandmother, immigrated to the United States in 1937. My grandmother had two brothers living in Kokomo, Indiana. When my grandmother arrived in Chicago, she immediately contacted her brothers to secure a sponsor for our family. I had my Bar Mitzvah on May 7, 1938, at the Borneplats Synagogue, which was burned to the ground on Kristallnacht. We just couldn't wait to leave.

The first week of June 1938, we took a train to Hamburg and upon arrival boarded the steamship U.S.S. *Harding* for our trip to the States. We traveled first class and had a wonderful trip. We stayed in New York for a couple of days to visit friends and relatives, and then took a train to Chicago where we settled permanently. Seeing the skyscrapers in New York and Chicago was awesome. A lot of our relatives who had preceded us to Chicago—all on my mother's side—had settled in Hyde Park. We found an apartment one block from where my uncle lived and two blocks from where my aunt and two cousins lived. Within the Hyde Park area we had about twenty families that were all uncles, aunts, and cousins. We had a big circle of friends and relatives, and life became very comfortable.

Walking up 53rd Street, it seemed as though everybody was from Germany. All of our family was able to leave Germany except my father's mother and his youngest sister and her family. They all perished in concentration camp, except my cousin who survived. I found her after the war, and my dad immediately started making arrangements to bring her to the United States.

My dad found a job in a factory and my mother did odd domestic work for the first couple of years. Then my dad started selling cigars and cigarettes and built up a very lucrative business, finally selling only cigars and tobacco.

We all knew before we left Germany that the war was coming. We saw the tremendous buildup of the army and air force. I will never forget the Sunday morning when we got up and found out that Pearl Harbor was attacked. My family was very surprised because we thought Germany would declare war on the United States first. I was still in high school when the war was declared. My brother and some of our friends made arrangements to enlist in the army. My brother was rejected due to his eyes. I personally wanted to finish high school first, but received my notice of induction the day after my birthday in April 1943, before I had a chance to finish my last semester.

I was inducted at Camp Grant in Illinois. From there, I was sent to Camp Fannin in Texas for basic training. I was placed in a specialized training battalion where I learned some interrogation techniques and communications. There were only five refugee boys in the interrogation class. Before being sent overseas, I became an American citizen. My biggest fear was being sent to the Pacific, as many of the soldiers I trained with were. We were trained as replacements and therefore not sent overseas as a unit. I kept reminding the first sergeant of my training company that I had the special training in interrogation and could be more effective in the European Theater.

I was finally sent to England to a replacement depot in January 1944. We crossed the Atlantic in a forty-ship convoy escorted by a small aircraft carrier, a destroyer, and several destroyer escorts. German U-boats attacked several times, and we lost two ships. I was on the U.S.S. *Heritage*. I continued to receive training both in communication and interrogation. There was a group of refugees in those classes, but I never saw any of them again after the invasion, as we were all sent to different units in France. We were shipped over without incident and landed at Omaha Beach; of course at that moment in time, the beachhead had already been secured a month before. I was assigned to the 3rd Armored Division. The organization was astounding. We hiked up the cliffs, where there were trucks waiting for us, and were immediately transported to where the division was located. There was a lot of anxiety because I was going to be in the thick of it very soon. The division was located just outside of St. Lo.

The 3rd Armored Division landed at Omaha Beach the last week in June and, on June 29, entered into combat. I was in the second replacement group when I joined. As a replacement, I was interviewed by the first sergeant and the company commander of the 1st Battalion, B Company, 36th Armored Infantry Regiment. I was told not to reveal to anyone in the company that I was a German refugee. They both felt that if I were captured, it was enough of a problem being Jewish. I saw my first combat near Marigny, Normandy, on July 24 as an assistant radio operator. On August 8, I was wounded by a mortar shell near Avranches (Normandy). The medics sent me to a field hospital near St. Lo. The Germans bombed the hospital every night, and after five days I requested to be sent back to my company. The company medics changed my bandages every couple of days for about three weeks to avoid infections. Four days after I returned to my unit, I passed out during an attack early in the morning. The prognosis was loss of blood due to constant drainage. The medics gave me a blood transfusion, and I was fine after that.

The division continued south in Normandy to Mayenne and then turned north to Fromentel, where we made contact with the British to close the Falaise Gap and cut off a considerable part of the German Army in Normandy. We were known as the "Spearhead Division" because instead of a frontal attack, we would cut a wedge in their lines and keep going until we could attack them from behind. The Germans would do the same to us. Once we traveled a hundred miles ahead and had to stop so the rest of the infantry could catch up with us. The 1st Division was assigned to the 3rd Armored Division, had to mop up in back of us, and had to fight its way up to where we were.

The division was commanded by Gen. Maurice Rose; he was a spit and polish West Pointer and had to go into combat in dress uniforms at all times. We shaved every day whenever possible. He was absolutely the epitome of a U.S. soldier; there was never a speck of dirt on his boots. It was unbelievable what he demanded of the troops, but he was respected immensely. General Rose made a point to hand out as many medals on the frontlines to the individuals in our unit. He felt that it should come from him instead of a company commander or a battalion commander. He was always on the frontlines because he felt that he couldn't ask of men what he wouldn't do himself. That endeared him to the division to say the least. I didn't know at the time that he was a Jew and the son of a rabbi who was in Denver, but when I did find out it gave me a tremendous sense of pride.

The division then turned east to Chartres. At Melun, south of Paris, we turned to the northeast toward Soissons with ultimate target Mons, Belgium. I was now the radio operator for the captain's jeep. We took Mons with only a few minor skirmishes. We started to clean our guns and equipment when the word came over the radio that a sizable German force was approaching the city. Our company captured two trucks full of German infantry. After I interrogated about ten prisoners—scouts who had come to look at our positions—all hell broke loose. On one of the main streets, a truck had approached with about fifty men and they were asked to put their hands up. When they didn't, we just shot them outright, killed them all in about a minute. We had no choice, for they came out of the truck with their guns blazing.

The Germans had not known that we had already taken the city. We sent an advance party with big white sheets (the Germans thought we were trying to surrender) to get the Germans to give up, but they refused. Needless to say, it was a massacre. Our tanks and antitank guns were in such good positions that there was no way they could hit us with any great impact. Of course, with the German Tiger and Panther tanks, we had to hit them with our 76mm guns on the side in their tracks because their armor was so good that our shells would bounce right off of them. Conversely, the Germans had heavier guns than what we had on our tanks, until we got the 105s later on.

It was on this day that I became very upset with some of my Jewish buddies, as several of them kept interfering with my interrogations and started asking the prisoners questions in Yiddish, which of course they did not understand. I must explain, under most circumstances we were able to separate the prisoners from our troops, but in Mons, things were happening so fast that it became quite a problem.

From Mons, we turned east to Liege, Belgium, and on September 13 to 15 penetrated the Siegfried Line. It was a very tough battle. We made a frontal attack with fifteen tanks and two infantry battalions; of the fifteen tanks, ten of them were knocked out in about two minutes. The Germans concentrated their fire on this one field, and there was no way our tanks could get through.

We then had to send the infantry in with Bangalore torpedoes, thirty-foot-long sticks of dynamite, which were shoved into their bunkers, killing everyone inside. That is how we took their pillboxes. It took us about a week to do this. Our battalion received the Presidential Unit Citation for this battle. The Siegfried Line had the infamous "dragon's teeth,"—concrete wedges in the ground—and we had to call in bulldozers to take them out, and then put sand down so we could get the tanks through. It was hard because there was so much steel and concrete.

While I felt a great deal of gratification that I was there with the American troops, I never felt that, "Here I am, back to fight you guys for what you did to me," because I became one of the GIs. I never gave revenge a second thought.

The entire division defended positions in the Aachen, Stolberg, Mausbach area from September until December. We had lost so much of our equipment that we were lucky to be almost completely re-equipped right before the Germans broke through in the Ardennes, during the Battle of the Bulge. In Stolberg we slept in houses, as a matter of fact, the Germans were so close—almost across the street in buildings opposite us—that we could talk to them without even shooting. They knew we had very little equipment and they didn't have much either. In fact one day I was standing on a teller mine, which was an antitank gun, so I couldn't get hurt and some Germans came out of a building and we shook hands. We had normal conversations like, "When are you guys going to leave without fighting us?" and that kind of stuff. I pretended like I spoke broken German and never let on that I was German. There was a kind of peace between us for a very short time.

On December 12, all units of the division were back to full strength, and we attacked the Germans near Echtz and Hoven, driving the enemy across the Roer River. It was during this battle when I became the company's communications chief, as we lost both our company commander and the communication sergeant. I also adopted a small Spits dog, which was about the only thing still alive in town at the end of the attack. On December 20, when the Germans broke through our lines in Belgium, the 3rd Armored was pulled out of Germany and sent south to Belgium.

We defended the Hotton–Soy area and stopped the enemy forces whose target was Liege. One morning, the temperature was ten degrees Fahrenheit. I took a patrol out consisting of one squad with a half track and four of us on a jeep to check out a town. As we were approaching the town coming down a sunken road, we saw an American column coming toward the town from the opposite side. Had we not been able to make immediate contact with battalion headquarters, we would have been killed or captured. It was the enemy using captured American equipment.

We retreated to the crest of the hill and stayed in the deep snow and cold. It was a frightening time because we never knew when the Germans would counterattack; it was tough and a lot of our units had many casualties. One unit had to abandon its vehicles and moved out at night on foot because it was totally surrounded. I asked for artillery fire, but was told we had to wait our turn, possibly for a few hours. The artillery forward observer at battalion headquarters said it was up to me to give the proper coordinates. We were so cold after about one hour that I asked for our group to be relieved, but company headquarters said that no one was available.

After two hours, we noticed that the enemy troops were starting to move. When I reported that everyone became concerned and we finally were cleared to receive our allocation of artillery fire. We were lucky with my calls and scored several direct hits on the equipment. This kept the enemy from attacking and overrunning us.

When I was in ROTC in high school, I had a map reading course, which came in handy that morning. After the Battle of the Bulge, we returned to Germany and, on March 5, made our way back to Cologne. On the approach we had to take a town and, as we approached, there were six German 88s sitting on the periphery of the town that started firing at us. There were no tanks with us either—half tracks and foot only. Out of 125 men, we ended up with 29, all the rest of them had either been killed or wounded.

The 88 was just the most wicked gun you can ever imagine. You could hear the blast from the gun, but by the time you heard it, it was almost too late. These were the kind of things that happened to us all the time. Our casualties were always tremendous because we just pushed through; we wouldn't let anything stop us. On this day, as I was running from one area to another, I saw a friend of mine standing in a foxhole. He had been hit and he was using an abandoned German foxhole because he had a leg wound. The next time I went by the foxhole, his head was blown off and I was just sick. I lost friends everyday.

Sometimes we got lucky and avoided ambush. On one approach, we heard talking in German and didn't realize there was a gulley in front of us; we climbed up this embankment, looked down, and saw a five-gun entire artillery unit with its guns trained over the hill toward us. Our guys stood up on command and the Germans put their hands up without firing a single shot.

TAKING COLOGNE AFTER THIS was a very rough battle. We hit the outskirts, and the Germans had made a concerted effort to defend the Ford factory. We attacked, and it took us four or five days to oust them from the factory, which was like a fortress. On the second attack, I lost the radio that was on my back while trying to dive into a house because of the way they were attacking us from the side. Once we got through that, we were close to the Rhine River when the Germans blew up the last bridge right in front of us.

Once a battle started it was total chaos. At a given point, everyone has to be on his own and try to eliminate whatever is in front of them. You coordinate what you can once a battle starts, but after that you're on your own and hope you can keep up with the rest of the troops.

We continued southeast to Herborn and then north to Paderborn. On March 30, south of Paderborn, General Rose was killed. It was a very strange day. Earlier that morning, we were on the left of a sunken road—on a hill— and we saw three of our tank destroyers being captured by Germans on one side of a hill. Our two lead companies that day were cut off and that was when the general made the decision to get out front with two armored cars and two jeeps and look for them. That was the last of him.

As he approached a sunken road, where the Germans had tanks in the gulley pointed at the road that his column was on, they stopped him. When he tried to surrender a trigger-happy German shot and killed him. It was devastating; we all said, "Why did he always have to get up in front?" We couldn't figure out why the man in a situation like that would want to take a chance, when we who had the tanks and the half tracks weren't going to take it. What made him think that two armored cars and jeeps could get across?

The next day we took several prisoners. During my interrogation, I found out that the SS Panzer training school was in Paderborn and they were not going to surrender. After a fierce two-day battle with heavy causalities on both sides, we took the city.

We continued pushing east, and on April 22–23 we took Dessau, where we met the Russians. I was glad the war was over and proud to be one of the guys who was kicked out of Germany and was able to become one of the conquerors. It was a revelation to see what we had done to Germany; I was elated when I saw the German cities destroyed, because I thought that it was justice and they got what they deserved. I felt that I did my job, but most importantly I was grateful that I had been given the opportunity to do this job.

When the war was over, I applied for a job with the military government. I was turned down because I was not yet twenty-one years old; I had been the youngest in my battalion. The military government was desperate for interpreters, however, so I was assigned a job in a unit that set up displaced persons camps for all the people escaping from the Russian zone. We set up three camps near Heidenheim and for three months I lived like a king. We had German servants that cooked, made our beds, polished our boots, did our laundry, and made us feel very comfortable.

I had enough points to be sent home at the end of August 1945. We were sent to Marseille, France, in the beginning of September for our journey home. Due to a dock strike on the East Coast of America, we were held up until the end of November. This obviously was very boring, as all we could do during this time was read, watch movies, and do calisthenics three times a day. I was in the best physical shape ever.

I received the following citations: European-African-Middle Eastern Campaign ribbon with five battle stars, Good Conduct Medal, Purple Heart, Bronze Star, Presidential Unit Citation, World War II Victory Medal, Expert Infantry Badge, and Combat Infantry Badge. The Jubilee of Liberty Medal was given to all soldiers who participated in the Normandy campaign.

When I returned home, I was told that I had become a different person. My brother, who said I had always been the joker of the family, noticed that now I couldn't joke anymore. Whenever I heard loud sounds like in war movies or a car backfiring, I jumped, but I got better over time.

When I think back, the 3rd Armored Division became a second family to me; we all lived together day and night and had been through and survived the most trying of circumstances to which few people can relate. Whenever I see them at reunions, it is like we have never been separated.

Ed Schloss was an optical executive for House of Vision Inc. for thirty-five years and moved with his wife, Elfriede, to San Diego, where he lives today.

Chapter 16

WALTER REED

MAINSTOCKHEIM, GERMANY

95th Infantry Division

Walter Reed was born Werner Rindsberg in the town of Mainstockheim. After Kristallnacht, he was sent to an orphanage in La Hille, France, where he remained until 1941. He arrived in the United States just three months before the Japanese attack on Pearl Harbor. He served in the 95th Infantry Division, Counter Intelligence Corps. He was the only member of his immediate family to escape Germany and survive the war. He is pictured above in 1944.

I've been able to trace the Rindsberg family origin to the mid 1700s. Since my father and mother were third-cousin Rindsbergs, it all goes back to one Feist Rindsberg, who lived in Uehlfeld in the mid to late 1700s (on Mid-Franconia in the Nuremberg area), a small farm village with a typical 8 to 10 percent Jewish population. So far I have never found any Rindsbergs in the world who did not descend from him.

As a young boy from seven to twelve years old, I always spent my summer vacations in Uehlfeld at my maternal grandfather's house with then unmarried aunts and uncles all living together, so I have many recollections of that village and its Jewish families. I have returned there regularly in the past fifteen years and know some contemporary families and the mayor.

My family lived in Mainstockheim, a similar Franconian farm village some fifty miles away near Wuerzburg. Mainstockheim was a typical small farming village where all of the non-Jews were small farmers, day laborers, and tradesmen like butchers, bakers, and haulers—no rich folks or intellectuals. Many of the Jewish heads of household were cattle dealers, some were wine merchants who traveled over a whole region to sell their wine to professional people and business owners, and others were small tradesmen.

My paternal grandfather Moritz Rindsberg (born in Uehlfeld) started a small wine making/selling business in Mainstockheim in the late 1890s, which my father, Siegfried, continued after Moritz died in the early 1920s. My father also cofounded the local adult soccer team around that same time and married my mother, Rika (from Uehlfeld), in 1923. I was born the next year and had two younger brothers, Herbert and Kurt. My father had two siblings who died in infancy, while my mother had four sisters and two brothers who all lived in Uehlfeld or two other communities, Gunzenhausen and Ellingen. All three villages were viciously anti-Semitic in the early Nazi years and therefore these relatives all immigrated to the United States before 1937, when it was still relatively easy, and survived the war.

Mainstockheim had a population just under one thousand, including some twenty-five Jewish families. Many of these were orthodox, including my immediate family, yet they were fully integrated into the community and were not subjected to visible discrimination before 1933. Although there had been a history of discrimination in the eighteenth and nineteenth centuries in all of Central Europe, that discrimination changed over time. Thus Mainstockheim once was a refuge for Jews from the nearby county seat of Kitzingen, where

Jews were not allowed to live in the early 1800s. In Mainstockheim, Jewish residents had to pay protection taxes to the nobleman landlord family in the 1700s. (A few years ago, a nearby nobleman descendant showed me the tax collection book of his ancestors.)

My grade school was a separate Jewish one-room elementary school and our teacher was Siegbert Friedman, who also was the cantor (quasi-rabbi) in the local synagogue. Additionally, he was the *Schochet* who came to family homes to perform ritual slaughter of congregation members' chickens and geese, since there was no kosher butcher shop in the village and Jews there would not buy meat from the regular butcher. Friedman's family members were my father's very close friends. His wife, Ida, was the sister of Henry Kissinger's father and Henry was said to have come to visit us at times. When he did, I apparently played soccer with him, which I do *not* remember (and I bet that he doesn't either). Friedman installed a keen desire for learning in me, and I probably was better educated by the age of ten than most of my contemporaries at the local public school.

At about age eleven or twelve, I transferred to the *Realschule* (middle school) in nearby Kitzingen, where I also did well and was on the soccer team. By then in 1935–1936, some teachers had become Nazis and showed it in the classroom in their pronouncements. Others, however, were still friendly to Jewish students, especially my French teacher. There was much name-calling and bullying of the Jewish students by our peers. By 1938, Jews could no longer attend public schools, and I was forced to commute to Wuerzburg, a twenty-minute train ride to the nearby larger city, to attend a Jewish seminary, which I did not like (too much religion).

As mentioned before, my family was orthodox Jewish, as were most Jews in our village, and we observed all the rituals, such as regular synagogue attendance and strict observation of the Sabbath and all the many holiday special practices. This included strict adherence to kosher food, not driving or riding a bicycle on the Sabbath, separate dairy and meat dishes/silverware, the complete cleaning of the house for Passover, building and using a *Sukkoh*, and on and on. Jewish men even wore a *Zylinder* (top hat) in the streets going to the synagogue for the high holidays. Herr Friedman instructed me for Bar Mitzvah, which took place in 1937. Unlike in America, it was a strictly religious ceremony, with no fancy party or lavish presents.

179

Until 1933 there was a close and normal relationship between Jews and other residents, especially through commercial transactions such as buying groceries and helping farmers with the harvest. There was also much community interaction; one Jew sat on the village council, my father was active in the local football club, and we employed local co-residents in the Jewish businesses and households and bought things from each other without really thinking about it.

As mentioned, my father was both a wine merchant and maker, though his business was small. He used a cellar in our house and one he rented from a local resident to process and bottle wine that he imported from outside (as Franconian wines were not the greatest). Since few people ever ate in restaurants in that time, he sold wine by the case to professional and business customers over a fairly wide region, which he covered by train as he never owned a car or truck. By today's standards, it was a very primitive business but many Jewish men in our region were competing with each other, though I do not recall much competitive friction. In fact, many of the Jews in our area were close or distant relatives of one sort or another.

The Nazi presence in our community began before 1933, in about 1930, with Stormtroopers parading on the village streets, swastika flags aloft, and singing militant songs, including those attacking Jews as "the enemy." By 1933 and after the Hitler takeover, few dared to show or voice opposition, as that would easily result in denunciation by ardent Nazi fellow residents and, from the beginning, the threat of being sent to Dachau. In fact our neighbor Sigmund Stern, the most prominent village Jew, was sent to Dachau "for protective custody" early on. This actually saved his life because it caused him to quickly immigrate with his family to the United States, where he survived in Pittsburgh.

In the first few years after 1933, the most disturbing anti-Jewish events were the constant nationwide vilification of Jews as criminals, bloodsuckers, inferior racial beings, and other propaganda. By 1935 racial laws, boycotts of Jewish businesses, and similar actions began to make life miserable, even in small villages like ours. Many other towns vowed to become *Judenrein* (free of Jews). This was true of Uehlfeld, and it saved my relatives' lives by making them speed up their emigration.

Much of the Nazi movement was based on evil, but skillfully manipulative and continuous, propaganda. Thus even young children were aware of the hassling of the Jews or the concepts of the "master race" and the drive to conquer the world under the scheme of the Third Reich. With radio as the main mass medium, Hitler and his principal cohorts were constantly shouting and preaching their skewed ideology on radio programs, and there were innumerable local parades and festivities, always draped in the Nazi and national flags. Sadly, the whole folderol of the 2008 U.S. presidential campaign, with its attacks, lies, and emotional hullaballoo (on both sides), is strangely reminiscent of the never-ceasing Nazi propaganda machine—and it truly worked!

I was nine to fourteen years old during that period and fully aware of these manifestations. It extended to the fact that many of my prior local friends and playmates had become members of the Hitler Youth and Bund Deutscher Maedchen (BDM, the female counterpart). They wore uniforms, camped out, and marched in parades. We were excluded, of course, but I am sure that had the Nazis not been enemies of the Jews, I probably would have been one of the most ardent Hitler Youths. It was the thing to do, unfortunately, and people fell for it. I was kind of a performer as a kid, and my parents expected me to work hard. If the Germans had not chosen the Jews as people to be put down and eliminated, I would have been one of the most active and enthusiastic Hitler Youth members in my community—I have no doubt about it. I would have marched, saluted, worn the uniform of the Fatherland, and probably would have been killed as a German soldier.

In our small village, interaction among kids was natural and without any special distinction between us and them. All of that changed quickly after 1933 and the Jewish kids in our village soon were bullied, attacked, and vilified by many of our contemporaries, usually three or four on one, as is customary in all bullying situations. It got worse, of course, as the Nazi anti-Jewish propaganda was intensified in the mid- 1930s.

I never witnessed attacks on adults, though they occurred in many places. However, as stated, kids often threatened or actually tried to beat up Jewish kids. While I do not remember specific attacks, a few years ago a retired German octogenarian dentist in nearby Kitzingen asked whether I recalled being attacked by two students in the *Kitzingen Realschule* (middle school), when he came to my aid. I said no, but when he mentioned the two attackers' names, I suddenly remembered them as bullies. The attack obviously occurred, but I had forgotten the incident. Until I met him by accident on a recent visit, I had also totally forgotten that I ever knew my dentist protector. Thus for me, time heals wounds and memories.

I believe that by 1933, *all* Jewish families and individuals "thought" about how to escape the Nazi persecution. The smart and lucky ones made quick decisions. Others, such as my parents, feared giving up their hard-earned possessions, businesses, and careers. In our village, few if any Jews had gone to college, and many only had elementary school educations. This meant that functioning in a foreign country with only German language knowledge was a daunting prospect, for they would have a hard time earning a living. There were also those, like my father, had aging parents (his invalid mother) living with them. They could not face leaving them behind and moving them out of the country seemed impossible.

Most of all, until 1938, there was always hope—foolish and wishful thinking, as it turned out—that the Nazis would not last. As friends, neighbors, and relatives left the country, emigration was a constant and urgent consideration, but unfortunately not acted upon by many. Finally, immigration was opposed by many countries and their citizens, the United States foremost among them. My parents simply waited too long, mostly, I believe, for the above-stated reasons.

I do not recall when my parents first took steps to obtain the required affidavits and U.S. visa applications, probably on or after Kristallnacht in 1938. On November 9, 1938, at seven o'clock or so, there was a loud knock on the door of our house and a truck outside with a whole bunch of Brownshirts yelling *"Raus raus!"* As it turned out, they wanted my father and me. I was fourteen years old. They arrested and hauled us, along with all of the other Jewish men and boys from our village, out of our houses to the county jail. We had no idea why, but we knew that things had really got bad because they arrested us and we thought they were going to shoot us. I had not broken any laws, smoked, violated traffic laws (because we didn't own a car), or stolen anything other than hazel nuts off a neighbor's bush. So, I really shouldn't have been arrested. I was in jail for three days.

When you're being persecuted, the main mental and psychological reaction is fear. You don't think of the things that people nowadays find easy to discuss, like "Why didn't you resist?" or "Why didn't you get a gun and shoot them?" That kind of thing, I think, was completely remote from our consciousness. Plus if you were in one of the twenty-seven Jewish families in a town of nine hundred, and all the other people had weapons and the law on their side, you would know there was absolutely nothing you could do. Unless you were revolutionaries, who nobody I lived with was, you were no different than the people who are currently fleeing Afghanistan for Pakistan because their lives are being threatened. Fear was the main emotion and nothing else.

The upshot was that all the boys were released after three days and all the men were all sent to Dachau. I remember the impact it had when my father came home five to six weeks later; he was in such bad health and horrible looking. He was told if he ever talked about what he saw or what went on in Dachau, they would bring him back in. This experience determined my parents' attempt to do what they could to save at least one of their children, which was me in this case, because I was the oldest at fifteen years old. They found out about the so-called Kindertransport, and in 1939 I was sent out alone.

By that time, my parents had a very high waiting list number at the U.S. consulate in Stuttgart (some of that record is actually in its Gestapo files, which I've managed to obtain), and they just never made it. They had, unfortunately, much company with those high waitlist numbers. I have learned that my relatives had provided the required affidavits, promising financial support to my family, but by late 1941 emigration was no longer permitted by the Nazis.

I actually remember nothing about leaving home or discussing the decision of my parents to send me to Belgium in June 1939. Of the journey I only recall changing trains in Cologne for Brussels, but nothing about my arrival in Belgium. In correspondence between my parents and my relatives in New York (which came into my possession after the relatives died), I found that my father wrote in May/June 1939: "We have been able to persuade Werner that he should leave." So apparently I was not eager to leave home, but I do not recall any of that.

I do, however, have a very clear recollection that coming to Belgium was, for me, like going to Disneyland. Coming from a small village to the Belgian capital, with its large and attractive buildings, cars, streetcars, museums, and parks, was indeed a big and exciting change. So, I was living in a boys' group home of about forty boys, even though at first everyone was a stranger. Most of all, being no longer the persecuted Jewish boy felt like breathing fresh air and coming out from under a dark cloud.

The good life in Belgium came to an abrupt halt in May 1940, when the German invasion put all of us once again in a jeopardy, which was so well known to all of us. Briefly put, the fifty or so boys from Home Speyer and a group of forty refugee girls from a similar girls' group home escaped to southern France on a freight train two days before the Germans marched into Brussels.

Life in the tiny village of Seyre, near Toulouse, in an unoccupied barn was very precarious, especially in the frigid cold during the winter of 1940 and worsened by food shortage, disease, and the increasingly hostile attitude of the Vichy French government toward Jews. Luckily, one of the Belgian woman protectors who had also fled to Vichy France persuaded a Swiss Red Cross affiliate, Secours Suisse aux Enfants, to take over our colony in October 1940. In the spring of 1941, these new Swiss protectors moved us into the Chateau de La Hille, a rundown property in a very remote location sixty miles from the Spanish border. By a stroke of luck my U.S. relatives' efforts to extricate me from France resulted in an immigration visa from the U.S. consulate in Marseille. I arrived in New York, via Spain and Lisbon, on September 2, 1941, just in the nick of time, for there were only a few more ships crossing the Atlantic with refugees after my arrival.

I like to say that when I've been to Las Vegas and to Reno, I've never lost a lot of money, but I've never won anything either. When I came to the United States, however, I won the lottery big time.

Getting to New York was the aspiration of all of us at La Hille, so naturally, I was extremely happy to have achieved that goal. More than that, America had always been considered in Europe as *das Land der unbegrenzten Moeglichkeiten* (the land of unlimited opportunities). I looked at the New York skyscrapers, the cars, the hustle and bustle, and especially the abundance of food and comforts, and saw a world totally different from the one in my recent past. It was indeed like a dream come true.

When I arrived I was taken in by my three aunts and one of their husbands, all of whom lived in one house in Brooklyn. It took awhile before I also realized that they were, like many of their friends, refugees of modest means, and a place higher on the economic scale had to be worked for and earned. Yet, at age seventeen, being able to put deprivation and persecution behind me was indeed like being reborn. At least for a short time, for Pearl Harbor occurred ninety days after I arrived in Brooklyn.

Soon after I arrived, I concluded that I should not be a burden to my loving and caring relatives. Somehow I remembered that my father had once indicated that I should not go into business like most Jews of our Bavarian surroundings, but that I should learn a trade; he suggested becoming a watchmaker. This possibly influenced me to get a job as an apprentice tool and die maker in a Manhattan shop owned by a Swiss-born craftsman. I commuted from my aunts' home in Brooklyn, worked six days a week, and attended Erasmus Hall High School in Brooklyn at night. My English teacher was a guy named Bernard Malamud, later a famous short story and novel writer. I had not been in school since I left Mainstockheim in 1939, except briefly in a vocational school in Brussels of which I recall very little. Working fulltime and going to school was probably quite a handful, but I was young and conscious of time I had lost and needed to be made up. Besides, it was wartime, and everyone was working hard.

The Brooklyn and Manhattan of those days was quite different from today. The Depression, although just about over by then, was on everyone's mind and expectations and lifestyles were still guided by it. Our expectations, especially as refugees, were scaled down because we always compared the present situation with what we had just escaped. In other words, we adapted quickly and enthusiastically to the American way of life, though always as outsiders. Baseball had to be learned, even by just listening to commentary on the radio, for we seldom would go to a game and TV had not yet been invented. American slang became a curiosity for the refugees and seemed like yet another foreign language. I soon strove to master all of that and become a "real" American, which was probably a typical teenage reaction, for my relatives and their many refugee friends were still always comparing things to their former lives.

Our house was in the Brighton Beach area of Brooklyn, then a mixture of Jews and working people of Italian origin, with elevated trains rumbling along behind our house. (In recent years, Brighton Beach has become a Russian Jewish immigrant section.) No one had air-conditioning and many did not have cars, so the subway was our lifeline and there were mostly neighborhood stores interspersed with the typical soda fountain places of that time. When it got too hot in the summer, we escaped to the beach at nearby crowded Coney Island.

I do not recall my relatives having any connection with people other than their relatives and other refugees. Non-refugee neighbors were strangers and many of the refugees still spoke only German. In other words, they were all typical first-generation immigrants, not yet integrated. The sole exception was my unmarried aunt Sarah, a nurse who owned our house and who had immigrated in the early 1920s as a young woman, thus she was the "American." After a while, this isolation from the mainstream began to grate on me and my annoyance heightened after I had been in the army for a while, beginning in 1943. Looking back decades later, I realized that this was the typical immigrant experience all over the world, not just in America.

My refugee family and I had, of course, a much more realistic understanding than any American of what was going on in Europe. I had a personal experience of what German invasion and domination meant from my time in Belgium and France. With the attack on Pearl Harbor and the total U.S. involvement in the war occurring immediately thereafter, we and other Americans soon were on the same footing—"They're attacking us, we're in danger, we got to fight." Having been in Europe and "knowing" the Nazis soon faded into the background and was replaced by the danger we all equally felt and were determined to fight against. Being a refugee from over there soon became less relevant; we now were all in the same boat.

In 1941–1942, America was still so geographically isolated that war coming to it was as unanticipated as the attacks of 9/11, and therefore a tremendous shock. Europe was far away and crossing the Atlantic (or Pacific) was still a remote possibility for the average person, so the direct involvement of the United States was not foreseen. Besides, I was too young to contemplate military strategy, I had no illusions about the Nazis' determination to conquer all of Europe, but the United States and most of its people did not get worried until Pearl Harbor. After that, Long Island went on U-boat alert.

At first, like everyone else I was surprised, but then I'd seen it all before—Austria, Czechoslovakia, Poland, the Western European countries, Russia—so it was not nearly as shocking to me as to native citizens. After all, I'd heard the Nazis singing about it in the streets of Mainstockheim and propaganda constantly blaring it over the radio when I was less than fifteen years old. Now, however, I felt more reassured knowing that the power and determination of America might have a chance to counteract and even end the Nazi terror against other nations.

All of the other German refugee boys I knew—all young guys of course—had been trying to assimilate and therefore felt that *their* country was being attacked, so they did not object to being drafted by the army. As for me, I definitely wanted to avoid the draft until after I had finished high school. I was now eighteen years old and that was more important to me at that time than going to war.

While many enlisted with enthusiasm, others were not that eager to be soldiers or sailors. At first I managed to get deferred so that I could finish school; also, tool and die makers were needed in defense plants, so deferment was granted to me once or twice throughout 1942.

Early defeats of the United States in the Pacific and questionable success in the early stages of the Africa campaign tightened U.S. requirements and draft board leniency. So I was drafted in March 1943 and soon found myself reporting to Fort Dix, New Jersey. Becoming a GI was inevitable—that's how I then looked at it. I was no screaming patriot, the way McCain seems to remember himself, though I doubt the accuracy of his recollection.

Although Brooklyn to Fort Dix is not very far, from the very first day, I understood that I had entered a totally different world. Refugee recruit Werner Rindsberg immediately became U.S. Army Private Rindsberg.

After a few days, I was sent to Fort Leonard Wood in Missouri's Ozarks for three months of basic training. GIs then tabbed it as "the hellhole of the world." This referred to the landscape, the accommodations, and the beastly summer heat without air conditioning. The slop, which was cooked by whom everyone claimed were truck-drivers-turned-chefs, and the purposely harsh drill sergeants contributed to the desperate description. I was now nineteen, but had not engaged in athletic activity since I was kicked off the soccer team in 1937. The obstacle course, crawling on my belly with rifle in crooked arm, or scaling the wooden wall via a rope net, singled me out as the typical awkward Jewish kid among the whooping and hollering natives. I felt inadequate and embarrassed. Fortunately, though it took time to discover this, there were other "city" types in the same boat.

Until I entered Fort Dix, I had never been west of the Hudson River, thus my America was limited to Brooklyn, Manhattan, the Bronx, and ubiquitous Washington Heights of Manhattan, dubbed the "Fourth Reich" because of its heavy Jewish refugee population. Since all troop travel was by train (first from Fort Dix to Missouri), I quickly realized both the enormous size of America and the diversity of its regions. This understanding increased when I was transferred from Fort Leonard Wood back east to Camp Holabird, outside Baltimore, where I was trained for three months as a Corps of Engineers bulldozer repair mechanic.

From there, I received another train transfer to the Ordnance Depot at Granite City, near East St. Louis, Illinois. Besides the landscape and the cities of St. Louis and Baltimore, I also became intermingled with all sorts of young Americans from many backgrounds and locations. This opened a whole new and daunting horizon, because many of my new co-soldiers came from all walks of life and attitudes. Shooting dice on a blanket, a frequent pastime and passion, was as strange as attending mass, which I also had never done before (and still haven't). I never really did learn the intricacy of gambling with dice. I quickly sensed my "otherness." I certainly did *not* seek out other refugee soldiers, or make special associations with them, and actually did not encounter that many until I was transferred to Military Intelligence in France in 1944. In that capacity I worked with many refugees, including those trained at Camp Ritchie. By then, I was more acclimated to being a U.S. GI than a guy who had been a refugee, so I probably was less timid about comparing notes with other refugees.

Frankly for me, it was never about "getting back at Hitler," or worrying about killing my former countrymen. People often ask me about that, especially students when I speak at schools. It was mostly "these Krauts are going to kill my buddies," "let's get them *first*," or "they killed our buddies, let's go get even." I do not recall anything about revenge or retribution from the point of view of a Jew. I was very young and easily influenced by my surroundings.

For quite a while, my different background and experiences definitely made me feel like the outsider. I just didn't quite "get" what it was like to go to high school in Ashtabula, Ohio, or to grow up on a farm in Indiana. Moreover, with a name like "Werner Rindsberg," coming from Brooklyn, I must have been a strange animal to many of my companions. Of course, many of them had the same problem, though from a different American perspective. They too were mingled with guys from different backgrounds and experiences from their own, but I didn't think about that until much later. I thought that I was the only odd one who had to watch and learn how I should react or conduct myself. Drinking and chasing women was another new aspect for me, at least from how the typical GI approached these topics. I tried to learn and sometimes faked interest when I didn't have any. It soon became part of my desire to blend in and also to have equal opportunity, even though I was not a native. Eventually, I had just as many friends as anyone else.

Among the Jewish refugee groups in New York, becoming a citizen was a universal objective, and all my relatives were proud to seek or obtain citizenship. Wanting "equal opportunity" for me certainly included wanting to be a citizen. So when I was notified at the camp in Granite City in the summer of 1943 that I was to appear in court to become a citizen the following week with other GI citizen candidates, I was glad to get ready. Someone apparently informed me that those who wanted to change their names could do so easily during the naturalization court procedure.

I was definitely embarrassed to go around as Private Rindsberg, because I felt that it instantly stereotyped me as a Jew and as a foreigner. This was the case not only with fellow soldiers and officers, but also with the girls we were usually chasing wherever we were hanging out. So I picked the new name about as quickly as McCain "selected" Sarah Palin; however I have stuck with "Walter Reed" all my life, which was not Palin's fate with McCain. I vividly recall that I had qualms about changing the name my parents had given me, so I intentionally kept the initials "W. R." and also selected my original first name of "Werner" to be my new middle name. I didn't know then that my parents would not survive to find out.

Once I had become Walter Reed, I wanted to be like everyone else (as I perceived it then). Having been persecuted for being "different," I was very intent on being considered as "equal" and "belonging." Like most immigrants, I have both felt proud to be an American, but also have always sensed an obligation to be a "good" citizen by voting and serving my community. I think my original background and experiences have put a special value on the privilege of being an American.

AFTER SIX MONTHS' TRAINING at Camp Holabird and in Granite City, I was assigned to a replacement battalion and sent to an assembly point north of Pittsburgh, Pennsylvania, and from there to England in March 1944. I do not have the slightest recollection of the guys in my unit, because we were intended as replacements. We would all be dispersed over time to replace casualties in other units. This produced a certain sense of fatalism among us, rather than cohesive team spirit or long-lasting relationships.

I am not implying that we had low morale. It was just not the "go, go" spirit of troops that would go into battle side-by-side and depend on each other. It was mostly fear of the unknown, heightened by the situation of being replacements. Unlike the usual propaganda about the military— "heroes," young people "making sacrifices," and so on—the life of a soldier is fear, discomfort, misery, and complaining. Those were mainly my, and our, emotions before we boarded the *Aquitania*, a converted ocean liner, to England. The former luxury liner had been outfitted for maximum occupancy, so all the luxury aspects had disappeared. The ship and crew were British, so the food was vilified and rejected by many GIs. I especially recall the troop version of a complete "English breakfast" included stewed peaches. These and other items were castigated as "limey food" ("limey" was our favorite negative moniker for British soldiers and their deficiencies). There was much seasickness, and no one knew where we were heading and how we would be deployed.

Anticipation therefore was limited to speculation, and there wasn't much basis for the reality we were about to face, as none of us had ever served in combat and few had ever crossed an ocean. We were indeed like sheep about to be shipped "somewhere." One of the hallmarks of the situation of ordinary soldiers in World War II was that we never knew what was going on, why we were doing what we did, and whether those in charge really knew what they were doing. Hence, the frequently used acronym SNAFU (situation normal, all fucked up).

Our ship arrived in Glasgow, Scotland, in March after a ten- or twelve-day crossing, and we were shipped by train to the Midlands near Chester. There, my military occupational specialty was changed from mechanic to "combat engineer," with training in hand-to-hand combat and building pontoon bridges. As far as I recall, we remained there until we were moved to southern England just before the invasion. One week after D-Day, our battalion landed in Normandy on Utah Beach. The battle had by then already moved about ten or fifteen miles inland. We camped in the Normandy fields surrounded by hedgerows until after the U.S. forces' breakthrough at St. Lo in July.

ONCE THE U.S. FORCES had begun their advance through northern France, our unit followed on trucks, usually at a safe distance from the fighting. After Paris was liberated, our unit ended up in the village of Auvers St. Georges, near Etampes, about thirty-five miles south of Paris. It was there where I became the unofficial French interpreter for the battalion commander and learned that the U.S. headquarters in Paris was in need of German speakers to interrogate prisoners. I applied, was transferred to a Paris suburb for about two weeks' intensive training, and assigned to a seven-man Military Intelligence Service (MIS) interrogator team of a captain, a lieutenant, and five noncoms. With only two weeks' training I surely was not prepared, but then in war even the best trained often have to improvise and I was well trained for other tasks before I was transferred to MIS. Most people quickly learned by doing, but war is not West Point or Annapolis.

Our MIS team was outfitted with two jeeps and a trailer and assigned to the newly arrived 95th Infantry Division, with two guys from our team assigned to each of the three regimental headquarters, where we did our work. Our task was to interrogate newly taken German prisoners and civilians who had crossed the battle lines about tactical information (location of their ammo dumps, number of troops, etc.) and to report that information to our officers and up the line to G-2 Section. We joined the 95th in September just east of Metz, where the division was already in battle. I'll never forget the sight when we came through at night of the smoke over the city totally in ruins. (That still-smoking, total devastation sprang into my mind immediately when I saw the second airplane plunge into the World Trade Center.)

We were often on the move as the battle shifted and usually close enough to action that anything could have happened. First we were in Normandy, where the sounds of war were always near, and we were warned that German infiltrators could be over the next hedgerow. I never saw or heard any of them, but when I arrived at the 95th Division regimental headquarters, an incoming mortar shell exploded a few feet away. That was my baptism of fire.

For a time, in December 1944, we were in Saarlautern where the advance had stalled. I think by that time I had already been upped to private first class and it was a short hop to staff sergeant, because interrogators needed a bit of rank to be effective with the German prisoners whom we interrogated for tactical information. I was never actually "fighting," but once I was driving our lieutenant in a jeep when shelling began. I panicked and ran the jeep smack into a tree.

Saarlautern was followed by the unexpected Battle of the Bulge, during which our division was shifted to the northern U.S. flank and I ended up briefly near Maastricht in the Netherlands; with bad luck we could have been captured, but we weren't. Once the U.S. troops resumed their advance and entered Germany, we advanced with our division to the vicinity of Aachen, which was in ruins. Now I must say that I deplore the destruction in all of those places—of the private citizens' homes, assets, and the factories—and the displacement of the people in them. On the other hand, I can mentally separate my regret of that from my realization that if the Nazis hadn't set out to destroy other places—such as Stalingrad, Soviet Union, or Coventry, England—their places wouldn't have been burned. They started it.

We then went toward Dusseldorf and into the Ruhr industrial area. We were in the area near Muenster when the Germans surrendered in May 1945. Shortly after that, I was reassigned to counterintelligence, working with U.S. military government units to help with the Denazification of local German governments and also the University of Marburg.

Some weeks after the armistice, I went back to Mainstockheim, primarily to look for my family. Local residents knew only that the Jews had been "sent to a labor camp in the East" several years before.

My parents and two younger brothers did not make it. All other relatives managed to immigrate to the United States. Recently, I saw the list with the names of twenty-seven Jewish persons deported from my village, and some of them were distant relatives.

I have a very peculiar viewpoint about how I feel about losing my family in all of that. I'm not unmindful that they were part of the six million that were murdered. I don't say they were deported, I say they were murdered by the Nazis, and that it was deliberate, it was on purpose. Obviously I feel a great feeling of desolation over the loss of my family and all the others. All through history man has been inhuman to man, and unfortunately I was born into a time and place where this took place again, and my family was among the unfortunate horrible victims.

For a time, I was stationed at Camp Dentyne near Kassel in Central Germany and later at Seventh Army headquarters in Heidelberg. From there, I was ordered back to the United States for eventual discharge in February 1946 at Camp Kilmer, New Jersey. I believe we boarded a Liberty ship in Marseille and came home after a stop in the harbor at Casablanca, Morocco. Once again, it was a primitive ride, with much seasickness on the wallowing ship, but the best part was that we were heading west and soon into civilian life.

AFTER THE WAR, I had totally camouflaged my past for the sake of avoiding discrimination and securing equal opportunity in life and in business. This means that on my business and vacation trips to Europe (including Germany), I always pretended that I was born in the United States and had studied French and German in school.

Beginning in 1997, I came out of the closet, including also on my visits and to my contacts in Europe. Since that time, I have enjoyed and created close relationships and friendships with many Germans, both individuals and officials, and I have been asked to speak to some German school classes and in public. My attitude is that horrible crimes against human beings were committed by the Nazi government and officials, as well as by many ordinary German men and women who were literally "drunk" with the idea that they were the master race. This idea led them to believe they had the mission and the right to take over other countries, take over individuals', companies', and countries' possessions, and harass and take lives at will, whenever the victims fit into their schemes for domination and extermination.

I feel that a vast majority of Nazi-era Germans either participated in, or proudly endorsed, these nightmarish crimes and misdeeds. I also feel equally strongly that the present-day descendants of these millions of perpetrators are in no way guilty or responsible for the deeds and crimes committed in the 1930s and 1940s. This is why I am committed to, and comfortable with, working alongside present-day Germans, Belgians, and French people to honor the memory and lives of the victims, and to do all that is possible to preserve their memories and their accomplishments, no matter how mundane.

My family and I have been most fortunate to collaborate and interact with many dozens of people in many German communities for this purpose and in this spirit. For example, in 2007 my wife, Jeanne, my son, Andrew, and I joined a pilgrimage of eighty local government officials and twenty-five high school students and their teachers. We traveled from my Franconian home area to southeastern Poland to erect a memorial to the victims from their region, visit three mass murder camps, and hold meaningful discussions about these victims' lives and sufferings.

In October 2008, Jeanne and I participated in a one-week commemoration of Holocaust victims as guests of the city of Dinslaken in the Rhineland, because some of the local children were refugees with me in Belgium and in France. I met new people there who were intent on paying homage to the victims from their area. Also, I spoke at a public gathering and at several high schools about the events and situation of the Nazi era.

Many similar activities in the United States and with Europeans have become an important part of my life in recent years and will continue to play an important role. As I said at the ceremony in Poland, reconciliation and commemoration are the only means available to us to honor the victims and their lives, as well as to join with the descendants of the perpetrators. Recrimination and vilification will not serve to honor them.

Walter Reed's lifelong occupation was public relations, and he was director of public relations for the National Automatic Merchandising Association (for the vending machine industry) in Chicago. As a lifetime member of Rotary International, he continues to travel the world and speak publicly about his experiences.

Chapter 17
MANFRED STEINFELD

JOSBACH, GERMANY

82nd Airborne, 504th Parachute Infantry Regiment
Operation Market Garden

Manfred Steinfeld lived in a small village of four hundred with six Jewish families. The oldest of three siblings, Steinfeld left Germany on the Kindertransport in the summer of 1938 and arrived in Chicago a few months later. Inducted nearly one year after finishing high school, after his basic training, Steinfeld was sent to the Army Specialized Training Program and then to Camp Ritchie for additional army intelligence training. At the time of the invasion of Normandy, he volunteered for paratroopers and was assigned to the 504th Parachute Infantry Regiment, G-2 Section, of the 82nd Airborne. His first action was in Holland. In the photograph above, Steinfeld (right) meets the Russians in Grabow, Germany, 1945.

I was born in Josbach, located one hundred kilometers north of Frankfurt. In the province where I was born, 492 communities had Jewish residents in 1933. This was in a province that is 100 miles by 100 miles, and they had been there since 1650, 1700, and some even before that. In World War I, most Jews were sent to the infantry and the number of fatalities among Jewish participants was twice as high as any other ethnic group. From my own family, one of my father's and one of my mother's brothers were killed. My father served in Macedonia.

We had a semi-successful general store and made a modest living. We lived in a town with six Jewish families. At the turn of the century, there were twelve Jewish families. The Sabbath was observed and they were all orthodox, but they also felt they were good Germans. I distinctly remember the election in 1933; Germans who fought in World War I all came to the election with their medals on because they had served in the war and felt as though nothing was going to happen to them.

I am sometimes amazed that we did not have radio or television, and yet information was quickly and widely disseminated by mouth. We knew what was taking place because some of the men were arrested, and they came back after severe beatings or after having been confined for six weeks to two months. In 1933 I was nine years old, my little brother was seven, and my sister was eleven. When the United States adopted a quota for the amount of Germans to be accepted in 1938, my mother applied for a quota number that indicated we would be able to get out by 1940 or 1941. She then decided to register me with the Hebrew Immigrant Aid Society (HIAS) that was responsible for getting children out, and in July 1938 I left with twelve other German Jewish children. At the same time she had registered my younger brother, Herbert, to go to Palestine, and he left in November 1939. My mother was more interested in saving her children. In fact, my sister was in Hamburg the day war broke out. She was supposed to go to England on the Kindertransport but she did not get out.

I arrived in New York, but traveled on to Chicago to join an aunt and uncle already living there. I certainly had to have been impressed by what I saw. I adapted very well and found part-time jobs while going to school. I was put in the eighth grade, graduated from primary school in 1939 and graduated from Hyde Park High School in 1942. All of my friends were American Jewish kids, though in Hyde Park there were many German Jews.

I realized in 1941 that when America entered the war that I, as a resident of the United States, was subject to the draft. I entered the service in March 1943.

I was certainly very anxious to do my part, and for the Allies to have a victory. I was sent to Scott Field, Illinois, and then to Camp Roberts, California, for basic infantry training. From there I went to the Army Specialized Training Program at the City College of New York. In January 1943, I went to Military Intelligence School at Camp Ritchie, Maryland. I completed a first course in interrogation of prisoners of war (IPW) and went on to become an order of battle specialist.

I became an expert in the German Army. In school we had American instructors speaking German and dressed up in German uniforms, and that was our only exposure to the German army until we got to Europe. My responsibility was to make an assessment based on the information we were getting from the POWs—for example, the breakdown of weapons, equipment, commanding officers, and the type units we were opposing. I found this quite easy because it was the same breakdown in the U.S. Army. It went as follows: squad to the platoon, platoon to company, company to battalion, battalion to regiment, regiment to brigade, brigade to division, and so on.

I sailed to Southampton, and then on to London to Military Intelligence headquarters, which was located at 40 Hyde Park Gate. The British were very accommodating, receiving us with open arms. My immediate assignment was to receive reports from the French underground, obtained by inmates of the brothels the Germans had established. With the usual German efficiency, every dog tag of a German soldier had name, rank, serial number, and the unit assignment. As these soldiers patronized the house of prostitution, all of these names were marked down by members of the French underground and sent to intelligence headquarters. Based on that information, we were able to make some assessment on the units we were facing on the coast of France.

At the same time the invasion was taking place, they requested volunteers for the airborne units, and I volunteered for the paratroopers, 82nd Airborne Division. This was exciting for a nineteen-year-old to jump out of airplanes. I was also patriotic and wanted to do my duty and win the war. Jump school was in England. We all had to be physically fit, which took about a week. It consisted of one hour of double time in the morning, stretching, landing, and then another evening of double time (full pack). It was total exhaustion. We also had to learn to climb ropes.

The first jump was on Monday, the second was on Tuesday, third was Wednesday night, the fourth was Thursday, and the fifth was on Friday.

Then I graduated from school on Saturday as qualified parachutist. I distinctly remember that I was the last man waiting to jump when the jump master came up to me and said, "Steinfeld, give me your wallet and watch. One out of every hundred parachutes won't open, and yours might be it."

I was trembling, but the chute opened automatically after he took my personal possessions and pushed me out of the plane. Certainly the next jumps were easier because I knew what to expect. When we got jump training we were jumping from fifteen hundred feet, so the total exercise from the time we were out of the plane until we landed was two minutes, so we wouldn't be an easy target on the way down.

I was assigned to the G-2 Section, as part of the order of battle team, number 16, which was commanded by Lieutenant Able, Sergeant Wynn, and me. Both of these soldiers did not speak German, so I had an advantage over them in carrying out certain responsibilities. We were responsible for all of the intelligence on which we based our campaign strategies.

The one campaign I was involved in from the beginning planning stages was the one in Holland. We were stationed in Leicester, England, and the campaign was announced fifteen days before the jump. It was hurriedly planned and I was involved from the beginning to the invasion, which was September 17, 1944. The 82nd jumped at Nijmegen, the 101st jumped at Eindhoven, and the 1st British Airborne jumped at Arnhem. The strategy was to seize all of the bridges over the Rhine and Waal River, and then make a shortcut into Germany.

Today, that campaign is considered one of the biggest military blunders. The 1st British failed at Arnhem. We remained at Nijmegen from September 17 to November 15, holding that part of the lines while the 1st British Airborne was wiped out. The Polish Brigade, which jumped five days later to assist the British, was also wiped out. The total campaign's casualties were about fifteen thousand.

I came in by glider. Normally, a unit would decide who was to jump and who would come in by glider. I was sitting in a jeep (in the glider) with Lieutenant Able, the chaplain of the 82nd Airborne, and we crashed. We all got hurt badly because the glider was totally demolished. I landed about fifty feet from the point of impact. There were more casualties caused by the glider landings than parachute jumps in Normandy and Holland. Jumping was comparatively safer than landing in a glider.

I was taken to a first aid station because I was banged up quite badly, with cuts and bruises. I finally made it to the G-2 Section on the day after D-Day. General

Gavin, commander of the 82nd Airborne Division, insisted those in headquarters live the same way as the soldiers on the frontlines. I lived in a foxhole for two months. We were not allowed the comfort of taking over buildings.

We did have the first Yom Kippur services in Holland, very close to the German border, in 1944.

I was in Holland until the middle of November. After being relieved from the frontlines, I was sent to a base camp in France until the Battle of the Bulge on December 18. I was responsible for posting the military situation map every day, as we received information from Supreme Headquarters Allied Expeditionary Force (SHAEF). I remember in the middle of December, we knew that the Germans were planning something. We knew there was a huge concentration of German forces and equipment, but no one was expecting anything.

We went by convoy to the Ardennes through the snow in the cold weather. Those nights during the bulge were quiet and terrifying. There were German soldiers infiltrating our lines dressed in American uniforms. I remember emptying a magazine into the night when I thought I had heard something. The next morning, I realized that I wasn't shooting at anything. My first actual contact with the enemy was during the bulge, when I interrogated a prisoner who was born and lived in the town next to my birthplace. Unless he was a member of the fanatical SS, the typical German soldier was glad to be captured.

After the German counteroffensive stopped, we were sent back to base camp in France. In the middle of March, we were assigned to the newly formed U.S. Ninth Army, then holding the west bank of the Rhine in the vicinity of Cologne. We were there until the middle of April, when the 82nd Airborne established the last bridgehead along the Elbe River.

On May 2, 1945, I was on the reconnaissance patrol that contacted the Russians. At the same time, I was involved in translating the unconditional surrender document; the 82nd Airborne Division accepted the surrender of about four hundred thousand Germans facing our sector on May 3, 1945. We also came across the Woebblin labor camp, a sub-camp of a larger Neuengamme concentration camp. I was certainly emotionally distraught in the camp, because there was always the possibility of seeing my mother and sister among the dead or half-dead. That was one fear I had. When we found the bodies in the camp, we decided to bury them in the nearby town square. I made the funeral arrangements and the American chaplain gave the eulogies. The Germans, of course, felt that we were doing an injustice to them by accusing them of these crimes, even though they lived only three miles away. They swore they had no knowledge of the atrocities. "We didn't know" was the typical German excuse.

When I was military governor of a town called Bossenberg in June, a woman came up to me in a concentration camp striped dress. She informed me that a man walking across the street was a criminal, and we arrested and interrogated him. It turned out that his name was Ludwig Ramdower and he was the assistant commander of the infamous Ravensburg concentration camp for women, where this woman was an inmate. We took him out for target practice and threatened him with our pistols before turning him over to the British military tribunal on June 10. He had a military trial and was hanged by the British three years later.

The interesting aspect of that incident is that the woman who came up to me was the former daughter-in-law of Martin Buber, the famous Austrian Jewish philosopher. Her name was Margarete Buber-Neumann; she divorced Professor Buber's son in 1930 and married Heinz Neumann, the head of the German Communist Party (he was executed in the Soviet Union by Stalin in 1937). When the war started, she was repatriated to Germany where she spent 1939–1945 in a camp.

By May 15, 1945, we knew what had taken place in the camps. When we moved back to France in June 1945, I received permission to go to my hometown. I arrived in Josbach on a Sunday morning and went to the *burgermeister's* (mayor's) office. News of my arrival came as people were leaving church. I soon found out the tragic fate of my mother and sister; they were deported in October 1941, sent to the Riga Ghetto until October 1944, when they were sent to Stutthof concentration camp near Danzig. My mother died December 30, 1944, and my sister died January 15, 1945.

When the war ended, the 82nd Airborne was selected to be the occupational force in Berlin. We entered Berlin in July and remained until October 15. I was discharged on October 29 from Camp McCoy in the United States.

Manfred Steinfeld is a philanthropist and the cofounder of Shelby Williams Furniture. With his wife, Fran, he most recently founded the Danny Cunniff Leukemia Research Laboratory at Hadassah Hospital in Jerusalem, in memory of their grandson, Danny Cunniff, who died of leukemia in 1997.

Chapter 18

JACK HOCHWALD

VIENNA, AUSTRIA

6860th HQ Detachment Assault Force, Seventh Army

*Jack Hochwald emigrated from Vienna, Austria, in 1938. Upon
induction, he was sent to train with an all-Austrian battalion,
which included exiled members of the Habsburg dynasty. After
the outfit was disbanded due to political pressure, Hochwald
was sent to a replacement depot in France and then to a frontline
intelligence unit, in which he served until the war ended. After
VE Day, he returned to Vienna to arrest Nazis he knew before
the war. A photo of Hochwald was unavailable; pictured above
is the 6860th insignia patch.*

In the fall of 1942, my draft board advised me that as a college student, I could get a deferred status until I completed my two semesters for which I had just signed up at City College New York. I told them I was ready to go anytime I was called, feeling very strongly that I should be in the military at this time, fighting the Nazis.

A month later I found myself on a train to Camp Upton, Long Island, for processing. Like all new recruits, I was given a short IQ test and interviewed by a classification officer, who did not seem very interested in my background or my knowledge of German, though he made a note of it. So, I was sent to Camp Grant, Illinois, for basic training, which was a very cold place during the winter of 1943.

After a few weeks into the year, a rather unusual thing happened. On a snowy morning, I was suddenly told to pick up my belongings and given my travel orders to transfer to the 83rd Division of the 101st Infantry at Camp Atterbury, Indiana. No reason was given for the transfer until I arrived there. I traveled by train to Chicago and changed to another train going to Indianapolis, arriving that same evening. At the railroad station, I called the number I had been given.

While waiting to be picked up, I noticed a few other soldiers waiting for transportation to the camp. Soon I discovered they too had been assigned to the outfit, but had no idea the reason for the transfer. Two of the men spoke with a German accent and the other two seemed to be American-born with Slavic-sounding names. When the driver came to take us to the camp, even he knew very little about the outfit, except that it had been activated recently and was located in a special compound of the camp. He thought it might be a commando/ranger outfit, but I would never have guessed that our assignment was to an "Austrian battalion." To this day, I wonder how many Americans—and for that matter, Austrians—ever knew that there was such a unit in the U.S. military.

As soon as we entered the room that seemed to be the headquarters of this new outfit, we were received by a good-looking, youthful captain who spoke in a southern drawl: "My name is Captain Schmidt, and that is spelled with a 'dt' on the end, and I'm a native Texan and proud of it. My parents came here before WWI from the Austrian province of Styria. We're a farm family or, as they say in Texas, 'ranchers with a spread.' The reason we're all here is to form an Austrian battalion, but an American outfit in every respect.

Hopefully, we will be able to participate in the invasion of Europe, and liberate Austria from the Nazis. This battalion will consist of four rifle companies and one heavy weapons platoon."

When I met my bunkmates, I found only a few more German refugee boys. The parents of the rest had come from the old Austria-Hungarian Empire prior to World War I. This had included Czechs, Slovaks, Hungarians, Poles, and Croatians—a real ethnic and religious mixture. As time went on, however, more and more recruits filled up our barracks—foreign and U.S. born. Many of them came directly from their reception centers and had no basic training at all. I soon learned that the originator of this outfit was none other than the Archduke Otto von Hapsburg. Upon fleeing occupied Europe, he met President Roosevelt and the First Lady for tea at the White House and proposed the idea of such a unit.

Secretary of War Harold Stimson, who was present, agreed and made the unit part of the U.S. Armed Forces. While the archduke himself was not allowed to join for various reasons, he sent his three younger brothers. I met one of them a few days after my arrival, when I was given kitchen duty. While working there, I heard the mess sergeant, who was of Czech descent, shout, "Damn it, Hapsburg! Put those hands deeper into the water. I want those dishes clean." Then in a somewhat lower voice, he turned toward us and said, "Boy, I sure wish my old man could see me now, giving orders to a Hapsburg. He sure didn't care for them and wouldn't like it at all for me to be in an Austrian battalion, but that's the fucking army for you."

During the next few weeks, more men began to arrive, and we all were given basic training, whether we had it before or not. This included the usual obstacle course and rifle training, as well as lots of marches and hikes. One time when we were returning from such an outing, we passed by a recently built compound for German prisoners, most of them from the Afrika Korps. Unknown to us, they must have heard us sing, which we usually did when on hikes. Not only did we sing American songs, but older German tunes, too, and so they rushed to the fence and cheered us wildly, thinking we were new arrivals, but when they saw our uniforms, they became silent and backed away. We then switched back to English songs, while some of us made obscene remarks and pointed rifles at them.

Apparently, word about this encounter got out to the camp commander, and we were told to avoid this area in the future. From then on, we never had any more contact with them.

One day in our mess hall, Colonel Conrad addressed us with the following remark: "Now we are almost at battalion strength, and soon we will receive the Edelweiss insignia to be worn on the upper sleeve of our uniforms. Wear it proudly, regardless of our national or religious background, and perform as a team." He emphasized the need for secrecy at this time, but hoped that there would eventually be favorable publicity about this outfit. He also believed that, in time, we might have outside visitors, such as reporters or local officials from the nearby city of Indianapolis.

Eventually, reporters from the *Indianapolis Star* came to the camp for interviews and took pictures of the battalion in training. At first, the publicity was favorably received, but eventually opposition came from two sides: from a socialist Austrian exile group which objected to the Hapsburg involvement, and from American voters of Slavic background who wanted the outfit abolished all together. So the end came pretty quickly. Even up to the final days, all members performed their duties well, having by then set aside much of their earlier antagonistic attitudes. In one of its last acts, the commander of the 83rd Division, General Milburn, presented the outfit with a citation, giving a medal to one of its soldiers who had saved another from drowning during a night exercise.

It was a sad day for many when our departure date became final. Some who had been expert skiers were sent to the newly formed mountain division in Colorado. Others like me were transferred to the 75th Division stationed at Fort Leonard Wood, Missouri. Many eventually did get a chance to go overseas and see action in Europe, and some even took part in the liberation of Austria. I am further convinced that had this outfit existed longer, it would have been a great credit to the U.S. military and to Austria.

UPON MY ARRIVAL at Fort Leonard Wood, I was assigned to Company B, 3rd Battalion, 289th Regiment of the 75th Division, a rifle company which had only recently been activated. Once more, I had to undergo basic training and spring maneuvers in Louisiana and the eastern portion of Texas, which lasted several weeks. After the D-Day invasion of Normandy resulting in more than the expected casualties, specifically among infantry divisions, the War Department quickly initiated a new policy to send individually trained enlisted men and officers as replacements, in what became known as "package shipments." To sweeten the deal, they gave both volunteers and selected GIs short furloughs.

Since I had not seen my folks in a year, I returned to New York. My parents were overjoyed to see me so tan and fit, except that my mother cried when she saw my partly shaven head. After making the usual rounds with relatives and a couple of friends, I reported to my new station, Fort George, Maryland. From there these "packages" going overseas to Europe were assembled in the East Coast.

After several days, we were ready, with full field packs and gears, to ship out to our final staging area, which was Camp Kilmer, New Jersey. Then we were taken to the docks and boarded the *Queen Mary*. It was pretty foggy and evening when we landed in Scotland, left the ship, and took a train with its windows blacked out. After several hours, we arrived at an army camp somewhere in the middle of England between Chester and Nottingham and stayed there while making final preparations for joining the Allied forces on the Continent. Then it was to Southampton, where we boarded a Norwegian fishing vessel with a Scandinavian crew. When dawn came, we were all anxious and ready to get off the boat, which would not come any closer than about half a mile from shore. Instead we climbed down nets with ropes, holding on tightly as we got into waiting LCTs. We stood around in silence, somewhat bewildered by what we saw.

Then we heard a voice and noticed a major with a bullhorn, making an announcement: "Welcome to Omaha Beach. As you can see, right where you are standing, many guys like you were wounded or died on D-Day. And there is still much fighting ahead, and our supply lines are stretched to the limits. While we need everything, there is a critical shortage of ammunition, mainly for the M1." Then he pointed to the nearby tents and said, "I want each of you to pick up at least one belt of ammunition or a box of cartridges, and carry it with you up the hill. And don't worry how long it takes, just follow the path as marked; rest if you have to, and you will find water cans along the way for drinking. And good luck to all of you."

We could now get a real feeling what it was like to be in a war zone. Our group, or "package," was taken to a partially bombed out railroad depot, where we huddled together to keep out of the rain. This was a "repple depple" (replacement depots), where we waited for assignment to our final destination. That turned out to be a place called St. Truiden in Belgium. This was not too far from the German border and was under the command of the Ninth Army. From now on, we were no longer considered a "package," but part of the 30th Division now engaged in the Eupen-Mastricht area. It also had recently participated in the battle for Aachen and sustained heavy causalities. One of my comrades remarked, "It really didn't make much difference where we were going or what the number of our outfit was, for we were still nothing but a fucking replacement for some poor bastard who had either been killed or wounded."

We were now headed to a regimental command post (CP) of the 30th Division, much closer to the frontlines. From there, we would be parceled out to one of the rifle companies as the need for replacement arose. The sky was gray and the whole landscape looked gloomy; our spirits were kind of low, too. None of us had much to say, even those who usually liked to make wisecracks to relieve a tense situation. As we were coming down the road near an intersection, we heard an explosion and saw a flashing light, thinking it could have come from an artillery shell or a mortar. In any case, the driver came to a stop, telling us we might be coming under an attack, so it was best we get out quickly and take cover on the side of the road. This being my first experience, I jumped out so fast that I fell very hard to the ground, and the butt of my rifle hit my mouth, knocking out a front upper tooth and breaking the next tooth in half.

I was in a great deal of pain (the doctor gave me a shot of morphine) and couldn't sleep that night. The next morning I sat in front of my tent and contemplated my fate while I watched replacements getting on trucks. I felt like the cartoon character Sad Sack, which appeared in the army newspaper, *Stars and Stripes*. On the other hand, this was the opportunity I had been waiting and training for—to fight the Nazis. Moreover, I realized that there were many native-born American soldiers who had less reason to be here than I had, and yet they seemed very courageous and often eager to battle the enemy. I also knew that they, too, had their anxieties and fears, but usually they were able to disguise it, by humor, making wisecracks like: "Ain't it great, our getting a free tour of Europe, thanks to Uncle Sam," or "Don't you feel sorry for the poor fucking civilians back home, who don't have steaks to eat every day!" and so on.

While deep in my thoughts, I heard someone call my name and touch my shoulder. "Private Hochwald, I've been looking for you all over," he said. "Get your gear together. I will be back in a few minutes with my jeep, which is parked in the CP motor pool." I figured it was my turn now to be sent "up front" and paid no attention to where we were going, trying also to get some sleep. I had gotten so used to the sound of gunfire that it took a while for me to notice the noise started to get less and less. All of a sudden, I realized we were heading back in the direction of St. Truiden, from where I had come a couple of days ago.

Now I was wide awake and asked the driver if by any chance he was taking me to Ninth Army headquarters, which he answered in the affirmative, but could not tell me why, since his job was mainly that of a courier. I figured it could be almost anything, but had a hunch it might have something to do with my German language and background. The moment we arrived, a first lieutenant came over to me, pointing to a folder he was holding, and said, "You are the last on my list, and as soon as you hop on the truck, which is across the road, we will be off."

When I climbed aboard, I saw several other soldiers already seated. They seemed glad to see me and shook hands with me. As they introduced themselves, I could tell that three of the six fellows there spoke with German accents, and I assumed that their backgrounds were similar to mine. The others sounded like native-born Americans with knowledge of the German language.

As soon as we got going, the lieutenant, who was sitting up front with the driver, turned around and, with a slight accent, spoke: "I know you all have been anxious to find out why you are here and where we are going. My name is Martin Rheinhammer, and I have only recently come to the ETO from Camp Ritchie, an intelligence school in Maryland. There is a critical need now for German-speaking personnel, and you have been selected based on your 101 file. The military only recently has decided to give you guys a shorter version of the Intelligence course that's been given back in the States. And as to where we are going, it's a town west of Paris called Le Vesinet, and we try to keep that secret."

Hardly had the lieutenant finished his sentence than we all jumped up from our seats and began cheering, for I could tell that they, too, were greatly relieved, having come from frontline units. Lieutenant Rheinhammer told us to sit down and remarked that we should not be so enthusiastic, for in about two weeks, which would be the length of our training program, we would either be back with the Ninth Army or be reassigned to one of the other army units in the field. He even mentioned the possibility that one of us could be sent on a mission behind enemy lines. Nevertheless, none of his comments could dampen our spirits, and for me the recent painful accident no longer seemed to bother me as it had earlier that morning.

We were told to exchange our M1 rifles for carbines, and those whose rank was sergeant or above were given watches and binoculars, which at that time excluded me. In between classes, we engaged in some physical training and target practice with the carbine and pistols, including a few weapons of German make. This lasted about ten days straight without any time off, but the following weekend we were given permission to spend a Saturday night out. We had to be back by Sunday morning the latest and, furthermore, were told to confine ourselves to the area of Le Vesinet.

And so, another fellow and I found ourselves walking down the road into town, when we came upon the railroad station. To this day I can't explain what made us do it, but we bought two tickets and before we knew it, we were on a train for Paris. When we returned to Le Vesinet the next morning, it wasn't long after we arrived that we stood in front of Lieutenant Colonel Rothschild. Standing at attention, he began to address us in a stern voice, telling us that we were facing disciplinary measures for disobeying orders and going AWOL, but he also had something else in mind.

He then gave the command "at ease" and, in a friendlier tone, waved a paper in front of us, which we tried to read quickly. It was a memo from SHAEF (Supreme Headquarters of the Allied Expeditionary Force), dated July 14, 1944, and signed by General Eisenhower, ordering the establishment of two T-Forces, their mission to participate with frontline units in the analyzing captured intelligence targets. "Since the two of you are anxious for action and excitement, I am sending both of you to these T-Forces, which are in need of more manpower. One of you will go to the Sixth Army Group, the other to the newly formed Twelfth Army Group. Your orders will be ready in a day or two. In the meantime, you are both confined to your quarters."

We were almost overjoyed, but tried not to show it. Sure enough, a couple of days later we had our travel orders, sending my comrade to the Twelfth and me to the Sixth Army Group, which was located in a place called Vittel, not far from Nancy.

The unit was commanded by Lieutenant Colonel Pumpelly and had about 250 men of whom one-third were intelligence personnel and the rest were support, such as ordnance and other logistical services. I also found out that T-Force, upon entering the town of Saarbourg, had sustained some casualties when it came under enemy fire. There had been one guy killed by the name of Arthur Remer, a former refugee like myself, and two others wounded by shrapnel. Also, two of the T-Force's jeeps and its mess truck were hit and completely destroyed. I was then told that the main body of the unit was relocating to the town of Savern in preparation for the Third Army's entry into Strasbourg, which could happen in the next few days.

It was December 1944, and we were all very optimistic that the Allied Armies would soon be crossing the Rhine and that shortly after the war would be over. We already had noticed the arrival of U.S. Navy personnel, along with engineering units, which brought with them various bridge-building equipment, including pontoons and rubber rafts. Both American and French Army units had reached the western bank of the Rhine and were making preparations to cross the river. One of the jumping off places was the town of Kehl, only a few miles east of Strasbourg, and where such activities were taking shape. However, this was not to be.

On December 16, news arrived that the Germans were attacking, not only in the north, breaking through the Ardennes, but also attempting to retake the Alsace region in an operation called Nordwind. Already, reports were reaching us that Nazi infiltrators and paratroopers, along with advance units of the German Army, had made surprise attacks deep into allied positions and territories.

There were a few occasions when we were stopped and suspected as being infiltrators. Our accents didn't help. Once, as we were coming back from one of the forward CPs, we were stopped by soldiers pointing their rifles at us. We showed them the IDs and even gave them the password for the day, but that wasn't sufficient, since infiltrators had been known to have forged papers and could have learned the passwords by listening in to telephone conversations over a walkie-talkie. The fact that our driver spoke with a heavy accent didn't help.

They asked us questions that almost any GI would at the time have known, such as who won the pennant and the World Series last year, who was the pitcher of the Yankees, Betty Grable's husband's name, etc. Fortunately, we had a fellow on our team who not only was able to give the correct answers, but as it turned out he and one of the soldiers were also from the same town. Not so lucky was another team in which all of them were taken to a stockade and questioned by MPs; they were not released until our colonel came and got them out.

There was another problem, unique to all of us former refugees who found ourselves once more on German soil. It was the realization that the Nazis might not consider us as regular soldiers, but as spies. Some thought about having the letter "H" (Hebrew) removed from our dog tags, which would help us—at least in the early phase of a potential capture—avoid interrogation by the Gestapo and we would be sent to a normal POW camp.

When we were finally able to push back the German advance in the Ardennes, our team was now mostly in the field in support of units that required assistance with captured documents and prisoners, but the supply of both had pretty much dried up in January. The German Army was in a defensive position and fighting pretty much on its own soil. On one occasion, when our team was with the G-2 Section of the 45th Division, Gen. Robert Frederick came into the tent hoping to find some captured Germans. Seeing none, he became angry and made the remark that it may not be a bad idea for us to get off our ass and go out and bring one in. This hiatus, however, also did not last very long, for once the big push started, the number of captured German soldiers increased rapidly and eventually became an avalanche.

At that point, too, T-Force became officially the 6860th HQ Detachment Assault Force, but for all practical purposes was referred to as Seventh Army T-Force. In the second week of March, all of our teams crossed the Rhine— thanks to the courage of an entire infantry company—at a place called Remagen, one of the last remaining bridges still intact. Also, under heavy fire, army engineers had constructed pontoon bridges in several other places on the Rhine, which would make for a swift advance into Germany.

In the second week of March, we were on the way to our first major intelligence target inside Germany. This was the I. G. Farben Complex in the twin cities of Ludwigshafen and Mannheim. We would find out that the Farben factory had been deeply involved in Germany's war effort and had also participated in the manufacture of Zyklon B gas used in concentration camps, but supposedly had not been aware of the great extent and usage in gas chambers operated by the Nazis. When we stormed into the administration building, we surprised the directors, who were having a board meeting.

We became overwhelmed with targets—anything of intelligence-related business—but we were moving so fast and being attached to units advancing quickly, this made it difficult to stay in one place for more than a day. We found ourselves with the 45th Division, which was closing in on Munich.

With the 42nd Division, the 45th was on its way in and entered the Dachau concentration camp. As it happens, I was fortunate to be assigned to a team leader, a Lieutenant Salzman, another refugee who suggested we go to the camp and offer our help.

By the late afternoon, we saw the barbed-wire fences and watchtowers, stopping at the main gate with its slogan above that said, *"Arbeit Macht Frei"* (Work will make you free). An officer came toward us as we were trying to get in saying that there was a real danger of a typhus epidemic and most army personnel were prohibited from coming in. So, we decided to ride along the fence for a while, where we now saw inmates in striped clothing standing around and waving to us. Upon seeing them, we left our jeep and walked toward a group of men huddled around a fire. We tried to speak to the group we had come upon; we had difficulty since they were Serbs and Croats. It wasn't very long before several other inmates joined in, and speaking in German and Yiddish we were able to communicate.

One of them, wearing the Star of David, asked us when the rabbis were coming, since he wanted to say Kaddish (Hebrew prayer for the dead). From him, we learned that the day before was when the first American troops had arrived, blasting their way in and mowing down with machined guns and rifles any of the German guards they first encountered. He then pointed to several boxcars standing on a rail siding, about a couple of hundred yards away, so we walked slowly over there. Soon the stench overcame us, but we managed to see in half-opened boxcars the remains of bodies, reduced to skeletons and bones. We were told that these were only part of a shipment of new arrivals from another camp who had not survived the trip due to disease and starvation.

As we were leaving, one of the Jewish inmates came over to us and, in a low voice, asked us who the Asiatic- and Mexican-looking soldiers were, whom he encountered the day before. We told him that all of them were good Americans and that among us, too, were former Nazi refugees who only a few years ago had escaped Germany. He looked dumbfounded but then understood who we were; he confided in us that he and a few others from his barrack had taken revenge on some of the *kapos* (block wardens and inmates acting as overseers), especially those who had been cruel. We assured him that he and his fellow prisoners did the right thing, and we would have done the same had we gotten there earlier.

When we got back to our jeep, we sat there in silence feeling emotionally drained after having witnessed actual hell on earth. After several days in Munich, I joined the team that our colonel had selected to proceed to the 101st Airborne, which had fully occupied the last bastion, Hitler's Alpine home and fortress in Berchtesgaden, or what was left of it. After a picturesque ride of several hours into higher elevations and over winding roads, we reached the renowned village of Berchtesgaden, where the Berghof was located. In what appeared to be a movie-set-like scenario, we saw GIs riding around in German staff cars and Mercedes Benz autos, blowing their horns (some wearing top hats and waving) and obviously drunk. We knew then for sure the war was over.

When I actually went into to the infamous Berghof and stepped into Hitler's office, I marveled that this was the place where he contemplated his strategies, and where in February 1938 Chancellor Schuschnigg was persuaded to make concessions to Austrian Nazis, which shortly thereafter led to the takeover of my country of birth, Austria. Here, too, came many other foreign dignitaries like Chamberlain and Mussolini, making deals and signing treaties. Now I stood here, too, and for a moment I felt a personal triumph. Even though my part in all of this was one of little significance, I could not help but picture myself as a conqueror. All I could think of was how the end of Hitler's evil empire was somewhat like Richard Wagner's opera, *Die Gotterdammerung (Twilight of the Gods)*.

When the war ended, we again joined the main body of the Seventh Army in Heidelberg. With pressure from the American public and the press, General Eisenhower ordered an operation called Tally-Ho— the code name for surprise raids of supposed hideouts, where we found SS men hiding in attics and barns in Bavaria. It may be of interest to note that most of those interviewed and asked where they were on November 9, 1938, on Kristallnacht, when many Jewish homes and shops were looted, synagogues burned, and thousands of Jews arrested and sent to concentration camps, all of them invariably replied that they had been "*zu hause*," which meant "at home." What bullshit.

AT THE END OF NOVEMBER 1945, I still had not been given any definite departure date for the States, so I thought I would take this opportunity to visit Vienna, which I had left in August 1938. While I was anxious to see how the city and the people fared during the war years, I had mixed feelings about the trip. At any rate, I got permission for a furlough and arrived there in the second week of December. My first impression was that the once-gay and romantic city had shed its glamour and seemed quite depressing, with its gray sky and blustering cold winds, which often brought snow. Additionally, I saw now how the ravages of war had left certain parts of the city with a lot of damage to buildings. Some of it was from Allied bombings, but much more was caused in the last days of the war, when Nazi officials refused to surrender to the Soviet Army, causing needless fighting and many casualties. Naturally, all this brought great hardship to the Viennese, and when the Soviets entered the city, in retaliation they did quite a lot of plundering and raping.

I did not have a lot of personal business to take care of, since there was no family owned property to claim. In those early days there was no restitution for Nazi victims, especially since the Austrians insisted that they had been Hitler's first conquest. Of course, everyone knew that the majority of the population was only too willing partners in the Nazi takeover in 1938. Eventually, Austria admitted guilt, though years later. However, I planned to find out what happened to some of my former classmates and teachers, and those I knew to have been ardent Nazis since I wanted to inform the local CIC, just in case any of them were wanted for war crimes or tried to apply for government jobs.

The one person I thought I found, Anton—my former classmate who had humiliated me in front of the others when he made me scrub all of the classroom desks—was not at home, but his father answered the phone. He told me that Anton had left the day before to look for a job in one of Austria's provinces, but he could not tell me in what town or when he was coming back. Since I knew that both his parents had been active party members and Anton a leader in the Hitler Youth, I wanted to make sure I had the right family before reporting them, and so I thought I should pay them a visit.

When I rang the bell, the parents reluctantly let me in; I saw two elderly people in their late sixties, both in poor health and quite nervous. They told me that Anton had been wounded twice on the Russian front and had achieved the rank of *Feldwebel* (sergeant), contrary to my belief that he would have been an SS man or a party official. I then was shown a photograph of him in his uniform, and I also recognized a drawing of his that he had made in class, since his desk had not been very far from mine. Though I knew that it was folks like them who were directly responsible for what happened in Austria and to the Jews, I almost felt sorry for them. When they realized who I was, they pleaded with me not to make any trouble for them or their son. I felt myself getting really agitated, and all I could say was that I had no choice but to turn over their names to the proper authorities, more to scare them than anything else. Then I left without saying goodbye.

The following day was Friday, and I thought I would attend services in the only synagogue left in the city, not because I was particularly religious, but more out of curiosity to see who would be there and perhaps by chance see someone I might have known. That did not happen. I also planned to visit the gravesites of my relatives, including that of my grandparents, knowing that my folks would have liked me to do so.

RETURNING TO HEIDELBERG, I finally heard what I had been anxiously awaiting. I was going home, back to New York, a proud U.S. soldier who had served his adopted country as best as I could. Upon being discharged in 1946, I was contacted by the Pentagon to work analyzing and screening important documents, not only those from our Seventh Army documents center, but also from other repositories located all throughout Germany. There seemed to be now a renewed interest, ever since the Iron Curtain had descended upon Europe, and there was a lot of information of special concern to Pentagon logistic staff. Just as important, and perhaps even more so, were the records and activity reports on foreign intelligence agents operating in the United States. Our office became known as the German Military Documents Center, and it soon attracted not only personnel from other government agencies, but also newspaper reporters, historians, and writers who—as William Shirer mentioned in his book, *The Rise and Fall of the Third Reich*—found a gold mine of material.

After working there for several years, we had fully screened most of the documents, and it was decided by the U.S. government to return many of these papers to Germany, as well as to U.S. Archives and other institutions that asked for them. From time to time, significant papers came to light, such as former Nazis living in the United States who had managed to enter the country under false pretenses. Also, various archives across the world exhibited these documents, particularly those that concerned the mass extermination of Jews in the Third Reich. A final repository for many of these papers was found when the U.S. Holocaust Memorial Museum in Washington, D.C., opened its doors in June 1993.

Therefore, even after the last holocaust survivors, victim and liberator alike, have passed on, these documents will bear everlasting testimony to one of the darkest events in the history of mankind. In some small measure, those of us who played a part in all this can have the satisfaction of knowing that our efforts and sacrifices were not in vain.

Jack Hochwald worked in law enforcement until retirement and lived in Hollywood, Florida, until he passed away in 2002.

Chapter 19
NORBERT GRUNWALD

VIENNA, AUSTRIA

106th Infantry

Bert Grunwald escaped from Austria by being smuggled across the Polish border. He lived in Krakow for three months before a cousin in London found a Quaker family to bring him over to England in 1938. After living in England for a while, his brother, who had made it to Baltimore, Maryland, arranged to bring him over to the States. A replacement sent to the 106th Division, Grunwald was one of thousands of troops captured by German forces during the Battle of the Bulge. He is pictured above in 1944.

The Enemy I Knew

Anti-Semitism became like a disease in Vienna by 1938. Our life became very miserable. I was riding my bike one day and a man, who knew I was Jewish, claimed that I was going the wrong way, got out of the car, and beat the hell out of me. That was the defining moment for me. I had my Bar Mitzvah in 1938, and in 1939 I went to my parents and said, "I'm not going to live here. I have looked at a lot of maps and I'm going to leave and cross the Austrian border." My uncle, who was very well connected, knew of some professional smugglers who used to smuggle before the Anschluss; he arranged for me to go across the border. I got on a train in Vienna, which was a very sad day for me and my parents, but I didn't have the imagination to be afraid. I crossed the Polish border, and a family from Krakow took me in with whom I lived for three months.

My cousin in London, who knew I had got out, took out an ad in the London newspaper asking if someone would sponsor a young boy from Austria, and she got an answer from a Quaker family that would take me in for a year. So, from Gdansk I went to Bloomsbury, in London, to stay in a Jewish community before I met my host family that lived right outside of Essex. They were wonderful people; they sent me to a Quaker school called Saffron Walden. Although my English wasn't too good, I made some friends on the soccer team and it was not a very bad time for me. They gave me a bicycle and I rode it to Cambridge.

The war started right after I got to England. Naturally I was very nervous about my mother and father still living in Vienna, but my brother in Baltimore made every conceivable effort and miraculously was able to get my parents out, via Trieste, before Italy got into the war. It wasn't before long that I, too, went to Baltimore. The experience was pretty overwhelming, but I assimilated quickly. I went to night school, and became an assistant welder in a shipyard where we built Liberty ships.

My brother went in the service in 1942, and I could not wait to also get in, for I still carried a lot of bitterness toward the Viennese. So in 1943 on my eighteenth birthday, I got into the army. I had the typical training at Camp Croft, South Carolina, where I was also nationalized as a citizen. While I was in the service, my father died, and since my mother was all alone, I was given the opportunity to get out of the service, but I chose not to.

From there, I went to Fort Benning for additional training. As there was an immediate need for infantrymen, I was shipped to the southeastern part of England. I was in the 106th Division, which was sent to Belgium;

the army put us where it thought there was going to be a quiet line so we would get experience right in the Ardennes region. When we were on the line, there wasn't much movement; the majority of fighting was south of us near Germany. We were supposed to hold that line and secure that front.

Then the Germans attacked us, which surprised everybody. We fought for a couple of days, but they threw everything at us and totally overran our position. We had lost connection with troops to the rear and could not retreat. There was fighting behind us, too. We had no idea where anybody was, so we dug in and fought the best that we could. It was cold but we just dug and dug because it was the only way to save ourselves. There was no where to run back to. I shared a foxhole with a friend of mine, to whom I got very close, and he was killed. I saw his body and I cried.

There was snow everywhere; we were surrounded and they shelled us. I got some shrapnel in my head; it was nothing serious, but I was bleeding. When the shelling finally stopped it was night, quiet and foggy. Using a bullhorn (they were close to us), they told us to surrender, and in the morning our officers met with them. They gave what was left of our battalion an ultimatum, and our major (our commanding officer was killed) decided it was hopeless and surrendered. Since I spoke German, I was the one that I was sent to "negotiate" the surrender with the German commander. I spoke with a very tough lieutenant; another officer offered me a cigarette and the lieutenant slapped his hand. I was taken by car to the commander, and all I could ask was if I could keep our blankets. When their officer asked me how come I spoke such good German, I told him that my father was an American doctor who studied in Vienna, so I had lived there as a little boy.

Most of us Jewish guys all threw away our dog tags because they had "H" for Hebrew on them; that really speaks to the caliber of the guys in the 106th who knew what could be done to us if the Nazis saw that we were Jews.

Fortunately for us, these were professional German military men and they told us to line up and bring our blankets and whatever we had. They were going to put us on a train. As we were marching one way and they another, I knew it was over for them; they had run out of petrol and had horse-drawn carriages. They put us on a train to go east, and when the weather cleared, our planes just strafed everything they could, include our cattle car, which held about fifty men and several were killed. I yelled in German, "Let us out, let us out!"

A guard responded, "Why should I let you out when you are killing our population?" Finally someone made the decision to let us out. I then went to the commander, told him that we didn't want to get back on the train, and requested to let us march.

My brother, who was by that time in military government, had heard I was missing and actually came looking for me. He nearly got captured a few months later.

In some sense, it was a relief for the Germans that somebody knew the language and could help them organize the prisoners. After marching a while, they put us back on the cattle car and sent us to Silesia. Stalag 11A and the American compound was very new; there were English captured in North Africa, as well as Serbs, French, Russians, Australians, New Zelanders, and nearly eighteen nationalities altogether in that Stalag. We didn't have much to eat there, but the British shared Red Cross parcels with us. I didn't have much luck with the French when I went from compound to compound to collect food for the American boys. The Stalag itself was not frightening; it was well organized and quite a friendly atmosphere. I was able to write letters to my mother on Red Cross stationary. The British who had been there for years made washing machines out of tin cans and even made a radio. The British, Aussies, New Zealanders, and Americans didn't communicate too much with the French. The Russians, who the Germans treated very badly, were bedraggled and separated from us.

I did my best to conceal that I was a Jew, but strangely enough I didn't care. When the Russians attacked, the Germans marched us west. Actually, not all of the guards were German; there were a lot of Latvians and other Slavics. Unfortunately, I never got their names.

They had hardly enough food for us, or even for themselves. One time, a few of us knocked on a German farmhouse, and the farmer gave us "speck"-fat-something we had never had. Later, I developed a fever and was diagnosed with yellow jaundice. I couldn't go on, and everybody knew that if the Germans who were in retreat found any Americans left behind, they would kill them. So, two Australians put me in a push cart and pushed me for two days until I got better.

Along with the help of my fellow prisoners, I think I was able to survive because I was initially so well trained, even though I had lost all of this weight. We did lose some people along the way. We were marched to Hof, near the Czechoslovakian border.

One frightening experience was when we came across a group of concentration camp inmates on a work force. A couple of us wanted to go over to them, because they looked so awful. I realized they were Jewish inmates; when I started walking to them, a German guard pointed a rifle at me and I thought he was going to shoot me. A couple of guys dragged me back. That was when I decided to lay low, because if they found out I was a Jew, I would share a similar fate.

When we got to Hof, it was about three or four days before the war ended. The guards took off, and we tried to make our way toward our own lines when we heard our artillery. I was told to be the leader of our column, in case they were German troops and I had to tell them that we were prisoners. We almost got shot when we made it to our lines and were shouting that we were American prisoners. It was wonderful; the officers couldn't do enough for us and they fed us in their tents.

Then I got so sick because I hadn't anything in my stomach. I weighed 104 pounds and was not well, anyway. I couldn't retain food, so I was evacuated to a hospital in England. When I was shipped stateside, at Walter Reed Army Medical Center I was diagnosed with colitis, which was a result of my yellow jaundice, but I eventually got better. We were treated well; for the returning POWs from Europe, we were in much better condition than those prisoners coming back from being in Japanese captivity.

Bert Grunwald earned his master's degree in Russian economics from American University. For nine years, he worked for the Central Intelligence Group (later renamed the CIA) before entering the brokerage business. In 1967, Grunwald founded Man Alive, Maryland's first methadone treatment program.

Chapter 20

ERIC BOEHM

HOF, GERMANY

In 1934, Eric Boehm's parents sent their sixteen-year-old son ahead to the United States. His older brother, Werner, had left Germany a year beforehand, and came to the United States in 1937. His parents did not emigrate from Germany until 1941. From 1936 to 1940 Boehm attended the College of Wooster in Ohio. During and shortly after the war, he was an Army Air Corps officer in intelligence, ending up in Germany and helping to dissolve the Supreme Command of the German Luftwaffe. Later, he was a War Department employee, involved in building up the German press, at the headquarters of U. S. Military Government in Berlin.

I was a lieutenant in the U.S. Army Air Corps. While stationed in Wiesbaden, Germany, I was told to report to Reims, France, to SHAEF and Eisenhower's HQ. The assignment was to serve as the intelligence/interrogation officer, on the occasion of the dissolution of the Oberkommando der Luftwaffe (OKL), Supreme Command of the Luftwaffe. The headquarters of the Luftwaffe was in Flensburg. SHAEF had the assignment of dissolving the Oberkommando der Wehrmacht (OKW)—Supreme Command of the German Wehrmact—and its navy, along with it the OKL. The reason for the mission to Flensburg was that the successor government to Hitler, headed by Admiral Doenitz, was located there (just south of the Danish border) whence they had fled from Berlin.

I was one of four officers sent there on the air force side. Altogether, the total mission had maybe twenty-five to thirty officers and a small number of noncommissioned officers. All of us were flown to Flensburg and actually landed with the help of the Luftwaffe unit that had been controlled by a Royal Air Force (RAF) regiment. The RAF regiment, I was told, went through the battle lines and persuaded the commander of a German SS division that it would go north "to establish order." I remember that an RAF regiment that arrived at the end of the war did its job well. There must have been about one hundred operational aircraft at the Flensburg airbase. They were inoperative since all of them had their propeller removed, and they were stored in a warehouse under RAF regiment guard.

The senior officer of the four officers, who were attending the air force side of the SHAEF control mission, was an American, General Schramm. The next in rank was Air Commodore H. W. Mermagen; third was RAF Group Captain J. McComb, and lastly was me, 1st Lt. Eric Boehm. I had the assignment based on a briefing by A-2 (Intelligence) of SHAEF; specifically the "order of battle," that is, the disposition of units and equipment of the Luftwaffe.

The A-2 of SHAEF told me that he had hoped that my commanding officer, Lt. Col. Eric M. Warburg, would represent A-2, but he was then busy interrogating Field Marshall Goering, so he sent me instead. The A-2 told me that my rank was too low for the job, and that I might have to get the support of General Schramm to overcome that handicap.

It was clear to me shortly after arrival that the two German headquarters, OKW and OKL, were pretty much operating on their old wartime mode and were not yet controlled by the SHAEF Control Party.

Eric Boehm

It is part of the standard operating procedure to take control of all files. The German military units had burned many of the files, and thus denied the occupying forces useful and often important information. I intended to go to the OKL headquarters to take charge of the files, have them sealed and turned over to us, and do this unannounced to avoid selective burning.

When I discussed the process with General Schramm, he said that I should simply ask them to select what is important and turn that material over to us. This violated common sense, as it stands to reason that we would have no control over their selection. We were the ones who should guide the selection process and have them work for us on a controlled basis. I tried to persuade this general that A-2 of SHAEF would look askance at his suggested mode of operation and that I was accountable to A-2 who sent me on this mission. I should physically be there while they were packing the OKL records, which I had previously ascertained that the OKL had done a certain amount of selection for itself when it fled Berlin, and what was left was quite manageable for us. The general would not budge, no matter how hard I tried. He thought it was too offensive to "pounce on them" to take charge of the files and I had to find another way.

I knew that General Schramm was interested in getting a German pistol, a Luger or a Mauser. So I went to Flensburg to the air raid bunker, where I knew huge amounts of small arms were stored. I was able to get a laundry basket full of Mausers and Lugers and presented this basket to the general. Obviously he was pleased and, with a smile, said, "Now I've got to do my duty as I've been taught, and you win, Lieutenant." So, I did my duty there, no records were burned, and A-2 of SHAEF was satisfied. I did get the order of battle of all the Luftwaffe units, and SHAEF was able to take control of the Luftwaffe units in a knowledgeable way.

At the time when Field Marshall Wilhelm Keitel was sent from Flensburg, I was the interpreting officer for that particular assignment. It must have been that he was taken in Luxemburg, though I was not entirely certain. He was, in fact, arrested and became a prisoner of war, and was detained in anticipation of the Nuremberg Trial.

On a ship called the *Patria*, I interrogated Luftwaffe General Eckhard Christian from Hitler's HQ, and he was crying when he talked about the last days of "*Der Fuhrer*." The reason for that became transparent later when I found out that one of Hitler's secretaries was General Christian's wife. It was embarrassing to see this man in tears. We weren't sure whether we could interpret this to mean that he was an ardent Nazi deploring what happened to

Hitler, or otherwise. During the interrogation of Otto Koller, who was then the chief of staff of the Luftwaffe, he was incredibly uncooperative because he was not being interrogated by a more senior officer.

As victorious armies, we were of course in a state of exhilaration—the war was over and we had won. Moreover, I enjoyed the personal satisfaction as a Jew from Germany of our having defeated the Nazi juggernaut and wiped the Nazi evil from the face of the earth. I was, however, very careful to make sure that I would never appear to be vindictive in any way. Nevertheless, it was very gratifying to be saluted by Admiral Doenitz, then the head of the German government. As a token of recognition of their defeated status, all Germans, regardless of rank, saluted the Allied soldiers of the SHAEF party first. We acknowledged, though I did it with reluctance.

Since there was a shortage of German-speaking officers, I was loaned to the army side as the interpreting officer for the arrest of Field Marshall Keitel. General Rooks, Eisenhower's representative, called Field Marshall Keitel to the ship in which we were operating to tell him to pack and be ready to be flown away from Flensburg several hours later.

About 2 p.m. that afternoon, a Lieutenant Colonel Boehm-Tettelbach and the aide de camp, or adjutant, on Field Marshall Keitel's staff came to the gangplank of the ship and picked me up, so that we could drive to OKW headquarters. We talked very briefly about the coincidence in name; I found out subsequently from my father that the family is from Upper Franconia, the area of Bavaria where I was born. I was rather disinclined to make small talk in any case, because I had some strong feelings, particularly about Field Marshall Keitel. He was known as the lackey of Hitler, but I did not know at the time that he was being arrested in anticipation of being held for the Nuremberg Trials, where he would be sentenced to be hanged—deserving this fate—because he was one of the most evil types serving Hitler.

At the OKW, the military guard was still behaving as in wartime—"by the numbers." Its soldier's behavior was as if they had come straight out of a military school. The guard looked formidable, comprising men who had evidently been selected for their extraordinary height. Some of the military police had a big metal shield on their chest. No other American or British officer came with me to get Keitel.

Keitel was allowed a fairly large number of accompanying generals to see him off at the airport, and our General Rooks had provided four staff cars. I was surprised at the amount of baggage that Keitel took with him, a weapons carrier full of at least half a dozen suitcases, some of them quite large in size. I remember one box that approached the size of a steamer trunk.

We all took off for the airport, which was about a thirty-minute drive from there. General Detleffsen rode with me in one of the staff cars. As we were making small talk, I asked him if he was a career officer. He replied in the affirmative. I then asked him what he would be doing in the future. He said there would always be a need for persons to polish shoes. His behavior was quite in contrast to Keitel, as there was no evidence of arrogance. I heard some five years later that this General Detleffsen had gotten a position in the Ruhr industry as a general manager of a large company—so much for polishing shoes.

When we arrived at the airport, it turned out that the plane, which was to take Keitel to his destination, had landed and then took off to do some sightseeing of Copenhagen from the air. It was uncertain when it would be back. Since it was an unusually warm day, I arranged that the whole group be taken to one of the barracks. Keitel was visibly taken aback by the fact that he had to wait. Since he lacked good understanding as to his new position, he was stupid enough to say to me something to the effect that he had to rush to pack and now he had to wait. I ignored him and certainly did not apologize, but wished in retrospect that I had said something to him to the effect that we had been waiting six years for him, so he could certainly wait a few hours for us.

Eventually, the American C-47 crew had come back and they were ready to transfer Keitel. He was wisely removed to take away the top authority from the OKW. He became a prisoner of war and was placed in one of the holding fortresses, which we honored by such names as "the Dustbin." I again saw Keitel at the Nuremberg Trails when I was in the audience. Keitel, whom I would estimate to have been 6 foot 4 inches, and weighing 250 pounds, looked visibly diminished both in size and importance in the court of war criminals.

This is the end of my encounter with history in 1945.

After the war, Eric Boehm completed his doctoral studies in international relations at Yale. In 1960, he and his wife, Inge. founded ABC-CLIO, an internationally known publisher of reference books now headquartered in Santa Barbara, California. He is the author of We Survived: Fourteen Histories of the Hidden and Hunted of Nazi Germany.

Chapter 21

FRED FIELDS

UEHLFELD, GERMANY

XX Corps, Third Army

Fred Fields was born Siegfried Dingfelder and fled Germany with his family just after Kristallnacht. They arrived in the United States in 1940 and lived in Brooklyn, where Fields worked as a baker until getting drafted into the army. A graduate of Camp Ritchie, Maryland, he shipped out to the ETO as an interrogator and joined his unit 69th IPW in Metz.

In the whole village where I grew up, there were eight hundred people and eighty of us were Jews, roughly 10 percent. There were three breweries in the town. On Saturday nights, everybody got together in town, Jew and non-Jews, and played cards. Then Hitler came in and everybody started to alienate themselves from the Jews.

I remember one man got up and made a speech in a beer garden where everybody met. He said, "I don't understand what they want from the Jews here, they've never done us any harm. They're just like we are." The next day he disappeared and ended up in a concentration camp. He came back six weeks later and never spoke another word about it. He was cured. The guy who was the political leader and ran the dairy, Mueller, organized the pogrom, in which all of the Brownshirts roused the Jews out and destroyed houses. They dragged the men out and burned the synagogue (just three blocks from our house) that had a beautiful Byzantine dome.

I was nine years old when the Brownshirts staged a demonstration outside our house; they banged on the walls, shattered our windows, and were throwing rocks. My family and I jumped over our back fence, and I led them through the barn, where we boarded horses once a year, and into our vegetable garden. We were sheltered overnight by a farmer who my father did business with and who lived about three miles away. I stayed with a second cousin in Fürth and went to school—an orphan school—for a while until I joined my family later.

In 1933, I was nine and couldn't fathom what was going on. There was no reason for it. I was scared. The week Hitler came to power my uncle, along with three buddies, came into our village from Nuremberg and marched down the street with a red flag, and that sealed his fate right there. When he fled, the Germans caught up with him in southern France and nobody ever heard from them again.

We resettled in Bamberg in 1935; my father and I took English lessons because he thought there was no future left for me in Germany. On the other hand, he felt that while he couldn't do business, he had saved a little money and thought he'd be able to survive. He was completely wrong. Ultimately, I was the motivator in getting our family to leave. My father said, "No, we'll stay," and I said, "Let's go."

Then on Kristallnacht, he and my uncle were arrested and sent to Dachau, like everyone else. If prisoners could prove to the authorities that they had a way out of the country they would let them out. When they let him out the end of August, he didn't look too good. He would not mention a word about what happened for fear it would get back to the Gestapo and they would take him back. He wouldn't even tell us about it at home. Anyway, we had a short time to get out of the country and we had to turn over our house, acres of land and meadows that we leased to other farmers. We sold everything for 1,000 marks, the price of two cars at that time.

We couldn't get into the United States because our quota number had not come through yet, so we had to go to England. Ten days before Germany invaded Poland, we were on a train to Frankfurt with very little: three suitcases and whatever was on our backs. Then we took a plane to England. At that age, I can only describe certain numbness in me and an apprehension about the future.

The place we stayed in London was an enclave of refugees. I worked in a button factory and learned all about London. Just before I turned sixteen in May 1940, we went to the United States on a Dutch ship and arrived at the port in Hoboken. My cousins met us and took us by subway to Brooklyn. It was strange taking the ferry and then the subway, and pretty scary. My cousin had a job waiting for me at a bakery. At sixteen I can't say that I was that introspective. I was making 38 dollars a week and I went to Ebbets Field to watch the Dodgers.

The refugee neighborhood in New York was Washington Heights, but where I was there were no refugees. The baker who I worked for was a Galizianer—an Eastern Jew—and he said, "Listen, you're a 'greenhorn' and I'm going to learn you everything I know." I didn't go to school, I only worked in the bakery. Whatever I learned, I learned from the streets, and before long there was no German left in me.

BEFORE THE WAR STARTED, I had the feeling that Hitler had to be stopped—that much I felt at that time. Chamberlain did the most idiotic thing when he shook hands with Hitler and turned over the Sudetenland, Czechoslovakia. You can't make deals with a dictator; that much I knew.

What I remember about Pearl Harbor was shock and disbelief, as well as disappointment that we weren't alert enough. How could squadron after squadron of airplanes catch the entire Pacific fleet with its pants down? I cannot say that I was too eager to go and fight, but when Uncle Sam wants you, you accept it. So, just before I was nineteen, I received my notice and was drafted. When the recruiters asked me for my preference, I requested mounted cavalry because of my experience in Germany with horses. They laughed at me because, aside from one outfit in Kansas (for ceremonial purposes), there no longer was a cavalry.

I went to Fort Drum, New York, and then to basic training like all of the other shlubs, where we did what we were told, marched, sweat, and trained. After that, I was sent to "bakers and cook" school at Camp Barkley, Texas. In my training company, there were real Georgia rebels, ignorant guys who thought Jews had horns on their heads. My sergeant was a real-rum head ex-boxer who didn't particularly like the guys from New York, especially the Jews. After eight weeks, I was asked to battalion headquarters and told to pack my duffel bag. I thought I had done something wrong.

I was sent to an intelligence school in Fort Ritchie in Hagerstown, Maryland. We always made fun of the cadre at Camp Ritchie, as we had Turks, Egyptians, French, Russians, Poles, and nearly every other ethnic group. We were in classrooms a lot of the time and there was just a lot of training. I was trained as an interrogator. In the training battalion, there were dozens of German Jews in my class.

On a Sunday, I became a citizen before I got shipped out. I was taken in a covered jeep to Washington, D.C., to be sworn in; before they brought the judge in, my commanding officer requested that I change my name because I was eventually going to Germany and it would be better for the nature of the work I would have to do. I was Siegfried Dingfelder, and you couldn't get more German than that. So I changed it to Fred Fields.

We were taken to a British freezer ship known to transport meat and joined a convoy of fifty other ships to Europe, but we couldn't see them because they were spread out so far. We lost ships, but we didn't even know it. I liked the idea that I was going back to fight Germany; it was in my plans that I could get back to where I came from and get some Nazis, but I was there to do the job I was trained to do, not just to settle old scores.

From a replacement depot in England, I went across the channel to another replacement depot in Paris and then to a suburb called Le Vésinet, where I got my shipping orders. I was sent the French-German border to join my unit, 69th IPW in Domville, Alsace-Lorraine, outside Metz. We did our work there under the XX Corps. The men in my unit were Capt. Al Lithen, Lieutenant Wallach, Staff Sergeant W. Marry, Staff Sgt. Bornstein, and Cpl. Fred Reich. From there we went up to Luxembourg, then Belgium, and then up to the Remagen Bridge breakthrough, where we got closest to the action. My first interrogation was in Metz, and I was certainly exhilarated to be able to do something of importance.

I felt that my training was sufficient enough; our unit officer, a captain, was of German parentage and came from Wisconsin. His German wasn't very good, so much of the work was left to us refugees, while he was more in charge of administration. Certainly, my German background was pivotal to my ability to do an effective job. From the Germans, we had to get information on the strength of their unit, how many men they had, how many they lost, and where their last campaign was. We found out that a lot of men came from the Eastern Front, running tail from the Russians and were coming to the west to gain some kind of foothold and drive us back.

Before the Remagen breakthrough, one of our guys found out that the Germans were pulling every regiment, every division they had from Strasbourg (southern France), to where the breakthrough was going to occur—all the heavy stuff. Our unit turned it over to our commanding officer, General Walker with the XX Corp, and Omar Bradley with the First Army. I did start to believe that a lot of troops had no use for our intelligence units at times, no matter how valuable it was. Commanders often liked to talk to their officers in the field to tell them what was in front of us.

It felt damn good to interrogate Nazis, especially when we had a pistol (usually one of their Lugers) in a holster on us. We knew that the average German soldiers just followed orders, so getting information out of them wasn't difficult. Name, rank, and serial number didn't mean much to them, so if we could put them at ease, it usually worked to our advantage. With SS and officers, however, it was drastically different; we had to be rough with them, psychologically (and sometimes physically) and threatened them with everything under the sun. On more than one occasion we would say, "If you don't talk, we are going to put a bullet in your head." With one guy, we had him dig his own grave, measure it, and then made him lie in it before bringing him back to the interrogation table. During one interrogation, I let my anger fly when I knocked a Sturmhauptführer's teeth out. I was stupid for not wearing a glove, because I hurt my hand.

At one interrogation, we had a platoon of Greek guys from New York who had their own anger for the Germans and who loved to get their hands hand on the prisoners.

WHEN WE GOT INTO GERMANY, I went to Buchenwald concentration camp two days after the war. We saw the skeletons in the ovens, and the skeletons were still walking, barely alive. There were dozens alive out of god knows how many thousands of people who were killed. As a German Jew, I felt anger and helplessness over what had happened to these people—you couldn't make good with what had already happened to these people and it was frustrating.

No matter what I have read or heard, it doesn't tell a damn thing compared to what I saw. I saw the ovens, the bunks where they packed people in like sardines. The ordinary person cannot fathom that. After the persecution we had experienced, I didn't expect that much more—but the concentration camp left us speechless. The eastern camps were worse, but I don't know how it could get much worse than what I saw.

Instinctively, I knew that whatever relatives I left behind ended up dead. Of my fathers seven siblings, three never made it out. My mother lost her twin brother, who was a communist. So, I had no love left for the Germans. When we caught Germans, suspected Nazis, their response to our questions was always, "*Ich bin nur ein kleiner Mann*" (I'm only a little man).

After that, we were turned south from there. When we got near my hometown of Uehlfeld I got permission from my captain to go back there. My cousin, Henry Schwab, who was in another unit, 57th IPW, operating nearby, took a jeep—a day and a half side trip—and we went back to Uehlfeld to look for the Nazis who we remembered. I asked around and they said they disappeared into a neighboring village. Unfortunately, when someone takes off their uniform and slips into a pair of overalls, they are very hard to identify out of a group of people. In Uehlfeld, I also made it a point to visit the cemetery to see if my relatives' stones were still there.

I was in Tutzing when the war was over. I applied for a civilian administrative job after the war but was turned down because of my limited education, even though I had all of this experience. All of us trained interrogators were well . . . suited to run an administration to ferret out any Nazis from a town.

Fred Fields is a retired butcher living in Riverdale, New York.

Chapter 22
PETER MASTERS

VIENNA, AUSTRIA

6 Commando
Normandy

Born Peter Arany in Vienna, Peter Masters left Vienna after the Anschluss and made it to England in 1938. He was interned with other friendly Enemy Aliens before volunteering for the Pioneer Corps. Anxious to get out of his unarmed labor outfit, Masters volunteered and was accepted into 3 Troop, 10 Inter-Allied Commando, and trained as a frontline interrogator. He joined 6 Commando right before the invasion of France and landed at Sword Beach on D-Day. He is pictured above in 1943.

I feel I have a mission. The mission is to say that the Holocaust took place, but not all Jews went like lambs to the slaughter. All of them would have preferred not to have been gassed defenselessly and hopelessly, and would have fought back if they'd been given the chance, but untrained and starving people can't mount a revolt efficiently. They did it in desperation in the Warsaw Ghetto and so on, but by and large their chances are very, very small. Partisan warfare is very difficult because it is unlikely to have any substantial success unless it is meritoriously and materially aided from the outside. The French Maquis could not have functioned if they hadn't had weapon drops from the Allies, and that goes for every occupied country. There has to be a hope of relief, of support, and ultimately of an invasion. When the Allies invaded Italy, the partisans rose up right, left, and center to fight against the Germans and helped in the toppling of Mussolini, who was hung by the feet.

I have always suggested that the partisans in the forests or the ghetto fighters would have done the same thing that we did: get out, get trained, get equipped, come back, and strike back. We were lucky to have that chance.

When the Anschluss came in 1938, my sister was eighteen and I was sixteen. We heard Nazi broadcasting and it was a memorable experience. We were watching the entry of the German forces, and then their tanks and infantry and motorcycles. It was a tremendous visual job, and of course they paraded at the slightest provocation.

Soon after, my aunt, who was away working in London, got fourteen people out of whom I am one. My father tried to ski into Switzerland and failed because there were too many German patrols out, but he managed to get to Switzerland by posing as a teacher with little kids, who were being marched across the Austrian border. From there, my father left for Belgium and tried to get into Britain because my sister and I were there by that time with my mother. He had no papers all along, so he had a problem because the British wouldn't let him in without papers.

My father, being a rather eccentric yet enterprising person carved a bust of George Bernard Shaw and sent it to him with a letter saying, "Please help me to get into the U.K., where my children already are living." Shaw responded, "Thank you for the very spirited bust. I have no influence at the Home Office, but I have forwarded your letter further. Good luck." Eventually, he stowed away on a Polish steamer to England with the collusion of one of the ship's officers, hid under a heap of coal when the customs and immigration people came aboard, and after they left, embarked and hitchhiked to London.

The aunt who got us out of Austria got me a job on a farm near Henley-on-Thames, and I worked there for a year and a half as a farmhand. It was mostly unpaid, but it meant that I was not a burden to my mother in London. When I would go across the fields in my rubber boots at night to shut up the chickens in their houses, I would pretend I was stalking Nazis. My sister came to visit me one weekend, and we hitchhiked to town. There was a crowd around a car and the car radio was on. There, we heard the Chamberlain speech, declaration of war, in Henley-on-Thames, in the street from a car radio. And as far as we were concerned, this was the only hope to end Hitler.

Being pacifists, I shudder to have to admit we were still praying for war. Why? Because we realized no one could negotiate with Hitler, as had been aptly demonstrated in Munich when Chamberlain thought they could get "peace in our time." That was nonsense.

Jewish refugees who had lived under the Nazis were motivated to fight them. I've always made the point that if I'd lived under them for six hours or six days, it would have been sufficient to motivate one to volunteer to fight them. I had no doubt Hitler planned to kill us all, and that if he invaded England, we certainly would have been killed.

So we tried to volunteer in any way we could, but it was extremely difficult. The age limit for joining the army was twenty and I was eighteen at this time. Suddenly, the army lowered its age limit to eighteen, and I immediately enlisted and got sent to the Pioneer Corp unloading trains, shoveling coal or ashes, and building roads. I kept volunteering to do something more active, because I said this war is mine.

In the Pioneer Corp, we were really frustrated. We tried to make the most of the situation; for instance, we tried to get onto task work. For example, we would say, "Give us a task, like unloading so many freight cars, and if we do it faster than you think we can, we're off, right?" When they gave us three freight cars to unload, and we did it by two or three o'clock in the afternoon, they would give us four cars next day and we were done by 2:30. So they were cheating us and we were showing off that we could lick the system. Essentially, we wanted to get out and get into a fighting situation.

Many of us volunteered very seriously, and eventually I responded to a notice in the Labour Corps requesting volunteers for special and hazardous duty. I was interviewed and accepted by an officer in disguise, who turned out to be the commanding officer of the commando unit that had been formed of eighty-seven refugees from the Nazis. All of them spoke fluent German and were subsequently trained in all methods pertaining to German forces.

When I got to North Wales where they sent us for training, we were surrounded by guys in green berets. Some of them were people I had known who had disappeared from the Pioneer Corp, since they weren't allowed to communicate once they'd been accepted. We didn't even know they had volunteered, they had just disappeared; it had been done very hush-hush.

We changed our names, dog tags were changed, and we had apparently volunteered not from the Pioneer Corp, because it would've looked funny if all of us were ex-Pioneer Corp people. So we had volunteered from an assortment of elite infantry units with which we'd never had any association in reality. I had volunteered from the Queen's Own Royal West Kent Regiment. In the commandos, you don't have a badge of the commandos, you have a badge of the unit from which you volunteered, so I had the white horse of Kent on my beret.

On my dog tag, it said 637025, which is a West Kent Number, Private First Masters COE (Church of England), to protect us in case of capture and to build a cover story. Born in London was inserted in my pay book, as was next of kin: mother, Mrs. C. Masters. We were not supposed to communicate with anyone with a foreign name, so I sent a couple of my friends, who were on leave, to my mother to explain the whole thing to her, because I couldn't tell or write to her about it.

The commander of 3 Troop, 10 Commando, was Brian Hilton Jones, who we called "the Skipper." He was a Welsh officer who spoke flawless German and flawless French and was the best athlete I'd ever seen. He was an unbelievably fit man, and whatever had to be done, he would not only do it first, but he would also do it first to show us how "easy" it was, which it wasn't. He would climb up the wall of a building where you could barely get a finger into a crack to pull yourself up, and he would say, "This is easy." He would come to a little ledge and say, "This ledge is big enough; you could have lunch here." We learned it was not smart to walk by a rock wall and say, like we did in the beginning, "Hey, I hope the Skipper doesn't see this rock wall or he'll make us climb up and jump down." If he heard it he would do exactly that.

We had all gone through a metamorphosis in which, to begin with, we were secular or religious Jewish or half German kids in Germany, Austria, or

Hungary. When the Nazis came, we were a hate object, which was a traumatic impact. Then we became refugees, and next, in my case, a farmhand—all the things I had never dreamt of being. After that we became soldiers in the Pioneer Corp in the labor unit. And now, like a butterfly out of a cocoon, we were the elite of the elite—in my case, a commando parachutist, having volunteered also for parachuting, which is another story.

With this metamorphosis comes a whole new identity. There is something exciting and welcoming about this, because we were discarding all the aspects that were deprecated and abused. In the doldrums of the war, the depression that was felt by many people was because the bombardment came without them being able to hit back much. As a new person, I was legitimately assuming another identity and it happened to be an elite identity. I would ride the London underground, and people would point and say, "Look, commandos." Try and tell me that this isn't affirming to a young guy. All of a sudden I had respect, and that's what it's all about.

They split 3 Troop up into teams about six weeks before D-Day. I was sent to the bicycle troop of 6 Commando, which had been to the desert in North Africa, so some of the guys were decorated. D-Day was my first action. In the initial briefing, we were all told we were going to do the initial assault and come home, to which one of the old hands in Troop 6 Commando (he'd been in North Africa) said, "Don't fuckin' believe it. Which colonel is going to let you go when he was an elite unit under his command?"

Of everybody in the bicycle troop, I was the only 3 Trooper. There were four others who were in other troops of 6 Commando, but we were all rather isolated and did not operate as a unit. We embarked in about four o'clock in the afternoon before all the craft were gathered together. It was getting dark, and we sailed with everybody singing and cheering each other from one craft to the next. We sailed from Southampton and went across the channel. It took all night and we were to land at six o'clock in the morning.

My wave was to land at 7:15 and 7:45. Two infantry regiments were to land first, the East Yorks and the South Lancasters, and they were to take the beach, then the commandos were to push inland. We were to be proceeded by gliders to take the vital bridges, and then we would cross over the bridges and take the high ground from which the Nazis would be shelling the beach.

During the crossing, I decided I should get all the rest I could because I would need all my energy the next day, so I lay in one of the hammocks in the hold. I was trying to read a book called *Cold Comfort Farm* and gave up. I said to myself, "This could very likely be the last thing I do." And then I said, "Well, I can't complain because I've had a rich full life." I was twenty-two years old, and it seemed to me I'd done almost everything. Sure I was afraid—there was plenty of reason to be afraid—but I said to myself, "I'm here because I wanted to be here." The point was to do what I had to do and, in a reasonably businesslike attitude, do what I had been programmed to do.

The sea was extremely rough and we were on the rough channel all night long. So almost everybody was seasick, which meant that the hold, in parts, was ankle deep in vomit. We all had seasickness pills, which I refused to take because I thought it was a numbing pill and I didn't want to be numbed. I wanted to be alert and with it. Going to the head, to the toilet, literally meant having to wade through pink vomit, which was a great encouragement to be even more seasick. What everyone really wanted to was get it over with, or at least be on deck where people could be sick over the side, but the captain of that craft said, "I want my decks clear for action. Get the hell out of here and keep below until I tell you."

Finally, he let us up; we picked up our bikes that had been piled up on deck. The bikes folded in half, but we had them assembled because we didn't even have the time to tighten the wing nuts. I was carrying a full-size pickaxe, a two-hundred-foot rope, a rucksack with a change of clothing and a blanket, a water bottle, eight hand grenades, and about five hundred rounds of ammunition We didn't carry a gas mask, as we appreciated they would not use gas, or a steel helmet. I also carried a Tommy gun. We didn't run up the beach, we staggered.

I had a couple of sayings; one of them was that in Austria, or in Europe in general, when there's a traffic accident involving a cyclist, it's always his fault—he always gets the blame. Another was in the British army, if somebody is in trouble it's usually the lance corporal, the lowest on commission track. I don't need to say that the world over, it is said if there's some problem, it's because of the Jews. On D-Day, I said the Nazis didn't have a chance because I, being one person, was a Jewish lance corporal cyclist, so the odds were stacked against them.

Sword Beach was the leftmost beach, which was subdivided into alphabetic subdivisions. I landed on Queen Beach, and Queen was subdivided into Queen Red on the left and Queen Green on the right; I landed on Queen Red.

The ship practically landed aground at Sword Beach, and I was the second person off the landing craft. On the beach, I saw the Skipper who had landed in the craft next to mine, and I didn't know what to do so I saluted. It was probably the only salute on the beach on D-Day.

The Germans were shelling and things were exploding around us. Oil bombs sailed through the sky like balls of fire, shot in rapid succession from six-barreled launchers called Moaning Minnies or sobbing sisters. Wherever they hit these incendiary rockets ignited large fires.

There were guys from the infantry sweeping mines with a mine detector and we were right in front of them. One of them said, "Wait! I haven't swept there yet."

We said, "Too bad, we can't wait. We have to get on," and went around him. Then we took a short rest in the dunes before it was time to get on our bikes and cycle. When we were on bicycles riding inland, we passed the parachutists and the gliders wearing the maroon beret of airborne units. They cheered when they saw us come up, because we were their first assurance that troops were coming by sea to reinforce them. Until that time, they were the only ones there. They had landed before H-Hour on D-Day: H-Hour was six o'clock in the morning, and they had landed the night before at H-minus.

When we passed, they would say, "Give them hell!" I remember to this day reflecting that it was a strange way of putting it, because it wasn't like we were literally going to give them hell. We were going to Varaville, six miles inland, to hold it until further notice. If German troops tried to stop us from getting there, we would stop them from stopping us, so it seemed incongruous to say "give them hell." In retrospect, I think they were quite right, for it was the spirit of the thing, but I was too focused on doing what I had been programmed to do to consider this at the time.

As we continued inland, we were under sporadic fire from German riflemen sniping at us from the woods. When we came to the forming up point, our brigadier, Lord Lovat, was walking around urging people on, and he seemed to be a man perfectly at ease. The shots and the noise didn't seem to bother him at all. "Good show," he said as Piper Bill Millen, the bagpiper who had piped us ashore, came dashing up. Millen was panting and catching his breath while carrying the bagpipes as well as his other equipment. "Come, get a move on. This is no different than any exercise," said Lord Lovat. He was very calm and carried no other weapon but a .45

Colt in his holster and a Scottish wading stick, normally used to keep one's balance when fishing.

There were a couple of prisoners at the assembly point. Lovat commented to me, "Oh, you're the chap with the languages. Ask them where their howitzers are." So I started to interrogate one of the prisoners. He was a great big guy who didn't respond. There was mumbling in the crowd: "Look at that Nazi bastard, he doesn't even answer our guy when he's talking to him." Meanwhile I was looking at his paperwork and saw that he was a Pole. He didn't understand a word I said in German. So I tried French, because many Poles learned French in school, and his face lit up in recognition, but he said he didn't know anything. Lord Lovat, who was standing next to me and spoke much better French, started to take over the interrogation. I felt very disappointed because I'd been upstaged by a better linguist.

Behind the woods of the forming up area, we encountered our first road, which was a pleasant change from what we'd been riding through so far, and prepared to start riding our bicycles. We were to cycle to the village of Varaville to relieve the Canadian parachutists, who were supposed to have taken the bridges.

There was death all around us. Dead cattle lay belly up along the roads, their bodies bloated. Dead parachutists were hanging from the trees. For most of us, it was the first action we'd seen, and it was shocking. The mortar and artillery shells exploding all around would have been even more frightening if we had really understood the situation. I kept telling myself that they were our shells, that it was all supporting fire. Of course, when the shells hit nearby and bullets whizzed past my ears, I had to admit we were under enemy fire, an enemy that was trying their hardest to kill us.

We had been instructed by the Skipper to make sure that we were used properly by the officers commanding the troops to which we were attached. He had said, "They'll be very busy and preoccupied with their own things, but don't you come back afterwards and tell me that they were too busy to use you. Pester them. Ask whether you may go when they're sending out reconnaissance patrols. Make sure that all your training didn't go to waste." So I contentiously did precisely that.

My captain, however, was indeed preoccupied and considered me a nuisance. Whenever I asked to go on a patrol, Captain Robinson simply said no and sent one of the people with whom he had been training for the last several years and had greater confidence than this kid with a funny accent who had joined his troop at the last minute.

Suddenly there was a burst of machine gun fire close by, and as I rode up I saw one of our people, a red-haired commando, lying dead by the road next to his bicycle. Robinson had us dismount and deployed us behind a little block overlooking the downhill road and grassy slopes on either side. On the left, there was a solid hedgerow and down below there was a village called Laporte, adjacent to Benouville, where there were two bridges that constituted our first objective. They were to have been taken by the British 6th Airborne Division gliders. I carried two hemp ropes in case the bridges were destroyed by the Germans or under heavy fire, in which case the ropes were to be used to ferry troops across the river in rubber dinghies, which some other people carried.

Finally, Captain Robinson said, "Now there's something you can do, Corporal Masters. Go down to this village where the bridges are and see what's going on." It wasn't difficult to tell what was going on. All hell seemed to have broken loose, with odd bursts of fire in every which direction, but it was hard to tell where the fire was coming from. I thought a reconnaissance patrol would be accompanying me, and I asked, "How many people should I take?"

He said, "No, I just want you to go by yourself," which didn't bother me.

I looked around at the scenery and said, "Yes sir. I will go in the left and come back in a sweep around the right hand side."

"You still don't understand what I want you to do," replied Captain Robinson. "I want you to walk down the road and see what is going on."

Now it was quite clear what he wanted to do—I was to be the target. He wanted to draw fire to see where the machine gun that had killed the cyclist was firing from. Rather than send some of his own men, he preferred to send this recently attached stranger. It felt rather like mounting the scaffold of the guillotine. I had been trained to figure out angles and to be more useful than that, so I frantically looked for some angle or option of improving the situation for which there was none. There were no ditches of any kind or cover, and it was broad daylight.

Then I remembered the movie *Gunga Din*, where Victor McLaglen, Douglas Fairbanks Jr., and Cary Grant get overwhelmed by Indians on the

Khyber Pass and inadvertently find themselves in a hopeless situation. Just before they get overwhelmed by two thousand rebels, Cary Grant delivered a line I always thought was funny: "You're all under arrest." And then an angle came to me at this precise moment.

As I walked down the road with my finger on the trigger of my Tommy gun, I yelled at the top of my voice, *"Ergebt Euch alle! Alle raus! Ihr seid volkommen unsingelt-Ihr habt keine Chance. Werft Eure Waffen fort und kommt mit den Handen hoch raus wenn Ihr weiter leben wolt. Der Krieg ist aus fur Euch!"* (Surrender all of you! Come out! You are completely surrounded and you don't have a chance. Throw away your weapons and come out with your hands up if you want to go on living. The war is over for you!) I tried to sound as Prussian as possible.

Nobody came out, but they held their fire, probably because they wondered what lunacy was going on. They'd seen the armada landing, they'd been bombed and shelled, they saw a bunch of soldiers on bicycles, which was a surprise, so they shot the first cyclist. And now a pedestrian soldier was walking toward them in broad daylight on D-Day morning. They must have figured, "Maybe he has an armor division right behind him. Maybe we are smarter to wait. We can always shoot him, but let's not betray our position." So they held fire for a while. Finally, a guy got up and fired at me. I fired at him but my gun jammed.

Now Captain Robinson had seen what he wanted to see, so he had the riflemen fix bayonets and charge. In the lead was Cpl. George Thompson, a former grenadier guardsman, firing his Bren machine gun from the shoulder, which was the usual method of shooting when charging. As I marveled at the charge, I saw Thompson suddenly move ninety degrees to his left and fire his entire magazine at a low target I could not see, practically at his feet. I got up to join the charge, and when I got there I saw his target. There were two Austrian machine gunners who had been shot. One of them was pretty much out of it. The other one was wounded but conscious. When I began to question them, they told me they were fifteen and seventeen years old.

Corporal Thompson came over to me. "You speak their language, don't you?" he said. "How do you say 'I'm sorry' in German? I've never shot anybody before." He added, "I took their life. I'm sorry, forgive me." The next day Thompson led another bayonet charge and was killed. I still get emotional when I think of him.

During the Normandy campaign, I was constantly out in no man's land as a sort of early warning system to see if the Germans were doing anything that would signal they were about to mount an attack. I went out every morning to creep up to where the Germans were and watch them. I knew individual Germans by sight.

We would interrogate prisoners or deserters as soon as we caught them. Being taken prisoner is a risky business for that person. If they are deserters, it's a doubly risky, because they might get shot from either side; The troops from which they are deserting are likely to shoot them in the back if they see them, so they would just barely escaped with their lives. What's more, they've been programmed to think that they will be executed and tortured and are afraid of what will happen to them. The usual question they'd ask was, "Are you going to kill me?" I would respond, "Not for the time being."

At times, I feel dissatisfied that I didn't do enough. I started out as a pacifist when I was a kid. Essentially, I yearned for peace, but I found the old saying, "If you want peace you must prepare for war" was extremely valid then, and is still valid to this day. I feel that people who haven't experienced persecution and war tend to come up with a pacifist notion that is completely misplaced.

Some of my friends said the important thing was to eliminate as many of the enemy as possible, as quickly as possible. At times, there was another question that came up in discussions among us commandos many years after the war, when the Palestinians assassinated the Israeli team in Munich in 1972. We thought they did that to make an impact, and I understand that. If we were asked, "Would you have done that?" The answer would be, "No way!"

If we heard that a plane was taking off from Germany to Spain with the soccer team from Frankfurt, and we had the opportunity to shoot that plane down, would we have done it? No, we would not have done it, because what do we have against the soccer team? These are sports people. However, if we had heard that on the plane was the Gestapo leadership, or even one or two SS types, would we have shot the plane? You bet we would have shot the plane down.

Peter Masters left England to go to the United States on a Fulbright Scholarship to study design. He eventually became a prominent television art director in Washington, D.C. In 1997, Presidio Press published Peter's autobiography entitled Striking Back: A Jewish Commando's War against the Nazis.

Chapter 23
JOHN BRUNSWICK

BOCHOLT, GERMANY

XV Corps, Third Army

*John Brunswick was born Hans Braunschweig in Bocholt,
Germany. Having arrived in the United States in 1937, he was
inducted into the army in 1943 and was trained as an interrogator
of prisoners of war (IPW) at Camp Ritchie. He served much
of the war in an IPW team attached to the Free French 2nd
Armored Division. In the photograph above, Brunswick (center),
serving as translator, sits between Lt. Gen. Von Foertsch (left),
Commanding General, German First Army, and Gen. Jacob L.
Devers, Commanding General, American Sixth Army Group,
as Von Foertsch signs the unconditional surrender of German
Army Group "G."*

W hen I received my draft notice, I had very mixed feelings. On one hand, I felt that I should have volunteered to fight Hitler and his Stormtroopers who had caused such unbelievable suffering to so many people and had ruined their lives. If not stopped soon, they would probably be unstoppable and cause more trouble throughout the world. On the other hand, I hated to leave my wife. At the age of thirty-two, having already been in the United States for six years, I was making a little more money and I was able to support my parents.

While I had no choice, deep down I knew that by serving my new adopted country, like everybody else, I was doing the right thing and would have felt guilty if I had not done so. I was inducted in March 1943 and, after about a week, landed in Camp Croft, an infantry training camp near Spartanburg, South Carolina. I slept in the barracks with about fifty other inductees, nearly all of them eighteen to twenty-one years old—I was the "old man." We came from all over the country; I had trouble understanding some of the farm boys from Mississippi and Louisiana with their thick southern drawl.

The first part of basic training consisted of six weeks of physical hardening, drilling lessons in discipline and commands and, above all, instructions in shooting the M1 rifle. The sergeants instructing and commanding us apparently did not expect the old man, who had an accent and was a New York Jew, would make a very good soldier. However, I surprised them all by qualifying as an "expert rifleman," which was the highest grade a marksman could achieve. After six weeks of basic training came another seven weeks of advanced infantry training. We had to hike up and down the South Carolina red clay hills with full, 50-pound packs on 20-mile marches in the 90-degree heat.

During that part of training, my wife, Hilde, visited me in Spartanburg for the weekend. Her arrival and search for a furnished room was quite shocking to us, as well as revealing about the attitudes still existing in the old South at the time. Even though I was in uniform, one woman informed us, "We do not want you Jews," and another one slammed the door in our faces.

I WAS SOON SUMMONED in such a hurry, but was not too surprised to find out that Class Number 16, consisting of about four hundred men, would not start for about six weeks. I became a "night-weeper." As the classrooms were being used during the day, they had to be cleaned at night—the stoves had to be cleaned out and stoked for the fire to be lit for the morning classes, etc. We were busy and slept a good part of the day. I met my friend from Germany, Rolf Wartenberg, there; he had been accepted in Fort Benning, Georgia, which was the Infantry Officer Training School and hard to get into.

At the end of our training, May 1943, I tried the same. There was an opening for five vacancies, and there were about fifty applicants from our class. I was among the last eight or ten, after the others had been weeded out, showing off my skills drilling and commanding about forty people under the watchful eyes of superior officers. My infantry training from Camp Croft would have come in very handy, and I believe that I would have been selected. I was doing very well when suddenly, to my great disappointment, I was called off. The next day I found out why.

Out of our whole class of about four hundred, the top fifty graduates had been selected for an immediate promotion to second lieutenant, I among them. It seemed like a miracle. When I called home and said, "This is Lieutenant Brunswick speaking," it sounded like a big joke, however, this is what happened. It not only made a tremendous difference in my status, but it also gave me a big boost to my morale, and it especially made a tremendous difference to my family's economic situation. All of the sudden, instead of having the basic salary of $50 a month, it became $300 a month, and I was now able to really provide for my family and my parents.

In June 1944, I had my final leave, said goodbye to all my loved ones, and held my little boy for the last time. Then I and many others found ourselves on a troop transport leaving from Boston Harbor. The crossing, in a converted large freighter, was an experience in itself. We slept deep down in the hold in hammocks, with three or four on top of each other like canned sardines. There were thousands of troops onboard, and there were probably ten or fifteen troop ships that crossed the Atlantic in convoys shadowed by war ships, zigzagging and trying to elude the ever-present German submarines, which had sent so many ships to the bottom.

We finally made it to a port near Edinburgh, Scotland. From there, we took a train to Broadway, a quaint little town, into the Midlands of England, not far from Birmingham. Once there, I was selected for an additional period of advanced intelligence training in Swindon. When I returned to Broadway, intelligence teams were formed, each consisting of two officers and four enlisted men, as well as two jeeps and a small trailer for the equipment. Towards the end of August, we crossed the channel and landed in Normandy. We saw what unbelievable odds they had fought, climbing those steep cliffs while being subjected to enemy bombardment and constant machine gun fire from fortified bunkers. They had been so brave, facing almost certain death.

In Normandy we saw additional evidence of all the destruction the war had caused; it was a new experience for us. We landed that day at the headquarters of General Patton, commander of the Third Army. It was not far from Paris, which had just been liberated. We set up our little tents in a meadow where we could see the city in the distance. It was the usual army thing: Hurry up and wait.

The other officer on my team was Lt. Herbert Heldt. He had been an engineering officer before being sent into the intelligence camp, obviously because he knew some German (his parents had been born in Germany). He was short and, in civilian life, had been a jockey and a midget automobile racer. He wasn't the smartest person, but what he lacked in brains, he made up in bravado. We complemented each other well because we were so different. Then there was Henry Block who had been promoted to master sergeant, the highest grade of noncommissioned officer. There were two lower grade sergeants and a corporal, used as drivers and clerks, to compete our little organization.

We had named our two jeeps Hilde 1 and Hilde 2, which was stenciled on the side below the official number. After that, we had no particular duties except to wait to go into Paris for the first time. We saw the church steeples from a distance, but the city was "off limits" to unauthorized personnel like us. Then Heldt got the idea: "Why don't we take one of our jeeps and look at what Paris is like?" So we did. It turned out to be what I might call the weirdest night of my life.

As army personnel we had no trouble clearing the various check points. Once in Paris, we parked our jeep in a garage that, we were assured, was under constant guard. This was very necessary, as the many French Forces of the Interior (FFI) were in need of equipment, so there were lots of looting and stealing going on. To be extra careful, we also took the rotor out of the motor without which the ignition would not work. We had our pistols in our belts and the four enlisted men carried their carbines.

Paris had no electricity or running water, however, there was no shortage of liquid refreshments; the Parisians cheered every Allied soldier they saw.

Then it got dark. There was still shooting going on by German stragglers, who were apparently trying to escape under cover of darkness. Suddenly, a shot rang out from behind me, grazing my left ear on the inside between ear and head, and some blood from my ear was visible. It was nothing serious, even though another inch farther to the right probably would have ended my story at the age of thirty-three.

For many years I claimed that the only reason I did not get the Purple Heart decoration for a wound received in action was because I could not report it, being AWOL at the time. In the interest of truthfulness, I have to report that the shot had been fired by my friend Henry Block, who had been walking behind me and, in the excitement and turmoil, squeezed off a shot in the wrong direction.

ABOUT A WEEK LATER, we were called to Third Army headquarters. One of the jeeps belonging to an IPW team with one of the divisions had hit a mine on the road. Three of the six team members had been killed, so we replaced this team. We got our instructions, received our orders, and were directed to the headquarters of the XV Corps to report to the colonel in charge of the Intelligence Division at Corps Headquarters. He assigned us to the HQ of the 2nd French Armored Division, which was one of the three divisions that belonged to the Corps. It turned out to be a good assignment.

The commander, General LeClerk, and his officer corps were professional soldiers who had served in North Africa and had all along been staunch supporters of General de Gaulle. From North Africa, they had been shipped to England to be re-equipped with American tanks and then had come from Normandy to Paris and beyond. The whole division consisted of volunteers of whom 20 percent were known to be Jewish. The French division was much less tightly controlled than the American ones; in fact, they were somewhat too independent for the American generals under whose command they fought. We were advised not only to furnish the division commander and Corps Headquarters with intelligence from interrogations, but also to provide the Corps with our own reports about the French division's movements.

As AMERICAN OFFICERS, we ate in the mess with the general and his staff. Conversation was naturally in French only. Even with our knowledge of

251

French, I understood only about 25 percent when they were talking among themselves rapidly and using a lot of North African patois.

The French operated differently from American units. The American units would prepare each tank advance with a lot of artillery preparation to hold down casualties. The French were less cautious; they hated the Germans more than the Americans did, having been subjugated by them, and were most anxious to liberate all of France as fast as possible. They advanced faster than the cautious Americans, thus suffered a great many casualties.

Our first battle was at a town called Andelot. It was a small town in a valley, surrounded by woods and hills, and we took it by evening. We were told that there were about four hundred prisoners whom we could see in the morning. At night, there was a lot of shooting in the hills. In the morning when we wanted to interrogate the prisoners, none could be found. We drew our own conclusions as to what had happened to them. In the town itself, a civilian mob had taken justice into its own hands to punish some collaborators. There were a bunch of men with pants around their feet and bloody genitals, there were women who had their hair cut off, and it was not a pretty sight.

WE WERE KEPT BUSY, as the troops advanced through France toward the Alsace, sometimes very fast, sometimes held up for a week or longer, either by German resistance, or supply problems, or other reasons that I did not know. I tried to write Hilde and my parents whenever possible. I knew they worried about me. I thought about Hilde and my son, Freddie, a lot. I missed them, feeling somewhat lonely and blue at times, and hoped that I would see them again, in good shape and soon. The other soldiers also felt the same way, especially the somewhat older ones who had families.

Due to heavy German resistance that slowed our advance, we stayed for about two weeks in a little town named Gerbevillers, but we were kept very busy at times with the German prisoners brought to our HQ for interrogation. Then one day something strange happened. I sat on one side of a table together with one of our men and a prisoner who was brought into the room. Before interrogating him, he had to empty his pockets and show his German army papers, which gave his name and serial number. This man was Martin Look, who said he was born in Bocholt. I had gone to school with Martin Look for four years, from age six to ten, and had even been in his parents' house.

Now I met him again, about twenty-five years later, and wouldn't have recognized him without seeing his papers. I doubted that he recognized me, and he was certainly not in position to ask an American officer any questions, but for half a minute I was tempted to ask him if he still had the wood-burning stove in his family's kitchen. Then I decided that not only did I not know whether or not he'd been a Nazi Party member, but that I also did not want any gossip among other POWs, so I sent him on his way, just like everyone else. I later found out from my old neighbors in Bocholt that Martin Look had told somebody that "Hans Braunschweig was the American officer that interrogated me." I still regret not having revealed myself during the interrogation.

BEING WITH THE 2ND FRENCH ARMORED DIVISION was very exciting. Between that division and the XV Corps, I believe we were some of the most independent American soldiers in the army. When the division expected to be in reserve and stationary, we asked for passes (Ordre De Mission) for the six of us, and permission was granted to go to Paris and return, "when mission was finished"—in other words, an indefinite time order. All we had to do was ask every day at headquarters in Paris when we would be needed back. We took off in our jeep, reported to French HQ and were assigned to first class hotels. It was a welcomed change and lasted for about a week. By this time, living conditions in Paris were a lot closer to normal than they had been during our first visit. There was electricity most of the time, running water, and no more snipers.

THE THIRD ARMY, along with the XV Corps and our French division, continued its advance through France southeast via Metz, where our team "liberated" a Panhard car. The headlights did not work but, nevertheless, it permitted IPW Team Number 92 to travel in style with one car and two jeeps. We could do things like this only with the French division, which was in every sense a very unusual outfit. It also comprised a battalion of Ghoums, native North African troops clad in black burnooses that surrounded them like big tents. They were very good at creeping up to enemy lines at night with a long knife in hand and creating havoc.

Our French division eventually advanced to Saverne, a town in the hills overlooking the plains and the roads leading to Strasbourg. The hills were snowed in, which the Germans were defending rather vigorously, and the pass through Saverne was considered the only passable one during winter for heavy tanks. However, the French could not be held back; they knew of some back roads that were not as heavily defended by the Germans.

They surprised the defenders, enabling the French 2nd Armored Division to break through. Then, against all orders from the XV Corps and Third Army HQ, it proceeded to advance with lightning speed for about sixty miles to Strasbourg, much to the consternation, as we later found out, of the American command, which by no means were ready to advance that fast on the whole front. We were promptly cut off by Germans, whom we had left behind us on both sides of the Alsatian plain.

Germans were also shelling us from across the Rhine, especially at the Gestapo building where the division headquarters had been installed. We were given a room on the top floor from which there was an excellent view of the Rhine and of the German positions. We also had an excellent chance of being hit by one of the artillery shells. We therefore decided that it would be much more prudent to change rooms and move into the basement.

One of the journalists of the newspaper *Yank* had heard of this story, and subsequently it appeared as one of the news articles in the paper with our names. The Gestapo building, however, was listed as a hotel in the newspaper, for security reasons. The Germans must have left in a tremendous hurry, for the drawers in the desks were still full. In one of them, I found a beautiful Walther pistol, which I brought home and had for many years.

OUR DIVISION WAS CUT OFF in Strasbourg for several days, as the U.S. Army had expended more ammunition than anticipated and had to stop its advance until supplies could catch up while being transported over the terrible and devastated roads of the French countryside. Our division had to withdraw to protect its flanks. When we eventually advanced again into Strasbourg and the Alsace, it was for good.

We spent quite some time in the Alsatian plain. This was where the news of President Roosevelt's death reached and surprised us. I remember that I was not the only one who cried at the time. Not only was I grateful to him that I and many others had been able to come to America during his presidency, but above all I believe that without his foresight, Hitler might have ruled the world. Roosevelt had to fight a tremendous amount of reactionary opposition in helping England and engineering the lend-lease destroyer deal, which made it possible for England to survive the unlimited U-boat war of the Germans. He had also supported the rearmament program of the United States before we actually entered the war, realizing that our help would be needed eventually.

There had been, at the time, the very influential German American Bund, as well as the pro-German and anti-Semitic propaganda of the radio priest Father Charles Coughlin and antiwar involvement speeches of Republican senators like Senators William Edgar Borah and Gerald Nye of Idaho and North Dakota, respectively. Roosevelt was not perfect. Turning away the seven hundred Jewish refugees from the S.S. *St. Louis* when it came into New York Harbor (many of whom perished after returning to Europe) and not bombing the rail lines to the Auschwitz-Birkenau extermination camp will forever be blots on his record, but on balance he had been a great leader. Without him, the world would have been a much worse place today than it is already.

IN THE ALSACE, we found heavy resistance but being with the French troops, our living conditions were generally much better than if we had been with an outfit under direct American control. We usually found an abandoned house from which the Germans living there had fled and made ourselves as comfortable as possible. Of course, there was no electricity, and there was no heat in the midst of a severe snowy winter, but there were usually beds and nice down comforters.

I was always amazed at the courage displayed by, and the seemingly nervelessness of, the French officers. I remember particularly one time when the command post was in a little village, and the German artillery was constantly shooting at the nearby church steeple from which their positions could be observed. There could have been someone hit at any minute and the noise was deafening, but everybody went about their business as if nothing else mattered and everything was peaceful. I don't know whether inside they were scared—I'll admit, I was.

Somehow, however, their attitude must have rubbed off on me to a certain extent. I recall interrogating a German major who had just been taken captive. We were in a building, the front of which had already collapsed, and we were on the second floor. There was constant artillery bombardment, apparently from two or three different gun positions. It was extremely important for us to know where these positions were, but he did not want to say anything other than his name, rank, and serial number. I finally said to him, "You won't get out of here until you give the information. You know that you Germans have lost the war, and it's just a period of time before it's finished. If you want to get yourself killed at this late date, go ahead. I have all the time in the world." He must have seen my point, because he finally told me what I needed to know and that ended this episode, not a minute too early for me.

Another interrogation that I remember vividly had taken place under more quiet conditions sometime earlier in the fall of 1944. The man I interrogated seemed intelligent and reliable. He was with what might be best translated as a punishment company. After he gave me all the information I wanted, like armaments, officers, and opposing regiments, I asked him why he was in a punishment outfit. He said, "I was on the eastern front near Riga, Latvia, where the SS rounded up thousands of Jewish men women and children. They made the Jews dig ditches, undress, and stand so that, when they were shot, they would fall into the ditches. This went on every day. There were so many that the SS needed help and requested regular army troops to help kill the Jews. I refused and that is why I'm in the punishment battalion."

While I had heard rumors of concentration camps, being cut off from all current news, mass murders surpassed anything I had imagined. I forwarded my interrogation report immediately to the division and also directly to Corps Headquarters, where I hoped it would be going up to higher headquarters. I have a copy of this interrogation still in my files because I was so shocked, even though this was against all army orders.

In December 1944, I was promoted to first lieutenant, but then all good things have to come to an end. One day we were advised that our XV Corps had been transferred from the Third to the Seventh Army, but the 2nd French Armored Division was to remain with the Third Army. When we were called back to HQ, we received a very nice letter of recommendation from General LeClerk. I personally was told that I would receive the Croix de Guerre for the valuable information I had provided the division. The 2nd French Armored Division received a Distinguished Unit Citation from the American High Command for its heroic campaign, entitling the participants in the campaign, naturally including us, to wear a fourragere, a corded ribbon, on the left breast of our dress uniform thereafter.

All of the above may sound as if being in the war was a lot of fun. I can assure you that it was not. We were very busy on most days, driving, looking for a place to sleep, setting up equipment, worrying about mines on the road, or roads under enemy fire. In the evenings, we were typing our reports, mostly in a cold room by the light of a gas lantern. I, like most everybody else, was waiting for letters from home; the mail reached us very irregularly. I wrote to Hilde whenever I had a chance, and to my parents and sister about once a week. My wife was doing her part for the war by accepting a job with the Office of Censorship. Since she could read German script, this enabled her to read the mail coming to German prisoners who had been brought to the United States. Quite a bit of valuable information could be gleaned from these letters—had our planes hit a bridge or missed it, was food scarce as a railway line was out of commission, was morale good, and so on.

I also worried about the future. I was thirty-three years old with lots of obligations and no means to speak of or any specialized knowledge of any kind to put to use after my return.

AFTER A WHILE, we were assigned to the 106th Cavalry, which was a reconnaissance outfit with light tanks and armored cars. We arrived there shortly before Hitler's last offensive in the area of the Vosges Mountains in the winter of 1944. At the time, we were in some village not too far from the Saar River, south of the Vosges Mountains. Of course, we didn't know about the offensive. We had quartered ourselves in some abandoned house when at about 2 a.m. we were awakened: "Get out of here within fifteen minutes, the Germans have broken through." We had never packed up as fast in our lives and were gone in ten minutes or less.

After Hitler's surprise offensive had finally been beaten back, the Allied advance took us up to the Siegfried Line, a continuous line of fortified bunkers, antitank ditches, and clear fields of fire for the German artillery. In our sector, once again luck was with me. I interrogated a very young captured SS officer who had been in the frontlines of fortifications. It was extremely important for us to know where some of the main gun positions were situated, but he would not talk.

Eventually, I got him involved in a conversation about Hitler, the master race, and ethnic purity. We also talked about the fact that Germany could not win this war anymore, to which he reluctantly agreed halfheartedly. I convinced him eventually that, in the interest of the Fatherland, it would be the best thing for Germany if the war would finish quickly and that he could save precious German blood and lives if he would cooperate. With tears in his eyes, he showed me on a detailed map the location of two of the gun positions with which he was familiar.

OUR UNIT FINALLY CROSSED THE RHINE near Mannheim on a pontoon bridge. The regular bridges over the Rhine had all been destroyed by either the retreating Germans or our aerial bombardments. From there, we gradually advanced to the Danube River, then to Wuerzburg, and on to Nuremberg. Most of Nuremberg was in ruins, with many of buildings still smoking. From Nuremberg, we advanced to a little town named Dachau. A few miles away was a camp, though we did not know what kind, whether POW or labor, which at this time was being penetrated by the first of our troops.

A strange odor hung over the town. When I inquired about it, several people pretended not to know where it came from. We soon found out. We drove to the camp the next morning, but were totally unprepared for the sights that awaited us. Right outside the camp stood about fifty open freight cars. Lying in them were dead starved people, severed limbs, which had fallen off bodies when some of the starving survivors had tried to throw out the dead people. They apparently had been able to climb out, but had been too weak to go any farther.

We found out later that this train had come from a camp in Poland, probably Auschwitz, which the SS had evacuated before the advancing Russians would overrun it. The unprotected human cargo had apparently been on the way for several weeks with no food and delayed by bombed out tracks. They finally ended up at Dachau, where guards apparently had had no more time to unload them and to destroy the evidence. The stench which permeated the whole area was unbelievable. It was so horrible that for months afterwards, whenever I thought of Dachau, the stench still seemed to fill my nostrils.

Inside the camp, more horrible sights awaited us. The SS guards had all fled but for a few who had been killed by our troops. Inside the barbed wire were thousands of emaciated inmates, their black and white striped uniforms hanging loosely on their bones. The ovens where the corpses were being burned were still warm. Outside the building were heaps of clothing and inside bodies, just skin and bones with a numbered tag on the big toe, were lying in heaps, maybe five or six feet high. If I live to be a hundred years old, I will never forget this unbelievable sight. Our American soldiers, mostly unsophisticated young boys from all over the United States, were completely unprepared for the sights they encountered. Until now, they had not really known what Nazism meant.

Two weeks later, we captured Julius Streicher. He had been a particularly sadistic anti-Semite. His newspaper *Der Stuermer* showed the most vicious caricatures of Jews, said the most outrageous lies about Jews, and incited the people to violence against them. The paper was read all over Germany and Austria. The man himself used to strut around with a horse whip in his hand. At any rate, he was jailed and I interrogated him in his cell before he was shipped back for more detailed questioning over many days.

It was amazing to see how ordinary a balding, middle-aged man looked when seeing him without his glamorous uniform and how his arrogant bearing changes when seeing him in a jail cell. He had posed as a bombed-out artist hiding in the mountains and painting pictures. I was amazed to hear that he was actually a friend of the Jews and, like the Zionists, just wanted them to go to Palestine. I questioned, listened to his answers in amazement, and took notes. He sounded so ridiculous and pathetic that I could not even hate him. He was sentenced to death as a war criminal during the Nuremberg Trials and eventually hanged.

I received orders to report early on May 5 to headquarters of the XV Corps, right outside Munich. Subsequently, I found out that I had been selected to be the official interpreter at the surrender of all the southern German armies. The German Gen. Von Foertsch was the chief of staff of Gen. Albert Kesselring, who was the commander of all German armies that had been in Italy, Austria, and southern Germany. There were six American generals, including Gen. Jake Devers, who was the commander of the two

American armies in the southern part of France and Germany. Then there was also one lowly First Lieutenant Brunswick.

The picture in the *New York Times*, as well as those in the other metropolitan newspapers throughout the United States, had the caption, "Surrender at Munich," and listed all the generals by name plus "an unidentified American officer." People at home who knew me recognized me in the picture—for once Hilde knew where her husband was. In any case, it was a moment in my life that I will relish as long as I live. There were long negotiations with the Germans—the officers wanted to stay in charge of the troops, they wanted to keep their side arms, and so on—all to no avail. Finally, this Jewish refugee who, eight years earlier had to leave his homeland, asked this high-ranking German general: "Do you understand that this means, 'unconditional surrender?'" To this, with utmost reluctance, the general eventually spat out, "Yes, I understand."

HAVING BEEN IN THE ARMY during World War II and proven my worth, this had greatly increased my self confidence and done away with the feeling of being inferior to native-born Americans. All through my youth, even before Hitler, Jews supposedly were equal citizens, but they were still perceived by many Germans as unequal. There had always been a lot of anti-Semitism. When I played with other children in Bocholt, I believed subconsciously that I was always wilder than they. I remember climbing on the outside of our house into the second story window, or climbing a tree high enough so that I could get on a factory roof, always trying to impress my friends.

In my army years, at times the same motives must have been at work; when in basic training I tried to excel, or when I interrogated the German major under artillery fire, I continued until he gave up. In any case I had often been a "reluctant" Jew, asking myself whether it was worthwhile to belong to a small minority and being exposed to discrimination by so many unenlightened people. Being in Israel changed my outlook. I greatly admired what Jews had accomplished there in such a short amount of time and I admired their spirit. While I had not contributed to their achievements and therefore had nothing of which to be proud personally, I came to feel that I was fortunate to have been born a member of this small group of people. In five thousand years of recorded history, Jews have suffered so much, yet still have given the world so much to advance it, in religion, philosophy, science, medicine, and many other fields of endeavor.

In short, over a period of time, this reluctant Jew became a rather proud Jew. Throughout the years, when someone questions me about my German accent, I'm always pleased to say, "No I'm not German; I escaped Hitler and I am Jewish."

IN 1992, WHEN HILDE AND I WENT TO AMSTERDAM, I rented a car for one day to show her Bocholt, where I had spent the first fifteen years of my life. It gave me a chance to spend some nostalgic moments thinking of the little boy and his sister who had roamed around here some sixty-five years earlier and of their parents. The house looked no longer as nice as it did then, nor did its visitor.

From there we drove to the Jewish cemetery on the outskirts of town. It was well maintained; monuments of my grandparents and other family were all still standing and in reasonably good shape. However, the memorial tablet at the entrance to the cemetery annoyed us. It said, in translation: "In memory of our Jewish citizens who had to lose their lives during the Hitler time. They died for their people and their religion." What nonsense! An upright statement as to what had happened would have read: "In memory of our Jewish citizens who were murdered during the Hitler years." It showed me that even well-meaning Germans, who had re-established the cemetery and were keeping it in good shape, still had a hard time, fifty years later, coming to grips with the awful truth.

In balance, I think that I have been extremely fortunate overall. My family, parents, sister, and I could have perished in the ovens of Auschwitz, like so many unfortunate others. We all escaped. I could have been killed or maimed during World War II, and again I escaped unharmed. I arrived in the U.S. penniless, with only a good education but no particular skills at the age of twenty-six. I was able to acquire the means to make a decent living for my family and myself and to give my kids a good education. I have been able to see my three sons marry and enjoy my seven grandchildren.

John Brunswick became a manufacturer of plastic shower curtains, tablecloths, and mattress covers.

Chapter 24
OTTO STERN

ROTH, GERMANY

70th Infantry Division

Otto Stern came from Roth, Germany, and settled in Chicago in 1936. After a brief stint in the Army Specialized Training Program, he was sent to the infantry. He returned to Europe as a rifleman in the 70th Infantry Division and remained on the frontline for eighty-six consecutive days of combat. In the photograph above, Stern is met by former neighbors upon returning to his hometown just after VE Day, May 1945.

Many young men, refugees from my neighborhood in Hyde Park, Chicago, were drafted. Some weren't even that young anymore. They drafted everyone from eighteen to thirty-five unless he was married. My brother, Julius, was also in the army. By that time, I spoke relatively good English, but with an accent that I still have. I had been in the United States for six years by the time I was drafted, so I was assimilated. The army knew I was German, but I let everyone know I was Jewish. In all of the three years I was in the service I only experienced anti-Semitism once.

I was sent to Camp McCoy on Monterey Bay in California for infantry training. Although I was in really good shape, training was hard, but I knew if I wanted to defeat Hitler I had to work very hard and I did. It entered my mind that I might be sent to the Pacific, but thank god I wasn't. My brother went through basic training with me and we were in same barracks, too. He had the upper bunk and I had the lower for three months, until the army split us up.

After basic training the army gave us an IQ test and sent me to Stanford for more tests and then to University in Idaho for the Army Specialized Training Program (ASTP). It was essentially college where we would be trained in a variety of concentrations that could be of use in military government during occupation. With the invasion of France coming, however, the need for man-power must have been great, for early in 1944 the program was disbanded. I was sent to Camp Adair, Oregon, to train with the 70th Infantry Division and then to Camp Leonard Wood, Missouri, where I ended up in what was going to be a frontline rifle company—three rifle platoons and a heavy weapons platoon that handled mortars. This was August 1944. I was an assistant Browning automatic rifleman and carried all of the ammunition.

The people I trained with were great guys. My platoon sergeant was a wonderful Korean man named Kim from Hawaii. I was a private first class, the only rank I wanted. Later when all of the officers and the first sergeant were killed, I was offered an immediate battle field commission, but I didn't want it. D-Day took place while I was still in Camp Adair. We left around December 5, 1944, for France, just before the Battle of the Bulge, on a ship called *The West Point*, which had all three regiments of the 70th Division, but no artillery.

We landed in Marseille in southern France. Since we arrived without artillery support from our own division, we were called "Task Force Herran," named for our commanding officer. We stayed in tents in a big, open, muddy field on the French Riviera for about five days. Then we were loaded onto freight trains, French 40 and 8s (forty men and eight horses), up the Rhone Valley, taking us as far as they could go. And then the trouble started.

We got on trucks and went farther north to Hagenau, where there was a terrible battle going on in a place called Wingen. The 4th Platoon, my platoon, was on the left and the others were on the right. Our platoon came under heavy artillery fire, and that is where I got my baptism of fire against the 6th SS Mountain Division. Fighting in the infantry was very tough; when you're under artillery fire, there's nothing you can do about it. It is a helpless feeling.

It was January and it was bitter cold. When we walked through the town after the battle, we were loading bodies onto trucks and they looked like pieces of wood. On the second afternoon, we patrolled through a forest of pine trees, and a German machine gun opened fire, killing a radio operator and his assistant instantly. We pulled back out of the pine trees and were ambushed by hand grenades flying everywhere. We couldn't dig in because the ground was frozen and had to pull back. The next day Sergeant Kim snuck us back up to the line by going a little to the left, where we had the higher ground overlooking at least four or five machine gun nests—twenty or so Germans—and we killed them all.

When we moved into a gulley not far from there, a German came out of nowhere with his hands up saying he wanted to surrender. Just as I was going to question him, the soldier next to me shot and killed him—a bullet right through the heart. I just hated that, and in fact, it is still on my mind. The last word the German said was, "*Mutter*" (Mother).

That same afternoon, we dug in the same area and the Germans devastated us with 88s. The same American soldier who shot the German was killed. I didn't know him very well.

We slept in the Maginot Line the next night and then we were moved up again to the Saar Basin. It was our task to take the high ground overlooking Saarbrucken. By now it was mid February and we were constantly on patrol up the hill and launching several attacks. This went on for about a month, as it was very difficult to get up there. My best friend, a German kid from Texas who was about eighteen years old, was killed. When we got up the hill, the whole thing was ridden with mines and six lieutenants lost their legs.

We advanced toward Forbach, where there was a castle we had taken. The German counterattack was fierce. The worst thing in the world is when there is a tank firing point-blank at you. We were told to dig in while the Germans attacked the castle. I Company was in the castle while we were outside dug in deep, which was good because our artillery opened up on the Germans who were coming up the hill, and we had no causalities. When it was over, there were about fifty dead Germans right near the front of the castle.

In the Battle of Forbach, we were divided by train tracks; the Germans were on one side and we were on the other. It was brutal fighting, mostly house to house where we had to run like hell every time we moved. When we took Forbach, I was chosen to lead a patrol to the Saar River, which was right across from Germany. We were able to see the Siegfried Line, railroad tracks, and the heavy fortifications. We quickly turned around and headed back to our lines, when all of the sudden eight Germans appeared with their hands up. We couldn't believe it. I talked to them and brought back to our unit, and I was awarded a Bronze Star for this.

In the Saar Basin we liberated some slave laborers who were working in coal mines. They were like skeletons. When I talked to one of the Polish workers who spoke German, I told him how terrible it was how the Nazis had treated him. He replied, "This is nothing. You should see what they've done to the Jews." Until that moment, I had absolutely no idea what was going on, and it was the first time I found out about the Holocaust.

Eventually, we were taken up to the Saar River and were going to make a crossing in assault boats. I knew then that we wouldn't survive that, especially if we were going to be in the first wave. The fortifications were such that we couldn't stand a chance, so we were pulled back for a few days until Patton's Third Army surrounded the Saar River Basin. On March 18, we were finally able to cross the river without a shot being fired and we took Saarbrucken. When we got there, a German came out, and the battalion commander asked my company commander, "You got anyone who speaks German in your company?"

When my commander said, "Yeah, we have a kid who speaks German," the battalion commander said, "Well, forget about him; he's now in 3rd Battalion Headquarters Company."

Then we marched about five miles into the first German town before we got to Kaiserslautern, When we saw all of the white flags and white bed sheets hanging outside the windows, I was proud as heck. It was the first night I slept in a bed for about one hundred days.

The war was over on May 8, and we were moved to Dietz, near the Rhine, for occupation duty. One of our jobs was to get the slave laborers back to their countries. I went to Fulda to talk to the railroad people about getting the French slave laborers back to France. My town was not far from there, so I decided to go back. Since I had to ask my captain for permission, I promised to get him five hundred fresh eggs, which was easy because I knew many of the farmers in all of the villages around there. I ended up coming back with one thousand eggs.

When I went back to Roth, the first thing I did was go to the cemetery where my father and grandparents were buried. It was in terrible shape. The stones were knocked down, and they had made a corn field out of it. For them, that was okay because no more Jews were going to be buried there. I saw the mayor, who I happened to know before the war, and said, "I want the cemetery cleaned up." When he gave me some excuse about not having enough men in the town to do the job, I said, "If it's not done by the time I come back, you'll do it personally while I point a rifle at you." Needless to say, by the time I did eventually return, the cemetery was in good shape, as it is to this day.

Otto Stern was a salesman for Shoe Repair Supplies in Chicago for nearly thirty-five years and retired in 1990. On September 16, 2004, his grandson, 1st Lt. Andrew K. Stern, platoon commander of the Third Platoon, B Company, 1st Tank Battalion, 1st Marine Division, was killed in action in Al Anbar Province, Iraq. Andy is buried at Arlington National Cemetery section 60, site 7999.

Chapter 25

KURT KLEIN

WALLDORF, GERMANY

5th Infantry Division

Kurt Klein immigrated without his parents to the United States in 1937 to join his sister in who had fled Germany one year earlier. His brother arrived in 1938. Klein was inducted into the U.S. Army in 1942 and eventually became an intelligence officer in the 5th Infantry Division. He is pictured above in France, 1944.

I was born in 1920 in the town of Walldorf, which is a small town outside of Heidelberg. I grew up, of course, during the turbulent time between the two great world wars. I saw what the weak economy lead to in Germany and how, step by step, the Nazis gained more power until it culminated in 1933 with Hitler becoming chancellor of Germany.

World War I was always present in my life. I read a great deal, not only in books, but in current magazines. Sometimes my father would tell me some stories about it, and there were pictures around the house as well. He did not particularly delude himself about the aims of that war, but he played his part. I must admit that to me, it seemed like ancient times, but while I was growing up it was ever-present and collective feelings of frustration remained, which Hitler very cleverly used to manipulate the German psyche.

I always sensed that there would be another war even then, because there were so many people who were frustrated by the outcome of World War I and wanted to remake history. During the postwar depression, my father was hard hit economically. He had a hops and tobacco brokerage business and it was very difficult to keep it going during the inflationary period, which added to the lot of his problems. Many businesses suffered because whatever they sold at a certain price that day had no meaning by the time the customer would pay them. It was a constant struggle during that period to keep businesses afloat.

THE JEWS IN GERMANY were more patriotic than possibly in any other country. They felt themselves totally a part of that society. Some would try to be more German than some Germans. I myself grew up before Hitler thinking that things would remain exactly the same as always, and I simply grew up German. I never knew that anybody would make the distinction between being Jewish and German.

Also, unlike in America, the Jews lived anywhere in any given city, not just one area. Even today in the United States, you find certain sections of any city that are predominately Jewish. You would not have found this in Germany before the war. There was an easy interchange with the German population back then. We had many non-Jewish friends and didn't make any distinction between each other.

By and large in our town, we felt it made no difference what religion we were; we simply celebrated different holidays. Sometimes we would share those holidays with our Christian friends. They would invite us around for

Christmastime or Easter and we would invite them for our Hanukkah celebrations. We did not observe anything they did and vice versa, but this seemingly made very little difference and there was a free and easy interchange. We were in each other's homes and sat at each other's tables, which was why it was such a blow to see that these very same people turned away from us. Some of my erstwhile friends with whom I had been very chummy were the very ones who, when I was already in the United States, invaded my parents' home on Kristallnacht and smashed all of their furniture. One of my very best friends was the ringleader.

I know of one friend who fought the propaganda that the Nazis was spreading. After Kristallnacht and at great risk to himself, he spoke to my parents on the street after I had already left the country. Another time he came on the train to their house, which was extremely risky in those days, especially in a small town where everybody knew everybody else, and expressed his indignation at what was going on.

When Hitler came into power, the Jews noticed the change immediately. When I came home from school one day, I found Stormtroopers guarding the door to our home and didn't know what to expect, but they let me pass because they obviously knew me. Early on, there was a boycott of Jewish homes and stores. The Nazis wanted to point out to the German population that they ought not to conduct business with Jews or be friendly with them in any way. And it had side effects.

It became very obvious, if not in 1933, then in 1935 when the Nuremburg Laws were passed. These laws disenfranchised Jews and deprived them of their official decisions in schools, hospitals, and government. They also deprived Jews of citizenship. It was quite clear that there was no future in Germany, especially for young people. That's when we made our first moves to see if we could get out. My sister was fortunate enough to be in nurses training at the time, which would help toward her emigration. Also, in 1936, we had relatives in Buffalo, New York, who sent the necessary affidavits that were required. So she was able to leave in 1936 and, in turn, made it possible for me to follow in 1937.

There were, of course, other people on that ship who were fleeing the Nazis. I met a young non-Jewish American man who had just finished his studies in Heidelberg and with whom I became quite friendly and engaged in a correspondence after I came to the United States. Although he liked his experience in Heidelberg, he predicted that Germany would have to pay a steep price for some of the things it was doing. He believed that the regime was far too militaristic and that the outrages against the Jews would have dire consequences.

I LANDED IN NEW YORK, and members of my family who had also lived in my hometown came to the pier to get me. I spent my first night with them in Brooklyn. They had gone to the States two years beforehand because their brother had been in the States since the mid 1920s, so they had an anchor there and were able to leave fairly early.

From the day I came to the United States I had the urge to become a mainstream American and wanted to become as Americanized as I possibly could. I did everything I could to follow. I soon developed friendships with American boys and others who had come from Europe, learned English, and acclimated. I would say that I could do all the things my American friends could do. It was a process that went on a great many years and has never really stopped.

I had seen New York City in films and photos, but I could hardly believe that I was there. Of course, to a young boy, the whole experience was an adventure not only because of the perils imposed on me and my family in Germany, but also because traveling to a place like that seemed immensely exciting to me. It meant that much more to me to see New York and discover all it could offer, but I didn't have all that much time to explore. Even a subway ride was exciting. I changed my mind in later years, as I was somewhat less enthusiastic about subway rides when I visited again. For quite a while, I persisted in seeing something I hadn't had in my former life and I found it exciting.

Naturally I rejoiced, for I now could lead a life of freedom. Unfortunately, the fact of the matter was that we had come at the tail end of the Depression in the United States, so it was not that easy to find jobs. When we did have a job, it was a menial one that paid very little. So the first couple of years were a struggle.

I knew, of course, that I was removed from the danger, but it weighed heavily on my mind that my parents were still in Germany. We sent papers several times and each time the events overtook us—some new catastrophe or disaster developed and we had to start from scratch. The first papers we were able to send them that would help them get out, the man who vouched for them died shortly thereafter, negating the papers, so we had to start from square one.

Then we had to look around for other relatives and when we found them, my parents were deported with an hour's notice to the south of France. Of course, that changed the situation entirely and we were up against new problems. France was still neutral, so we could have gotten them out by way of Lisbon or North Africa, but there was nothing but red tape.

Additionally, the prevailing attitude in the U.S. State Department was to let in as few Jewish immigrants as possible. At every turn, obstacles were put in the way of completing our papers, and we had to get additional papers and endless papers and had to find people who would vouch that my parents had not been active politically, which was absurd. Also, the ages of my parents (my father was sixty-two) presented another obstacle and were used as a reason to delay their getting a visa.

I had hoped that, once the war started in Europe, America would get involved because I saw it as the only way to stop that tremendous evil. All of the political developments were absolutely predictable to someone who knew the conditions in Germany and the brutality of the Nazis. So I did expect war to break out, although I didn't know when that would be. It was a great frustration for me to stand by and see all of these developments that I knew were going to happen without being able to do anything or help my parents more. So it came as a great relief when America entered the war, for as tragic and dramatic as that was for its people, it had to be done. Instead of being a powerless bystander, I found that now I could actually play a small role in the defeat of this monster.

I could not volunteer for the army, however, because I was considered an Enemy Alien. I registered with my draft board anyway and eventually it said that I qualified for induction into the army. By November 1942 I reported to the army.

The induction center for Buffalo was Fort Niagara, which was not far from Niagara Falls on Lake Ontario. I stayed there for a rather long time because no one knew what to do with me. I was called in to the intelligence officer, who tried to test my loyalty to America by saying things like he had in mind to send me as a paratrooper behind enemy lines; how did I feel about that? I said anything he saw fit for me to do I would be prepared to do it. I convinced him that I was, in fact, loyal, and from there he sent me to South

Carolina to Camp Croft to start my basic training. Being in the army came as a tremendous relief to me because I appreciated that America had given me the opportunity to serve as a soldier and possibly defeat evil. It was the first time that I felt good that I could help.

I didn't find that anyone discriminated against me or inquired too much into my background. Those who did didn't seem to have any feelings in particular against me for having come from Germany. I never found any overt signs of anti-Semitism wherever I was in the army, then or even later. A group of German Jews that included me, and was attached to various units, received some puzzlement from some of the troops who had never seen a Jew in their lives, perhaps because they lived in remote areas. I never found any feeling of hostility, however. They did inquire, and it was quite obvious that I was from Germany. Some of the German Jews had a stronger accent and some had less of one, but either way no one I knew ever found it to be a problem. I have heard stories from other GIs that they ran into anti-Semitism, but I personally never did.

I went to basic training in Camp Croft, and I was absolutely enthusiastic. I didn't find it a great hardship, for I expected worse after the stories I heard about basic training. Frankly, I was in good physical condition, though somewhat short at the time. For me, it was just part of the adventure and I was perfectly willing to see it through all the way.

After four weeks of basic training, I was called in by the commanding officer. He told me that since I spoke German I would be sent to the military intelligence center at Camp Ritchie, which turned out to be in Maryland, not far from where Camp David is today. This was in January 1943.

Obviously, my background was considered in my being sent to Ritchie. I was among the initial classes (the third class) they had for the courses in military intelligence, and the camp was still not perfectly in place. I remember we had to wade through mud in the winter because there were no roads yet between the barracks, but we had some extremely interesting courses. We learned everything to do with military intelligence, the makeup of battle, and everything about the German army that would be of value to us. We actually knew as much about the German army as we did about the American army at the time. The classes were between fifteen and twenty people of all ranks. A private could be sitting next to a major, because we were pulled in from all over, as we had some capabilities that were appropriate for military intelligence.

I suspect that a lot of it came through the British Army. It had a very good intelligence service. Although as an ordinary person, I wasn't aware of what intelligence gathering had gone on, I think for a long time it had compiled a lot of material on the German army, having been engaged with that army so much earlier than America. Whatever the British could find out was passed on to us. We also learned about the British army and its ranks and customs.

It gave us a certain sense of importance and satisfaction that such privileged information was accessible to us and to learn it all. Also, the rules were a lot more relaxed than they were in basic training, even if the conditions were a bit primitive while I was there. On the other hand, we would playfully refer to it as a country club because military protocol was not strictly observed and we had certain freedoms that others in an army camp didn't have. We had discipline, but in certain areas it was certainly more lax than others.

We went out on these maneuvers and had training both in the field and in classrooms. As a matter of fact, the program tried to make it realistic by having members of my team dress up in German uniforms with German equipment and speak in German. We taught the troops how to take apart a German machine gun and put it together again, along with what other kinds of weapons they could expect to find and how to deal with them. We learned quite a bit about German weaponry. They had some really effective guns, such as the 88s. I became quite adept at taking apart some of their weapons. We found that their rifles seemed to be inferior to our M1 rifles, but some of their other equipment was really better than what we had at the time.

I FORMED SOME GOOD FRIENDSHIPS there that still persist today. There were also notable people at Ritchie. There were some who had worked in Hollywood, which was extremely interesting to us. For example, my brother had Klaus Mann in his class, who was the son of Thomas Mann and was a writer like his father. There was also another well-known German writer, Hans Habe, who was there when I was. He organized something that was extremely fascinating to me at the time. We had a movie theater, and one day we were called to assemble in there. We found it decked out with all the paraphernalia that the Nazis had used for one of their party congresses in Nuremburg, including huge banners with swastikas. He gave a speech just as Hitler would have delivered. Everything was simulated to the highest degree that it could be.

Aside from that, we would go on field problems where some of us would dress up as German soldiers, and we had to capture and then interrogate them to show what we had learned in the courses. They would only respond to certain questions that were pertinent and had been pre-programmed. If we hit on the right combination, they would answer, otherwise they would refuse. That would prove we had learned our lessons in class. I had assumed a certain authority through my training and often thought it was the fulfillment of a dream to find myself in that position. Certainly it was a position in the army that I never expected to have, so I was very happy I could be in that place in that capacity.

We knew that we were preparing for invasion. Although we didn't know when that would be, we could see all the signs indicating that we would soon be leaving. In June 1943, after finishing our courses, we went on Louisiana maneuvers where they gave us simulated ranks. I was an acting master sergeant. After Louisiana maneuvers, which ended toward the end of July, most of us got the acting ranks confirmed back at Camp Ritchie, and I would be a master sergeant for most of the war. We were initially a six-man team attached to any given unit. That was cut down to four men, and some of our officers moved on, so I was in line to get a field commission. (Due to that fast forward movement, however, it wouldn't catch up with me until April 1945.) After Ritchie we were then sent to Fort Myers, outside of the Pentagon in Washington. There we were stationed waiting to go overseas, and they thought that we were important enough to fly us to Great Britain. That was quite an exciting trip that very few GIs got to take.

On September 14, we landed in Scotland and took a train to London. That, too, seemed like a great adventure. The bombing of London had diminished since I had been over there, but I could still hear the rumble of it and the sirens, which added a certain air to it that was, to a young man, quite exciting at the time. To meet and form friendships with the population who were quite friendly toward us was also exhilarating. In that sense, it was a great adventure, aside from our military duties. I realized that it took me places that I could not have traveled to at that time and I appreciated that.

After staying in London for a couple of weeks, we went to a pool, which was located in another camp in the Cotswolds. Again, we were split into teams or stayed in the teams to which we were originally assigned. From there, they assigned us to the various units in Britain. I was assigned to the 5th Infantry, which was stationed in Northern Ireland. I joined it in October 1943 and spent the following nine months with the 5th until the invasion in Northern Ireland.

I HAD ONE ROSH HASHANAH IN OXFORD, which was in a beautiful synagogue. I also had occasion to visit some relatives who lived in England at the time. I had a first cousin who lived with her English husband outside of London. Another more distant couple, who I had known in Germany quite well and had spent an unforgettable summer with them, lived in Chilton, which was very close to the camp I first went to in England.

While we were still in England, we went to a POW camp where we practiced interrogating real German prisoners. This experience gave us a little more of an inkling of what we would be up against once we were in the field. Two or three of us went into the interrogation room at a time. We were told not to have any short arms with us, because the prisoners could overpower us and use them against us, so we went in there without any weapons. It was sort of a funny feeling to be in there without being armed, but we got used to that.

Then we started to interrogate them. Some of them had been interrogated before, so they knew what to expect and would very often digress into something else. I remember one in particular because the digression happened to be in the field of my civilian endeavor of printing; one of them gave me a whole lecture on a typesetting machine and described every part just to detract from the other question I was going to ask him. I did cut him short and finally got to the point of the matter. Furthermore, they felt fairly secure in their position as prisoners. Some of them would answer quite easily. I found this quite funny: they would cooperate with us, but then, for example, would ask if we could end the interrogation by a certain time because they wanted to see a British film playing later and they didn't want to miss it.

During interrogations, it was quite a bit like what courtroom lawyers do: do not ask any leading questions, sort of circumscribe and get to the point in many other ways until they reveal something. This method doesn't seem as threatening to them.

I was always mindful of the fact that I would show my emotions, but I was able to control them sufficiently to do the job that I was meant to do and didn't let my personal feelings about them interfere with the interrogation.

What I thought of those prisoners was quite another matter, especially when I encountered the SS. We knew whether the prisoner had been in the SS even if he tried to hide it, because under their arms there was the SS tattoo—that was of course the giveaway. It wasn't known in full detail, but we knew enough to know that they were the worst of the bunch.

I was still in Northern Ireland waterproofing our jeep, which was a long, drawn-out process that took a week to accomplish. We had to put a special compound on all the wires in the jeep, because it was expected that we would not land on dry land and the jeep would have to go through water. This process is what stands out most in my mind. After that, they shipped us to a staging area near Liverpool in Salisbury, and from there we embarked on our trip to Normandy.

We had heard how tough it was in the beginning, and it was a very precarious situation, but then after a few days it stabilized. Although the units were stuck in the beach not far from where they landed, they were dug in and fighting for short stretches of land. It was from one hedgerow to another. By the time we arrived, there was still an occasional German plane, but the artillery had been knocked out well before then.

I landed late in June on Utah Beach and we relieved the 1st Infantry by taking over the positions it had held. We dug in there in foxholes and there was not much movement until the big breakthrough at St. Lo, the day when a thousand bombers came over and blazed the way for the infantry to go forward in the armor.

I was attached to the 2nd Infantry of the 5th Infantry Division. We were with the regimental headquarters. I had a carbine and a pistol, a .45. At one time, I also had a Browning semiautomatic rifle (BAR). One of the first places my unit was sent was about two hundred yards from the frontline, but we had to get out of there in a hurry when Germans spotted us and began a mortar barrage, which could be very deadly.

The most nerve-racking thing about being entrenched anywhere was the artillery barrages—the noise, the sweating out of where they would fall. You would hear the whistle and would never know exactly where they were going to hit, and when you were exposed to that at great lengths of time, it could get on your nerves. I saw a few of our guys start to crack, but never completely. Some of them certainly showed signs of that stress.

German prisoners were being taken right from the start. It was our job to find out what units they had come from because it was important to determine what units we were facing. We would ask if there were, in fact, several units that had been put together, as this would show a certain weakness on their part, whether they had taken remnants from all over and put them together; what their strength was and armor was. We tried to find out as much as we could.

In the beginning, they all in varying degrees assisted in interrogation, but we had ways of soliciting information by telling them that somebody else had told us something that we suspected, and then have them confirm it. We would also threaten that, since we knew what the facts were, they had better not lie to us. Later on, during the French campaign, we would resort to some tricks. For example, prisoners who refused to give any information at all would be segregated from the others. Then we would hang signs on them with big red letters that said, "I am being turned over to the Russians." In other words, we played psychological warfare on them.

Above all, they dreaded falling into the hands of the Russians. As we were to find out when we joined up with the Russians, they would hold out against the Russians much longer because they definitely didn't want to fall into their hands. The Germans knew what they had done to the people in Russia and how the Russians dealt with them, as opposed to the American troops who were much more lenient. The Americans would stick more to the rules of the Geneva Convention, with which the Russians were not too bothered.

Some prisoners would ask where we learned to speak such good German. The joke among the members of my unit was that some of them would say they had taken a blitz course from Berlitz. I once interrogated an officer who claimed that he had played tennis with me in Vienna, which of course was not so because I had never been in Vienna.

In the end, I would try to get as much information as possible without bringing a lot of personal emotions into it. I wouldn't say that it would have been wrong to bring it in. In retrospect, it might have had a stronger effect, but that was just my mode of operation at the time.

I enjoyed seeing Germans as prisoners because now the shoe was on the other foot. To see them bedraggled and kind of desperate to get out of the war felt very good. When I lived in Germany, they had the decision of life or death over us, and we could only stand with our hands tied. Now to see them in that state felt very good.

AT ONE TIME, we moved very fast with the advance; we were attached to Patton's Third Army, and his tanks moved quite rapidly. First, we spent some time at the French/German border, when we were bogged down and the tanks had run out of gas, which wasn't replenished right away because there was a shortage. After that, we took the town of Verdun, which was a significant city where a World War I battle took one of the heaviest tolls of the war. From there we went to Metz, which at one time had been German, but by the time we got there it was French though German-occupied. That's where we were bogged down because of the forts that surround the city. It was probably a tactical mistake to stay there and wait for the surrender of the forts, because we could have bypassed them, which might have required a detour, but the forts would have been ineffective. Somehow, though, it was decided that those forts had to be taken, and we spent an undue length of time in Metz because of that. I was instrumental as an interpreter in the surrender of Fort Driant, which was one of the major forts and had command of the roads that lead out of Metz.

I had to meet the German colonel and his officers and arrange for their surrender. Again, it was somewhat an odd feeling going in there unarmed, not knowing what they were still capable of doing, because even if they wanted to surrender, some were still quite upset that they were surrendering. I remember one of their sergeants who, after the surrender, had put his communications system out of commission. Unfortunately he had already left me by that time, but I had to stay where I was, so I couldn't reach him anymore. Once we found their message center and found that it had been decommissioned, I really wanted to get a hold of him for what he had done.

What really got me was that once they surrendered they were quite willing and, in fact, tried to get us to agree, to go against the Russians. I remember some high officers telling us that.

One time, I was walking outside of the fort with a German officer. We were going across the expanse around the fort and many horses had been hit. He expressed his regret that these poor animals had to die. I asked him if he had any regret that so many human beings died. I also asked him whether he had any regrets over what the Germans had done to the Jews. He gave me some nondescript answer, saying that there was always loss of life in any war and he had been trained to expect that.

AFTERWARDS, WE WENT TO ALSACE, which had constantly changed hands between Germany and France after every war. Now it was German again, and we moved into Alsace, but then when the Battle of the Bulge began, we were quickly pulled up north. It was quite a feat of logistics to move us as fast as they did. We went to Luxembourg to bolster our defenses and reinforce the units that were under siege there.

We left Luxembourg once the danger had been removed after the Battle of the Bulge. We went into Germany by way of Bitburg and then to a place near Trier, which was one of their major cities. At that time, I believe the Remagen Bridge had been found intact, but the 5th Division actually crossed the Rhine in a town called Nierstein, where our engineers had put up a pontoon bridge.

From there, we went south again and by 1945 we took the major town of Frankfurt. We then went into reserve and stayed there for at least a week or two. This break afforded me a chance to look for a cousin of mine who had lived in Frankfurt and whose wife was not Jewish, so I had some hope of finding perhaps the whole family, but if not, at least members. I was successful in locating his wife and two children, who were living on a farm twenty-five miles outside of Frankfurt. Some people began to filter back into Frankfurt after we took it; they were mostly members of mixed marriages, which was how they survived. I was able to find a place in Frankfurt for my cousin's family, which was at least one thing I could do.

My cousin's wife was immensely grateful that I had taken the trouble to track her down and was able to make life a little bit easier for her. Unfortunately, my cousin, late in the war, had been sent to some concentration camp, and she was doubtful of his fate. She hadn't given up hope, but she didn't know exactly what had happened. He was a doctor and presumably died on a death march in March 1945, so close to the end of the war.

It was an odd feeling to be back on German soil, but at the same time gratifying to be part of the American troops and be in power. At the same time, I was mindful of the great losses that we had personally sustained. So it was not unalloyed joy that I felt when I came back, because nothing was the same as it once had been. Nevertheless, it was better to be back in that capacity than the alternative possibility. I had a deep appreciation for the sacrifices that other GIs from remote areas in America—who had very little contact with European—had made in the name of defeating this tremendous evil.

THE WAR WAS OVER ON MAY 8, and after the city of Frankfurt, we advanced to the Czech border to the so-called Sudetenland, which was populated by Germans. Hitler had made the case of taking over Czechoslovakia because he considered that German territory, but it was just a pretext. I found it was odd to be in the place that he had used to start the war.

I was stationed in Bavaria after the war was over. I would scout the countryside after receiving some tips on where to find Nazis and jail them. It was not up to me to de-Nazify anyone that early in the game, it was done by other authorities, usually military governments, with which we worked closely, but that was not my domain.

Once we reached the border of Germany and Czechoslovakia, I happened to have what I call my rendezvous with destiny. We came across a group of what had been slave laborers, young Jewish women from Poland and Hungary. They had been abandoned by their SS guards in the town whose surrender we had taken just days before the end of the war. We had heard about them and knew we had to go there reinforced by our medical battalion and render some aid.

Once I walked into the factory where the SS had locked them up, I met a young woman who was standing at the entrance and who took me inside when I asked her. She left quite an impression on me. She was at the end of her strength and collapsed once. Our medics took them all to the field hospital that we found in town. Out of that encounter evolved a friendship with a person of rare caliber, which developed further and one year later we were married in Paris.

Now this makes me reflect on the fact that I had gone to Europe to fight the Nazis with hatred in my heart for all they had inflicted so gratuitously on Jews and the world. I had to witness the results of what they had done to my people. Also, I was 95 percent sure that my parents could not have survived the war. While all of that was true, for me personally the key to my own future was being able to go to back and be in that place at that time, which was connected to me by a tenuous thread.

If I had been born one day earlier none of this story I have told would have ever happened. When the war began, America had the first draft, and a while later it had the second draft that would take men of a certain vintage and it had a cutoff point of June 30 or July 1, 1938. I was born July 2, so I missed the second draft and was in the third draft instead. None of this would have happened if I had been in the second draft.

So you see how destiny can play tricks on us, but I am immensely grateful for this trick. We have always considered ourselves lucky that we met in the fashion we did. We supported each other in coming to terms with the losses we had sustained and felt that we could have continuity within our respective families by having children and grandchildren—in our case now a family of sixteen.

Being in the army proved to me that I could face tough situations and handle them adequately, which imbued a certain sense of self-assurance. Before going into the army, I could not know what I would run up against or how I would conduct myself, but I was glad to see how it affected me. Aside from serving, a great deal of army life is waiting around for something to happen. In that sense, during those periods, the army afforded me chances to see places and get to know people I would never have met otherwise. Even the Camp Ritchie experience was an extraordinary one. I was thrown together with people who were utterly fascinating to me, and I was able to form some friendships. It was certainly a relief from the routine of making a living back home. For me, it was somewhat akin to going to college, because I also formed a bond with the people with whom I was thrown together. Some of them lasted a lifetime, while others were of a temporary nature.

I felt proud that I could serve the United States in the capacity that I did. Nothing made me happier than being of some use to America after what it had given me, which was the idea that I could live in freedom. I live with the regret that my parents could not make it out, otherwise my happiness could have been complete.

Kurt Klein brought his wife, Gerda, home with him to Buffalo, New York, and worked for many years in the printing business. Gerda Klein's account of being liberated by her future husband was the subject of an Academy Award–winning documentary film, One Survivor Remembers, *and both became internationally known humanitarians and public speakers. Kurt Klein died in Guatemala while on a lecture tour in April 19, 2002.*

Chapter 26

HARRY LORCH

DIEBURG, GERMANY

29th Infantry Division

Hans "Harry" Lorch was born in 1921, fifty miles from Frankfurt, Germany, in a small town called Dieburg. There were fifty-five Jewish families out of a town of six thousand people. Lorch was kicked out of high school in 1934, and two years later he left for Holland where he lived before leaving for New York in 1939. He returned to Europe in 1944 as an infantry replacement in the 29th Infantry Division, 115th Regiment, D-Day plus-one. He remained with the division until it reached the Elbe River in Germany. After V-E Day, Lorch was reassigned to Military Intelligence Services and sent to Norway to work in postwar Denazification. He is pictured above in Germany, 1945.

October 23, 1939, was the day I left Holland for New York. I was on the *Westerdam*, part freighter and passenger ship. A group of other refugees and I were in the hold because we did not have cabins, and it was a really rough voyage. When we came close to England, we saw a lot of sunken ships and ours was escorted through a minefield. We picked up more people in England and then were off to the States.

When we landed in Hoboken, New Jersey, I looked down to the pier and saw my uncle and my cousin waiting for me. My uncle and aunt lived at 170th Street in Washington Heights. Walking down Broadway, I met quite a few people who I knew and it was quite exciting. Washington Heights was beautiful. Everywhere I looked I saw people I knew. I joined a synagogue and went regularly Friday and Saturday. I had a very hard time finding a job, but in time I started working as a mechanic.

I was playing soccer in West Newark, New Jersey, when I heard in the dressing room that Pearl Harbor was bombed. When the war came, I did some defense work and my boss didn't want me to go to the army. He said, "You're more important here than if you were in the army," but I didn't want to do that. I went to Whitehall Street to volunteer for the army, but I was told that I couldn't because I was an Enemy Alien. I replied, "This is ridiculous. I was thrown out by Hitler. How could you consider us enemies?"

In Washington Heights, there were a lot of stories coming out of Germany. The newspaper *Aufbau* was publishing articles all of the time about how horrible the Jews were being treated, so we all knew what was happening over there.

I WAS DRAFTED a little less than a year after I had originally tried to volunteer, and being drafted for me was an incredible sense of relief. When I went to Fort Dix, the entire coach on the train was full of refugees. We were all very anxious. My cousin Lou Wolf and I were inducted together and initially stayed in the same barracks.

Since we had to march in Germany in school, I was already good at marching and I got used to basic and advanced training very quickly. The only problem was that I hated Camp McClellan in Alabama, because it was in the middle of the rainy season, so there were thousands of mosquitoes and the dampness was horrible. However, I knew I was there for a purpose and that purpose was to train to fight a war. My only worry was being sent to fight the

Japanese, because I knew I could do more for America in Europe. Almost immediately I had great relationships with the other GIs; even though they used to call me a "Heinie," there was just wonderful camaraderie among these men.

After Alabama, I went to Wisconsin to join the 76th Infantry, a ski troop. Ski training was very tough. We had no experience prior to this, and it was extremely cold. We also trained in Michigan's Upper Penisula, where the snow was unreal. The first time I jumped off a truck, I fell into a ditch and others had to dig me out. Not long after the army broke up the 76th, we were shipped to Camp Shanks, New York, a camp for replacement troops, from which I was shipped out to England in April 1944.

There were quite a few ships in the convoy across the Atlantic. I was on an English transport, which was originally used for transporting meat from South America to Europe. The English kitchen left a lot to be desired, and when diarrhea broke out in the hold next to ours, I was blessed with it and it was a horror. All the way over, we were so sick.

From Liverpool, we were transported to a camp in Bath, England. Everywhere you looked you saw troops. When I saw that camps were restricted and heard bombers overhead day and night, I knew, along with everyone else, an invasion was going to happen.

On the morning of D-Day, we were on a hike. While we were marching, we looked up in the sky and saw plane after plane after plane. It was an unbelievable sight. That evening we packed our duffels and were prepared to go to France. I was thrilled because now it was my time to get into the fight, but I was also a little worried. I was afraid of being captured, but what really scared me was what would happen to me if I was challenged at night by a fellow soldier and responded in my very German accent.

I arrived in Normandy via Omaha Beach on June 7. The staging area was as busy as Times Square, with trucks, tanks, and troops moving inland in all directions. It was mind-boggling. There were stockpiles of equipment all over the beach and we could tell there had been one hell of a fight the day before.

I arrived in St. Mere-Eglise and was sent to a field surrounded on four sides by hedgerows. There were a couple of sergeants from the 29th Division who took role call. When they asked me what company I had been with and I replied, "I&R" (intelligence and reconnaissance), they said, "No room, go to D

Company." I told them that I knew nothing about heavy weapons and asked if I&R had an interpreter. They said no, so I was eventually put in I Company of the 115th Regiment, a reconnaissance troop.

Shortly after I got to my unit, I got into a fight with another soldier, a corporal who made a remark I didn't like. He and a noncom were walking by me and he said, "Now we got a Jew bastard in our outfit."

I looked up and said, "Corporal, what did you say?"

He said, "Now we got a Jew bastard in our outfit." I sprung up and hit him so hard in the face that it knocked him over. I couldn't box, so I took him down and we started wrestling. We got into a bear hug on an incline and started rolling down the hill; since I was on top I beat the hell out of him.

That day I was assigned to his squad, which was made up of about twenty-eight men. We didn't talk for several months and he never marched in front of me. "He's not going to shoot me in the back," I overheard him say once.

In Normandy we couldn't make it cross-country very well. There were so many sunken roads that made it difficult to bring in jeeps, so we reconnoitered on foot. The hedgerows were murder. The Germans had a habit of setting up machine-gun nests where four fields would meet, so they could control two fields with one machine gun. One of the biggest problems was all of the dead animals, such as horses and cows, that the Krauts shot and left everywhere. The smell of all of the decomposing animals was very hard to take, and the combination of maggots, flies, and heat was brutal. Bulldozers had to be brought in to clear all of it away.

On my first day of combat I saw two dead German soldiers who had been run over by tanks, and they were flat as pancakes. That didn't bother me. The same day, however, I saw a couple of dead American soldiers and got sick to my stomach. That bothered me terribly.

We spent more time behind German lines than we were behind our own. If it was a motorized patrol we went by jeep, otherwise there were foot patrols. In France we had roads with hasty minefields, where Germans in retreat hastily threw mines down on the roads. Our lieutenant had an idea that one of us would lie on the hood of a jeep to look out for mines while he drove very slowly. We were ambushed many times, when I was shot at and I fired my weapon.

AFTER ST. Lo, we advanced to Landels, in a county called Calvados, where the French produce a spirit—applejack—called Calvados. I'll never forget my first sip. When we came to this town we saw a burning tank that had hit a mine and our lieutenant, Elmer Hill, a prince of a guy, called in the combat engineers to clear the mines. It was the lieutenant who suggested we go into Landels.

In the center of town was a little country store, and I went in and spoke a little French to this little proprietor. I asked him why the county was called Calvados and, without answering me, he disappeared into the backroom. A few moments later he brought out a huge bottle of Calvados. Apparently he misunderstood me, but I decided to open the bottle and take a drink. When the guys in my platoon asked me if it tasted any good, I replied, "It's the best I've ever had." In about a half-hour, there were twenty-eight guys as drunk as can be.

Then our lieutenant said, "Boys, I'm sorry to spoil your little party, but we don't have time for the engineers. Let's go straddle those mines." So we straddled those mines and moved forward up the road. Somehow the Germans picked up our radio and they opened up on us with 88s. That was the beginning of a big battle in which we took a lot of prisoners.

A few days later we came to a town and I didn't see anybody alive: mostly dead women, children, and old men. A German division had come through the town, an SS division called Das Reich Regiment, Der Fuhrer.

AT THE END OF AUGUST, we moved up to Brest and fought there for three weeks. In Brest, there was an underground Wehrmacht hospital that we captured. We were extremely tired, so we decided to stay there overnight. The food and drink storage they had down there was incredible. There were some wounded and dead Germans, and some of their medics remained. Since I was the only German speaker, I told them to go upstairs and I separated the officers from enlisted men, so the officers were on the left and the enlisted men on the right.

Before marching them, I asked if any of them had ailments, but nobody volunteered that information. The reason I asked was if I put a sick man at the head of a column, it would slow the pace, so there wouldn't be any stragglers. The Germans didn't answer because they figured they would be shot, since that's the kind of thing they would do to their prisoners who couldn't walk.

The German prisoners were so meek. Very seldom did we see some of them acting the way they did prior to being captured.

We started marching and all of the sudden, I hear one of the prisoners saying, "Hans." I told them to be quiet. A little while later, someone said again, "Hans."

I asked, "Who's talking?"

"It's me," said the soldier, "don't you know me anymore, Lorch?"

I said, "How the hell should I know you?"

"We used to go to school together in Dieberg. I lived on Theobald Strasse and you lived on the corner of Frankfurt and Theabold."

Then, I knew immediately who he was. We brought all of them to a staging area and that's the last I ever saw of him. I was surprised that he recognized me, because I hadn't seen him in ten years since I was still a kid. I was sure I looked different with army clothes.

THE GERMANS IN BREST surrendered on September 19, which for me was significant because it was Rosh Hashanah. All of the Jewish boys jumped on trucks and were taken to services that were held in a nearby church.

I knew what the Germans were doing to Jewish people. While I didn't know to what extent, I knew that it wasn't good. So, I carried my hatred for the Germans with me into battle. I had some prisoners who admitted there were things happening to Jews in Russia that were unimaginable. Sometimes I told prisoners that they were talking to a Jew, and they would start to shake in their boots.

From Brest, we went to Rennes, which was a fairly large city. In Rennes we went to a café in which the waitresses couldn't speak English and we couldn't speak enough French. There was a civilian there who did speak a bit of English and asked, "Gentlemen, can I help?" So we asked him to translate for a few of us, which he did and then returned to his table to resume eating. I couldn't help but stare at this man because for some reason, I had a hunch that he was Jewish. I got up from my chair and made my way over to where he was sitting. He was too preoccupied with his meal to notice that I was standing over him, until I said in Hebrew, "*L'Shana Tova*" (Happy Jewish New Year). I startled him so much that he bit down on his fork. He slowly got up and the two of us embraced. He cried and so did I. Afterwards, I went back and told the guys that we had to do something for this man. I arranged for the fellows to get candy bars and cigarettes for him, but he disappeared after paying our whole tab.

WE MOVED TO BRUSSELS, and then to Maastricht and Valkenburg in Holland. I used to live twenty-five miles away from there when I left Germany. Since we were on the border between Holland and Germany, we made several night patrols from into Germany. The first time I stepped on German soil was on *Kol Nidre* night (eve of Yom Kippur).

While we were there, we lost an entire company. They were all taken prisoner with the exception of one man who came to our command post (CP) a nervous wreck. Apparently, there was a soldier in that company that was related to General Hodges. All of the sudden, division wanted to know what happened to that particular company. It was reported to S-2 Intelligence, Major Bruning (who was the nephew of former Reich chancellor, Heinrich Bruning, under Hindenburg); the major was a hell of a nice guy.

We were supposed to go out on a patrol and bring back prisoners to find out what happened to this company. Major Bruning suggested we go out in a horseshoe formation, get Germans in the horseshoe, and then close up and capture them. Lieutenant Neff, a Jew from Chicago, said, "Okay, men, I need two volunteers."

The fellow who had called me a Jew bastard when I first came to the field said, "Lieutenant, I'll take the lead on one end." So, I volunteered to take the other end, then walked up to the guy and said, "John, tonight for the first time I'm with the 29th, I respect you as a man, and as a soldier, and I want to forget what happened between us in the past." He threw his arms around me and kissed me, and from that point on we became best buddies.

MY FAMILY WAS ALWAYS ON MY MIND, especially as I got closer to Germany. When the division was in Holland, across from a coalmine (we used the coal to blacken our faces and hands during our night patrols) there was a bar where I encountered a German Jewish refugee who had been in hiding. At first he was petrified of me because I wore a uniform, as he didn't know the difference between an American uniform and a German one. I told the man not to worry, because I too was Jewish. When I told him that I was originally from Germany and had lived for a while in Holland, in Roermond, he said, "Come with me to my house. There is a Jewish family that had also lived in Roermond staying with me." It turned out the family was from the same region as me and knew my entire family. In fact, the son–in-law was a business competitor of my father.

The news they had for me was not good. They told me that the whole family, including my parents and sister, but with the exception of my uncle, aunt, and cousin, had been deported to Westerbork concentration camp. After our meeting, I kept these people supplied with rations until my company moved out.

My cousin Lou Wolf's outfit, the 2nd Armored Division, was attached to the 29th Division for a while, and our paths crossed from time to time. When I saw Lou, he told me about an older prisoner he had interrogated in Titz; the man's ID stated that he had come from Dieberg. Lou immediately asked the prisoner if he had known the Lorch family to which the old man replied, "There were a few Lorchs there, which ones?"

"Max and Ida," said Lou.

"They were very good friends of mine." Upon hearing Lou's last name, Wolf, he asked, "Are you the son of Hugo or Albert? It couldn't be Leopold because he had no sons." It turned out that this man was wonderful to my parents after I had left. He brought them food and took care of them before they were deported. I wish I could have thanked him.

When the division moved into Muenchen-Gladbach in March 1945, I had an experience that left quite an impression on me. On March 27, I was one of four hundred Jewish servicemen from the 29th Division and other outfits who attended a Passover Seder in a castle that had until recently belonged to Joseph Goebbels. As everybody began to gather in the dining room, I noticed some very large portraits of Hitler and Goering on the wall, so I immediately went to take them down. When the chaplain saw what I was doing, he said, "No, Harry, leave them up. I want them to see this."

Harry Lorch owned Empire State Leather, an importer/distributor of leather products, and now lives in Englewood, New Jersey.

Chapter 27

MANFRED GANS

BORKEN, GERMANY

3 Troop, 10 Commando

Manfred Gans was born in Borken, Germany, a town forty miles north of the Ruhr district and twelve miles from the Dutch frontier in Westphalia. Gans was sent to England in August 1938. When the war broke out, he first served in the Pioneer Corps, an unarmed labor unit of the British Army. He then volunteered for hazardous duty and was accepted into the 3 Troop, 10 (Inter-Allied) Commando/Special Services Brigade.

Gans changed his name to Freddy Gray and was attached to the 41 Royal Marine Commando as a frontline interrogator three weeks before the D-Day invasion. He landed at H-Hour on Gold Beach the morning of June 6, 1944, and fought in Normandy until the Allied breakout. He earned a battlefield

293

commission in the invasion of Holland, where he was wounded
twice in Walcheren landings. He remained at the frontline
until the occupation of Germany.

I was absolutely set on seeing the war through and making sure that I was there to see Germany liberated from the Nazi government. Very often, I thought about what might have happened to my parents and occasionally I got very depressed.

My father, Moritz Gans, and his four brothers had joined the German Army during World War I, and my father lost a leg and a lung. He was a decorated veteran, extremely well known. After the war he had joined the League for War Invalids War Orphans and War Widows. There was an organization like that in every town.

He soon became the president of his league. He used his office extensively to write letters on behalf of all the members and their plight for pensions to which they were entitled. At that time people could not afford lawyers, so my father's office was used for this purpose, in addition to his textile business. He never charged anybody for mailing a letter, and his staff did everything that was connected with it. My mother often complained about this free service because it interfered with his business too much. As a result of his efforts, he became extremely popular and when he ran for town council in our very catholic town, on a social democratic ticket, he was elected. He was the only Jew ever elected to the town council in 750 years of the town's history.

In 1934—the year after Hitler took power—the headquarters of that organization wrote him a very complimentary letter, expressing admiration for what he had done for the organization. In the letter they also wrote, "You know how things are going, and we would appreciate it if you would resign from the organization," which he did. He kept this letter in his artificial leg wherever he went and always had it on him, showing what he had done.

In the fall of 1944, I heard from my uncle in New York that he had received word from a family friend in Switzerland who had heard that my parents were rumored to be alive in Theresianstadt, the concentration camp outside of Prague. Well, as far as I was concerned, the war was over on May 7, and I persuaded my unit to let me go, give me a jeep and a driver, and go find my parents. Theresianstadt was 150 miles away, through unconquered southern Germany and into Czechoslovakia.

I tried to go through territory that was known to me. Essentially, I tried to hit the eastward autobahn as soon as I could. I wasn't really scared; I was more worried about the brakes on the jeep than about getting behind enemy lines. When my driver and I reached Aue, the town was undamaged and had not been looted. German police and thousands of German soldiers were on the street. Two and half German divisions had yet to surrender and were still intact. We passed a lot of positions that were still completely manned. There were roadblocks with perfectly good antitank guns guarding them, but no one went behind their guns or put their finger on their triggers. They actually let us through. Nobody had expected us.

Soon I picked up a wounded German soldier and his girlfriend because I felt safer having people like them in the jeep. All of the Germans who I encountered broached the subject of whether they could surrender to me and I said, "No, you can't. You are fighting the Russians and you'll surrender to them."

A German woman said, "You know, the Russians will rape everybody, they're so cruel. How can you do this to us?"

In a snappy reply, I said, "This is what you people did in Russia and Poland, too. You were very cruel."

Their reaction to that was, "There are bad people among all nations."

I remember thinking, "What the hell am I saying, here amongst the last two divisions of the German Army who have yet to officially surrender?" Imagine me accusing them of being cruel to Eastern Europe!

When we got down from the Sudeten Mountains into Czech territory, we ran into the Russian Army. That was a great experience. They were so happy to see us! You would not believe their enthusiasm—they had seen American and British liberated prisoners, but they had never met an officer in a vehicle who had weapons before, and they were beside themselves with joy. Most of the MPs directing the traffic were women, and they all embraced us. In fact, they practically raped us.

When we reached the Russians, I still had another hundred miles to go, but we were making good time. The Russian Army was coming in the opposite direction, but there was no heavy traffic. We continued to make good time, driving about a hundred miles in two and a half hours. Toward evening, we managed to get to Theresianstadt.

The camp was behind heavily barbed wire, with Russian guards outside. I walked up to the Russian guards at the gate, and once again everybody was delighted to see us. After all of the handshaking, congratulating, slapping each other on the back, and saying how happy we were to meet each other, I told him what I wanted. The beam went up and we drove into the camp. There were a massive number of people in there, all terribly crowded; most were too weak to get out of the way. People were practically crawling through our legs.

I did not know where to start looking. Somebody drew my attention to the fact that there was a central register, so I made my way there. The camp, having just been in German hands, was of course very organized as far as lists and things like that went.

There was a girl there who spoke English, and I told her that I was looking for my parents, Moritz and Else Gans. There was an endless list. After a few moments, she looked up and said, "You're lucky, they're still here. They are alive."

I said to her, "Well, there's no two ways about it. You're going to show me, and you're going to take me to them now."

She came with us on the jeep and took us to the house where my parents were registered to live. My parents were living on the second floor of a house in the Dutch section of the ghetto. I told the girl to go upstairs and tell them that their son was there, but to prepare them a little bit for it first. I just waited outside.

She went inside and said, "I have a very joyous message for you."

My mother asked, "Are we getting some extra food?"

The girl said, "No, your son is here."

I stood outside in the dark, and after maybe a minute, my parents came out. Of course, they were in an unbelievable state. My father was so decimated, if I had met him on the street, I would not have recognized him.

When they saw me, my parents were totally swept up—crying, shocked, I don't know how to describe it. They could hardly speak. I said, "Calm down, let's go and sit down somewhere." And then, of course, people collected. Everyone crowded around downstairs on the street and started singing. A group of Zionist girls came and gave my mother flowers; friends of my parents came to congratulate them on my arrival. My driver was just a kid. He said at one stage, "All this experience is no use to me. Nobody is going to believe it when I get home." He was right.

Afterward, we sat down and spent the night talking. They knew very little, almost nothing, of what had happened in the world. I knew more about places like Auschwitz than they did. They did not realize the full extent of the murder. They knew that a lot of people had disappeared from Theresianstadt and never came back, including my aunt and uncle, but they didn't know a thing about the gas chambers.

At one point, my father said, "We'll never get our own back after what the Germans did to us." I told him that we *had*, perhaps not in the way we would have liked, but we did get back at them. I gave him a rough idea about what fights I had been in on D-Day and the assaults we made in Normandy. I told him about seeing the dead bodies of three SS divisions in Falaise, killed by the air pressure of our bombers during the breakout in Normandy. Since our hometown was only twelve miles from Holland, the seat of the Gans family, my father was particularly interested in my participation in the Walcheren landings; I told him about the inner city of our hometown, that everything was gone. I said, "I can't even recognize the spot where our synagogue was standing. Everything was totally destroyed." I described to him my unit, which consisted largely of German Austrian Jews, and the qualification of getting into the unit.

Since I had gotten to the camp at five o'clock in the evening, by ten o'clock, I thought I would take my parents over to the commandant of the camp. He was delighted and with great sincerity said he was happy that I had found them. Then he turned around and said, "Look, I have to close both my eyes to allow you to be in this camp. There are diseases here, they are communicable, and you will go back to your army and carry these diseases with you."

The next morning I gave my parents all of my spare clothing, all the spare food, and everything that I had and set off. When we were leaving the gate, the guards stopped us again and I thought, "Now I'm getting into trouble." Actually, there was a bunch of officers who had not shaken my hand and who wanted to come out and celebrate. When this was over, I raced past the camp to show my parents that I did get out, and that was it. My parents told me later it gave them the will to live. Knowing that their three children had survived the war was a tremendous boost to rebuild their lives. Three days after I returned from Theresianstadt, I traveled to Breda to where the temporary Dutch government had been set up and met

with Princess Juliana, who was handling all Dutch returnees. She arranged a plane to take my parents from Prague to Holland, where they arrived three weeks later.

Manfred Gans is a retired engineer living in Fort Lee, New Jersey. He worked for Scientific Design Company for thirty-four years and rose from the rank of a process engineer to senior vice president in charge of technology, while the company expanded from a dozen employees to become a global engineering company. He recently completed a book about his life.